KISS and
Philosophy

Popular Culture and Philosophy®   Series Editor: George A. Reisch

For full details of all Popular Culture and Philosophy® books, visit www.opencourtbooks.com.

Popular Culture and Philosophy®

KISS and Philosophy

Wiser than Hell

EDITED BY

COURTLAND LEWIS

OPEN COURT
Chicago

Volume 134 in the series, Popular Culture and Philosophy®, edited by George A. Reisch

To find out more about Open Court books, visit our website at www.opencourtbooks.com.

Open Court Publishing Company is a division of Carus Publishing Company, dba Cricket Media.

KISS and Philosophy: Wiser than Hell

ISBN: 978-0-8126-9491-8

Library of Congress Control Number: 2020942574

This book is also available as an e-book (ISBN 978-0-8126-9495-6)

Contents

Contents

Contents

Corrupting the Youth Since 1974

COURTLAND LEWIS

You wanted the best, you got the best, and finally, philosophy is going to examine the best! The hottest band in the world, KISS!!!

KISS is one of the greatest forces in rock'n'roll. From their humble beginnings in New York, they transformed—and continue to transform—the landscape of music, performance, and society with their make-up, pyrotechnics, anthems, positive messages, and of course, their libido-centered songs and tour debauchery. You know, all the stuff young fans love and adults hate. Add to all of this the ridiculous claim that KISS are "Knights in Satan's Service," and for any rebellious youth looking for ways to distance themselves from "normal" folk, KISS is the greatest, most irresistible, outsider, freak-band ever. Love 'em or hate 'em, KISS is a rock band with the power of a Category Five hurricane that inspires just as much obsessive fandom and critical hatred. They can sell millions of albums, T-shirts, shoes, caskets, condoms, vaults, and just about everything else. They can tour the world multiple times, playing the same basic set-list for the past several decades, and millions of fans will show up every time. They can open restaurants, appear in movies, be artists, host cruises, start side bands, and write books. There is no limit to what they can do, but they've yet to delve into the world of philosophy. With *KISS and Philosophy*, that's about to change.

I can already hear the dissenters: "No way!" "KISS isn't deep enough for philosophy!" "It's just another way for KISS to take your money!" Just as they've always proved critics and dissenters wrong, KISS is about to blow your mind with how much philosophy is contained within their music and life. For diehard fans, you're about to read some of the most interesting and engaging philosophical writings on your favorite band. For casual fans, you're about to see a side of KISS you never knew existed. For any haters, get ready to have your mind blown. Whether you became a fan of KISS in 1974, your first album was *Asylum*, or you just like hearing "Rock and Roll and Nite" on the radio. Whether your first concert was in 1975, 1983's Creatures of the Night Tour, 1996's Reunion Tour, 2019–21's End of the Road Tour, or you've never seen them. Whether you're a Demon, Space Ace, Catman, Starchild, Ankh, Fox, or you don't wear make-up. No matter where you come from or how long you've been a fan, pro-Elder or not, *KISS and Philosophy* offers an explosion of philosophical ideas that will forever change the way you understand the greatest rock band in the world.

The Wisdom of KISS

According to Gene, "The philosophy of KISS in the beginning was to create magic and to encourage the suspension of disbelief. Eventually it was to get laid and make money." Like a pendulum swinging back and forth, KISS uses both philosophies to give fans a unique musical experience that is both mentally and physically exciting. The authors of *KISS and Philosophy* have done the same. Here's a taste of what you can expect.

Like each night KISS takes the stage, the following members get a section of the book to perform solo: The Demon, The Starchild, The Space Ace, The Catman, and of course, The Fox. Each section contains a variety of hit chapters that detail some of the deepest truths found in philosophy and KISS. These greatest hits include R. Alan Siler's examination of "the Message" of KISS, Matt Alschbach's historical account of KISS's impact on history and culture, along with Donald Presley's Knights in Satan's Service, which discusses how we should understand KISS in relation to the Dark Lord, and Peter Finocchiaro's answering of the question: can KISS survive without any original members?

Speaking of KISS's identity, Casey Rentmeester's "The Joyful Relativity of Kondoms and Kaskets" shows how we should understand KISS's philosophy of letting loose, Christopher Innes questions KISS's Bad Faith, and Shane Ralston tries to answer whether KISS is still KISS, even with the many line-up changes. Michael Forest and Matthew Mitchell delve into the individual perspectives of each member's memory of recording "Beth," showing how fans should make sense of the differing accounts offered in their respective autobiographies. How can four people experience the same event but see it completely differently? It's probably tied to their different character traits. So, to help us understand their characters, Randall Auxier offers readers an archetypal characterology of KISS's different personas—fascinating, indeed.

The hits continue with Robert Vuckovich's exploration of how KISS's sexual indulgencies provide insights into human self-fulfillment, with L.A. Recoder teaching readers about KISS's "destroyer" attitude, which inspires love and rejection, and offers insight into the often unexplainable devotion of KISS fans. Robert Grant Price ponders the possibility of KISS playing forever, then takes an intimate look at Paul Stanley's message of love. Mikko Puumala, then, looks at the concept of preservation in environmental ethics, in order to determine whether KISS is worthy of preservation for future generations.

As the biggest fan of KISS I know, I couldn't help but contribute a few tracks myself, including an examination of Paul's "Lick It Up" Philosophy, an explanation of how KISS Was Made For Lovin' You, avenues for KISS to Forgive and Make Up, and a controversial analysis of why "*The Elder*" is beautiful. Finally, the book closes with a bonus short compendium of KISStory. Fans can explore all the different incarnations of the band, notable contributors, official studio, live, and compilation album releases, including all of the songs, movies and videos, and of course, books. The hope is that the section will serve as a fun guide for fans and a handy reference while reading the book.

Are You Ready?!

I've been a KISS fan since the late 1980s, and like Paul says, "It is an honor to be with you" on this journey through *KISS and Philosophy*. My obsession with KISS caused me to hide tapes and T-shirts from my mother, wear lots of clown white greasepaint over the years, stand up to bullies who wanted me to conform, and even get kicked out of a KISS concert for "stalking Gene Simmons." Thanks to KISS, though I sometimes thought of quitting, or working a job I hated, or being a person I despised, I never gave up. I never listened to those who called me a failure, and I still refuse to hear the voices from those who say I can't do something. Nowadays, I get paid to Rock and Roll All Nite, and *Philosophize* every day. I just hope you've heard and listened to the same message from KISS. It helps keep you sane in the crazy, crazy world, and for me, it helps keep me *alive!*

With that said, I also hope you're ready to see what we all have in store for you. So, let's dim the lights, turn up the speakers, get our fire and blood ready, and start clapping our hands—'cause you know that's what rock'n'roll is all about!—and see what *KISS and Philosophy* is all about.

I

The Demon

1
The Message of KISS

R. ALAN SILER

To me, growing up in a small (like, "dirt roads and a post office with only about 50 boxes" small) town in Central Florida, KISS was literally everything.

It's a typical story: Shy, awkward kid finds escapism in the larger-than-life comic-book-isms and the over-the-top everything that KISS put forward. My bedroom was my KISS shrine—books, records, action figures, magazines, and more. And posters, of course. Lots of posters. All four walls, both doors, and eventually onto the ceiling. I knew exactly how many I had, and I affixed a special placard on the 100th one that I hung, and again on the 150th.

In the corner of my room was an old drum set from the 1940s with a finish coincidentally called Black Diamond on which I taught myself to play by listening to Peter Criss's part on "Christine Sixteen" from *Love Gun*. But even though I was an aspiring drummer, I most identified with lead guitarist Ace Frehley, whose whole otherworldly schtick really appealed to me, the kid who never seemed to fit in and felt like he was from somewhere else. And that's part of what drew me to KISS—the desire to fit in, to be accepted, while being kind of weird and a bit off-kilter at the same time. KISS seemed to be the ultimate expression of that.

But it was more than just that. There was a Message, found in both their music and in interviews, that spoke to me. It was a Message hidden in plain sight, overshadowed by the more hedonistic and bombastic aspects of their image and personalities. KISS's most important and most consistent Message to their fans—their philosophy, if you will—is one of self-belief: that if you work hard, believe in yourself, and never give up, then you can achieve your dreams. It may be an oversimplification, and it may come across as little more than shallow platitude, but this conviction was what drove Gene Simmons, Paul Stanley, Ace Frehley, and Peter Criss to all the successes they achieved.

They were preaching nothing that they didn't practice themselves. Paul and Gene have stated in interviews numerous times that from their earliest days playing crappy pubs and bars, many times not as the top-billed act, they attacked every stage as if they were headlining Madison Square Garden. As a kid just learning to play drums with my own nascent dreams of rock stardom, KISS represented everything that I thought I wanted in life, and they were laying out the secret formula for getting it.

Taking the Oath

In the early 1970s, KISS was mostly concerned with gaining an audience and convincing their listeners that they were already rock stars (as in 1975's "Room Service" from *Dressed to Kill*). The 1976 album *Destroyer* proved to be something of a new chapter for the band. Having experienced their first real taste of stardom with the success of their first live album, *Alive!*, KISS went back into the studio with a new confidence and exploring new musical textures (employing orchestra, piano, and choir). And it's here that their most sacred mantra makes its nascent appearances, couched within their standard hedonistic ramblings. "Shout it Out Loud" is really nothing more than a bog-standard KISS party anthem, but tucked away amongst the mandates to get the party started is the kick-in-the-pants reminder to "treat yourself like Number 1." A bit more on the nose is "Flaming Youth," an anti-establishment paean that encourages fans being held down by parents and teachers to break out of their cages, "'cause Flaming Youth will set the world on fire." There are a few other instances of The Message throughout the rest of the Seventies: in "Hard Times" on 1979's *Dynasty* album, for example, Ace tells a story of the hard knocks life he led before becoming a rock god, tacitly reassuring listeners that the same can happen for them, regardless of their background.

But it's in the Eighties where the "believe in yourself" creed really starts to take prominence. As the decade started, KISS was in the midst of its first career slump, having alienated their core American audience with the lightweight pop-infused *Dynasty* (1979) and *Unmasked* (1981). The costumed ones decided to make a back-to-basics hard rock album in a desperate attempt to reclaim their former standing as rock gods. And then . . . they didn't. In one of the most bizarre chapters in KISStory, they decided to make an art-rock concept album that was intended to be the soundtrack of a new sword and sorcery movie called *The Elder*. Rather than doubling down on their hard rock roots, they instead diverted onto yet another winding and thorny side path that even their European and Australian audiences, which had remained loyal up to this point, weren't willing to follow. A tour was planned, a stage set designed, but the album bombed so badly and the reaction so negative that all tour plans were cancelled. KISS had hit rock bottom.

In spite of the utter failure of *Music from 'The Elder'*, the album proved to be an important milestone in KISS's career. Peter Criss had left the band the previous year to be replaced by Eric Carr, and Ace Frehley already had one foot out the door (his disgust over *The Elder* and disagreements with Simmons and Stanley finally drew the line for him). They had for the most part completely lost their audience. The ship was sinking. But even though the band made a last-minute detour into an artsy new direction with *The Elder*, the philosophy that had made it possible for them to achieve worldwide success in the first place was still there.

The storyline that the album is based around is one of a boy who is chosen by the Council of Elders to take an Oath and undertake a quest and to fight evil. The boy doubts his abilities, seeing himself as too young to serve in such a capacity. The Council reassures him that "only you are the answer." Guided by a mentor called Morpheus, the boy realizes in the end that all he needs is "a will of my own and the balls to stand alone." The whole album is about overcoming doubts

5

in the face of challenge, to rise up and face destiny. With declarations of self-determination and fortitude, the final song, "I," is the clearest and boldest statement yet of KISS's Message: "I believe in me / I believe in something more than you can understand / yes I believe in me."

Scaling the Mountain

As the 1980s continued, KISS did indeed reclaim their rightful position in the rock'n'roll firmament, and became even more fervent in preaching their gospel to their throng of disciples. Numerous songs throughout the next decade were built around Gene and Paul's workplace motivational poster sentiments. *Animalize* in 1984 gave us "I've Had Enough" ("Wishin' and hopin' won't get you nothin' / Prayin' and schemin', no time for dreamin' / I've got the power, this is the hour now") and "Get All You Can Take" ("If you got half a chance you take it / You gotta get all you can take / Stop waitin' for your lucky break"). 1985's *Asylum* had "King of the Mountain" and "Trial By Fire" ("Can't listen to nobody else / you've just got to believe in yourself / They'll criticize you and lay down the law / They'll say 'just who do you think you are?'"). On 1987's *Crazy Nights*, Stanley told his listeners "I'm never gonna stop, I'm never gonna give up in the fight / 'Cause after the battle is done, all you've got left is your pride;" while also reassuring them that "Everybody's got a reason to live / Everybody's got a dream and a hunger inside" (in "My Way" and "Reason to Live," respectively). In 1989, KISS released the album *Hot in the Shade*, on which Stanley related a tale of reaching inside and tapping reserves of inner strength as a young man to gain the finer things in life ("Cadillac Dreams").

Despite hit singles like "Hide Your Heart" and the monster ballad "Forever," the highlight of *Hot in the Shade* album proved to be a song sung and co-written by drummer Eric Carr. Carr had co-written numerous songs for KISS albums with other members, including "All Hell's Breakin' Loose," the second single released from *Lick It Up*; he'd also been submitting his own songs throughout his time in KISS, such as "Dial L for Love," "Somebody's Waiting," and "Eyes of Love," but for various reasons none of them was ever used.

It wasn't until "Little Caesar," a song about a scrappy street-tough kid fighting to find his place in the world, that Carr was allowed to sing one of his own songs on a KISS album. The song reads as something of a chronicle of Carr's rise to stardom, reflecting his own pre-fame experiences. A young man, just one of ten million stories in the city, knows that it's going to be a fight if he wants to see his name in lights. Through steadfast belief in what he knows to be cool, he'll get his shot to show the world just what he can do. He knows that he has what it takes to make it, and the thing that separates him from those who can't is his determination and mindset: "they never rocked it hard enough." In drawing from his own experiences, Carr portrays himself as the ultimate example of KISS's Message: Work hard, believe in yourself, never give up, and you can achieve your dreams.

Following the *Hot in the Shade* tour, Eric Carr began to feel ill, and diagnosis eventually revealed that he had heart cancer. As his health declined, KISS tapped Alice Cooper's drummer, Eric Singer, to record a new song for the soundtrack of the movie *Bill and Ted's Bogus Journey*. The song, a rewrite of the Argent track "God Gave Rock'n'Roll to You II," became one of the great KISS anthems, boldly proclaiming the KISS Message in its most distilled and pure form:

> If you wanna be a singer, or play guitar
> Man, you gotta sweat or you won't get far
> 'Cause it's never too late to work nine-to-five.
> You can take a stand, or you can compromise
> You can work real hard or just fantasize
> But you don't start livin' 'till you realize . . .

Not well enough to play drums on the song, Carr did join the band in the studio to record backing vocals. When the time came to shoot a music video for the song, Carr had regained enough strength to resume his position behind the drum set for the filming. It was his last participation with KISS; he passed away three months later. Eric Carr's eleven-year career with KISS was bookended by two of the clearest statements of the band's principles: "I" from *The Elder* and "God Gave Rock'n'Roll to You II."

Living to Win

Following Eric Carr's death, KISS continued on with Eric Singer pounding the skins, eventually reforming with Frehley and Criss, then settling into a final line up with Singer and new guitarist Tommy Thayer. In the midst of all the tumult, KISS's Message found a bit less representation in their music during their later period.

On *Psycho Circus*, the 1998 reunion album, Stanley surveys his accomplishments, having achieved more than he ever expected: "I gave my blood and I gave my soul / I stood my ground and I took control" (from "I Pledge Allegiance to the State of Rock and Roll"). A song recorded for *Psycho Circus* but not used ("It's My Life"), proclaims Gene's staunch and rebellious individuality. Stanley summed up his personal philosophy in the title song of his 2006 solo album *Live to Win* ("You ask me how I took the pain / Crawled up from my lowest low / Day by day, kickin' all the way, I'm not giving in / Let another round begin—live to win"). KISS's next album, *Sonic Boom* (2009) includes "Never Enough," in which Stanley proclaims that he won't stop till he makes it to the top ("I'll do my sleepin' when I'm dead" / I'm gonna kick it up instead").

The Message gets little or no mention on KISS's final album, *Monster*, which leaves the Eighties as the prime source of KISS's philosophical Message. Is it possible to suss out the reason for this? Maybe it's because, having scaled the heights of success in the 1970s and subsequently nearly losing it all, KISS clawed its way back from obscurity and irrelevance, reinvented themselves, and regained their crown. Maybe it's because the 1980s was a decidedly less hedonistic time than the Seventies, giving the band a new focus. Maybe in the 1980s KISS was competing in a market with newer, hungrier bands that were influenced by them, like a heavyweight champion constantly having to defend his belt from younger opponents seeking to claim the prize. Or perhaps it was Eric Carr, that scrappy street-tough kid, wide-eyed at experiencing fame for the first time, that reignited Gene and Paul's fire, reminding them from whence they came. Perhaps.

Fighting the Fight

I never became a rock star. But that's okay, I don't think I was cut out for that lifestyle anyway. However, adhering to KISS's Message has held me in pretty good stead. I have achieved things in my life that I wouldn't have otherwise. By working hard, believing in myself, and never giving up, I have accomplishments that I'm proud of.

I will admit that it's a struggle to rock it hard enough every day, but by dropping the mp3 "needle" on one of the band's more inspirational songs, or by reminding myself of the example that Eric Carr set, the KISS Message rallies me to keep fighting.

2
KISStory and Kulture of the Hottest Band in the World

MATT ALSCHBACH

As a professor of history, I often meet college students who find it difficult to recognize the intrinsic value of history. They're either unable or unwilling to apply the lessons of the past to their own lives and the present. Stories of the past seem monochrome and distant to these students. I find this frustrating, because I do everything I can to paint a picture of the past that is vibrant in color and rich in nuance, complexity, and relevance.

History is a set of fascinating stories about the past, and as I'm quick to point out to students, the facts are usually far more compelling than some fictional account. There are few stories more compelling than that of the rock band KISS—one of the most colorful, bombastic, and influential bands of all time. As a historian and a product of the 1970s, I recognize that KISS is much more than just shock-rock Kabuki theater—they have inexorably shaped American culture over the last forty-five years, and continue to do so today.

So, here are the observations of one 1970s super-fan, placing those experiences within the broader narrative of KISStory and US culture, in order to make the history of KISS both fun and enlightening—as it should be.

Flaming Youth (and My Dad)

In November of 1979 KISS came to my hometown, San Diego, California. I was eleven years old, and a massive KISS fan. When I heard the news, I pleaded with my parents to take me, and I was surprised when my father, a police officer, agreed. I'm certain that he wasn't a KISS fan. On many occasions, he had directed me to "turn that down" when he arrived home from work. As with so many young men, my relationship with my father was difficult. He was a provider and a disciplinarian—we weren't friends. The idea of going with my father to a KISS concert was hardly ideal, but what choice did I have? I was eleven years old, and thankful that he was willing to take me to my first concert.

I have a vivid memory of walking into the San Diego Sports Arena on November 29th 1979 and being met with the aroma of marijuana smoke. There were many older fans indulging pre-show, as well as a number of scantily clad young women in KISS make-up moving about in anticipation of the band's performance. I remember thinking that my father was going to arrest everyone, thereby causing me to miss the show. To my astonishment, my father simply ignored the joints being passed around and did his best to ensure that I had a safe and enjoyable evening. I was mesmerized by the band's performance. The stage show, the fireworks, Paul Stanley's powerful vocals, Gene Simmons "flying" through the air during "God of Thunder"—it was a sensory overload for my young mind. This concert was a defining moment in my life, and still is forty years later.

The following day, my father asked me which KISS album contained the song "Shout it Out Loud," as he had enjoyed that tune the night previous. This was a rare moment when my father and I bonded over a shared interest in something that I loved, and I was thrilled to introduce him to the band and music I adored. There weren't many moments like that in my youth, but KISS provided a memorable one. KISStory became my history!

A World with Heroes

I was ten years old in 1978, and to a ten-year old boy living in southern California, KISS wasn't just the greatest band in my admittedly limited musical stratosphere, they were the *only* band that I cared about. My bedroom walls were adorned with images of the iconic rockers. Every chance I got, I walked to the local record store to peruse the KISS albums, or to the local ice cream shop to buy KISS cards. I knew the band members' names and the fictional back-stories of their characters. However, like so many kids my age, I had never gazed upon their unmasked faces. It's this fact that vexed me to my core. Many KISS fans who discovered the band after 1983 didn't get a chance to experience the magic and mystery associated with the "disguised" KISS, as the guys carefully guarded their identities, and there were no public photos of the band sans make-up.

I remember thumbing through a music magazine and seeing a photo of Gene Simmons leaving a restaurant whilst holding a cloth napkin just above his nose so that photographers only captured his eyes and steely gaze. When I saw that picture, my fascination with the band and this mythological man soared. I bought the magazine and shared the image with my peers at school, and their reaction was likewise one of astonishment, followed by speculation about what the lower two-thirds of his face might look like. Conversations with fellow KISS enthusiasts about the true identities of these masked men continued for years.

Paul, Ace, Peter, and Gene were "larger than life" figures to me and the legions of KISS fans that I encountered daily at school and in record stores. Their trademark images were carefully cultivated by the band and their management so that lads my age knew them as the Starchild (Paul), the Spaceman (Ace), the Cat (Peter), and the Demon (Gene). I loved this imagery and the outlandish mythos the band and fans had concocted. Seeing a photo of Gene (at that time my favorite member of the band) exiting a fancy restaurant, identity obscured, lovely lady in tow, should have somehow changed my perception of the band and the man—he was, in fact, a mere mortal. It didn't, because like all KISS fans, I had a love affair with the hottest band in the world—KISS!

It's our love affair with KISS that changed the world. For example, in 1978, KISS issued a best-of album called *Double Platinum*. The album sleeve was a glossy metallic cardboard. When the gatefold was opened, inside there were images of the band members pressed into the cardboard so that their likenesses were slightly raised from the background. My friends and I spent countless hours placing tracing paper over those raised images and shading with a pencil to reveal what the band might look like without make-up. It didn't work, but we kept at it, nonetheless.

We Are One

The cultural impact of KISS in the 1970s was irresistible. In elementary and middle school, most of my friendships started with a conversation about KISS. To my delight, many boys my age also adored the band. The typical conversation went something like this: "Do you like KISS?" "Of course I like KISS, who doesn't like KISS?" "Oh yeah, well then what is your favorite album?" If the respondent named two or more KISS albums, he was legitimately a KISS fan. If he could name all of the band members and albums, we were likely going to be friends. If he had actually seen KISS in concert, we might be friends for life. KISS was the unifying force in my youth that acquainted me to like-minded music fans, but also introduced me to the beautiful world of rock music in all its multi-faceted complexity.

Keep in mind that all I have described so far occurred long before anyone wore KISS shirts to school, so there were no visible markers of KISS fandom—we simply identified fellow KISS fans by engaging in conversation. Soon I found that there were many like me, harboring this fascination with four make-up-clad grown men in tight spandex and cod-pieces. We would debate during lunch hour which album was better, *Alive!* or *Alive II*? *Love Gun* or *Destroyer*? *Dressed to Kill* or the eponymous debut LP? Decades prior to the Internet, it was a chance to showcase our knowledge of the band, the songs, and the albums. KISS brought us together in friendly competition and comradery. Remarkably, KISS was, and continues to be, a unifying cultural force in the lives of both hardcore and casual fans. How did this happen, you ask? You could say it was "A Million to One."

The rise of KISS as a cultural pillar in America in the 1970s is particularly remarkable when you consider that the band was hardly a household name. While it's true that the band had a devoted cult following, most adults and many young people viewed KISS as a novelty act that would fade after a few years. I have vivid memories of classmates mocking my affection for KISS, and telling me that I should listen to "good music" produced by the more popular artists of the day. At best, parents viewed KISS as a fad that would fade in a few years. At worst, they saw a fire-breathing, blood-spitting Gene Simmons as evil incarnate, and scrambled to shelter their kids from such unholy entertainment.

KISS received meager financial support from their record label, Casablanca, and limited airplay on American rock radio. Casablanca was an upstart record label, and KISS was the first act signed by the company's founder, Neil Bogart. The label continued in starts and fits throughout the 70s, with little capital to spend on promoting a shock rock band with a devoted following, but limited popular and commercial appeal. In September of 1975, Casablanca released *KISS: Alive!*, a double live LP that enjoyed strong sales. It's often argued that the success of this album rescued Casablanca records from bankruptcy and showed the record industry that you could make money on a live album. There must be something to this, because the label began to spend money in support of KISS over the next few years. KISS fans were treated to TV commercials touting new albums (see YouTube for the commercial spots advertising the solo albums and *Dynasty*), or a radio spot announcing that the band was headed to your town. What's ironic about the radio spots is that most American rock stations refused to play KISS songs. We heard promotions for a rock band that the stations wouldn't play! Further, the handful of stations that did choose to play KISS decided upon the single "Beth," KISS's first ballad. This annoyed many hardcore KISS fans, as the track is a total departure from every other song in KISS's catalog to that point in their career! To add to the irony, "Beth" was also their most successful single to that point in the band's career.

KISS received occasional exposure on national television because, despite the lack of airplay and financial support, they were becoming cultural icons in the latter half of the 1970s. Gene, Paul, Peter, and Ace appeared on *The Mike Douglas Show*, *Rowan and Martin's Laugh-In*, *Don Kirshner's Rock Concert*, and *The Tomorrow Show with Tom Snyder*. The reason I recall these appearances from memory is because my friends and I waited for them with frenzied anticipation. After scouring the *TV Guide* booklet and spotting the band's name (and usually circling the channel, day, and time with a pen), we proclaimed the news at school. KISS fans attempted to move heaven and earth to ensure that we would be able to watch the band's appearance live and in real time.

Prior to the VHS player/recorder, there was no way to record television—you simply had to tune in and wait. This was particularly difficult for a ten-year-old with a bedtime, as *Don Kirshner's Rock Concert* aired at one in the morning on the West coast.

When we finally saw them perform on TV, it was magical, and only reinforced their mystique. Most of these appearances were no more than four to five minutes, just enough to fire our curiosity, but too little to slake our thirst for the band and their music. It only made us want to know more about this outlandish, irreverent, and cryptic rock act.

Cadillac Dreams

Although most KISS fans likely didn't realize it in the 1970s, it's clear now that founding members Gene and Paul had a vision to make KISS a global success from the beginning. The aims of the duo were different from how fans viewed them in the 1970s—fans loved KISS precisely because they were an oddity, far from the mainstream. The lack of radio airplay, the fact that parents recoiled at seeing their album covers, and the backlash from religious groups—a few claimed that "KISS" stood for "Knights in Satan's Service"—these were all reasons to love the band. In other words, fans didn't want them to be too successful, and we certainly didn't want them to become popular with the masses. Gene and Paul disagreed.

In retrospect, there was a preponderance of evidence to suggest that Gene and Paul always intended to make KISS the biggest band in the world, and that their true motivations were fame and wealth. Consider, for example, the 1976 song "Do You Love Me?," where Paul croons "You like the credit cards and private planes, money can really take you far. You like the hotels and fancy clothes . . . You really like rock'n'roll, all of the fame and the masquerade, you like the concerts and studios, and all the money, honey, that I make, but . . . Do you love me?" Similar themes venerating fame, fortune, and excess can be found in the band's early catalog. In the mid-1980s, KISS achieved global success, in no small part due to the direction and ambition of Paul Stanley and Gene Simmons, but not without setbacks.

By 1983, KISS had lost two original members, with drummer Peter Criss and lead guitarist Ace Frehley departing the band. This prompted founding members Paul and Gene to do what many thought would never happen—they took off the make-up! MTV televised the grand unmasking and tried to make an event of it, but it was in many ways anti-climactic. KISS was on the decline after losing two members and producing a couple of sub-par records over the previous few years. They still had a devoted following, but many of KISS's hardcore fans from the Seventies had moved on to heavier, darker, more serious music. KISS, sadly, had become a parody for many of their longtime fans. Paul and Gene, astute businessmen always, recognized this, and they did something bold. They completely reinvented the band.

KISS in the 1980s was a dramatically different band than the one I had followed with cult-like devotion just a few years before. Gone was the make-up, black leather, and studs. Instead, it was sequins, bright and fluorescent colors, scarves and sashes, animal print pants (and guitars), and Paul Stanley pirouetting on stage like Travolta in the movie "Stayin' Alive." This was NOT the KISS I grew up loving, and I wasn't happy. I began to explore heavier music in the 1980s. In my view, KISS had sold out. I didn't realize at the time that this is what Gene and Paul intended—to grow their fan base and amass a global following.

Paul and Gene wanted not only to recapture their former glory of the late-1970s, they wanted to exceed it, and they did just that. The era of MTV provided a vehicle for the band to connect with an entirely new generation of fans (teens with disposable income), and to refashion the KISS brand. In the Eighties KISS went mainstream with a string of radio-friendly hits like "Heavens on Fire," "Tears are Falling," and "Forever." So, while they lost (albeit temporarily in many cases) the attention and devotion of many long-time fans, they immediately became accessible to younger fans, and just as importantly, women.

In an example of the band's growing cultural influence, in 1987, *The Oprah Winfrey Show* featured Gene and Paul in an episode that examined rock stars and their sexual exploits. The duo were all too happy to both defend and revel in their unbridled promiscuity. They made no apologies— Paul made womanizing and casual sex sound downright patriotic! What was more astonishing about this episode is that many of the women in the audience agreed with Paul and Gene's "Love 'Em and Leave 'Em" outlook on life. Far from finding the pair's behavior abhorrent, many female audience members stated that they wanted to approach their intimate relationships with the same cavalier attitude, but without the double standards and stigma so often associated with sexually adventurous women. In other words, Gene and Paul were living lives that both men *and* women found exhilarating and satisfying, at least in the imagining, if not in practice. Once again, KISS played a major role in shaping the cultural narrative.

A bit of historical context here: in 1987, KISS was hardly the biggest rock act in the US. Van Halen, Mötley Crüe, Def Leppard, and Poison were massive commercial successes within the genre, to name just a few. What's more, these bands were legendary for their debauchery and sexual exploits. Van Halen's David Lee Roth and Mötley Crüe's Tommy Lee were well-known for their sexual proclivities and relationships with high-profile celebrities and super models. Further, by 1987, David Lee Roth (by that time a solo artist) was a far more recognizable entertainer and rock star than Gene or Paul. Yet the producers at Oprah's show reached out to the founding members of KISS to serve as "experts" and spokespersons for an entire genre of music and the subculture it spawned! You can view the full episode of *The Oprah Winfrey Show* featuring Gene and Paul on YouTube.

The "Remasking" of KISS

The band produced a run of commercially successful albums in the Eighties, and in the process, a multitude of new converts were inducted into the KISS Army. However, the Nineties were a dark time for bands like KISS. Grunge, pop, hip-hop, and rap were the flavor of the decade, and hard rock and heavy metal were out. Nevertheless, in 1994–95, the band attempted to reinvent their sound yet again by producing an Alice in Chains–style grunge album. *Carnival of Souls: The Final Sessions* was eventually released by the band with little fanfare in 1997. Ironically, this album illustrated that the band was capable of more complex arrangements, serious themes, and a much heavier direction. Unfortunately, Gene and Paul had mixed feelings regarding the material, and chose to part ways with Bruce Kulick, their brilliant guitar player in the Eighties and Nineties, and major contributor to *Carnival of Souls*. Many staunch KISS fans hold this album and Bruce Kulick in high regard precisely because it is so different from all of their other material. The delay in releasing the album was the result of Gene's and Paul's decision to shelve the completed record, in order to reunite with founding members Ace and Peter, which from a business perspective was a stroke of genius.

The band's decision to reunite in 1996–97 and embark on a world tour in make-up was received by both classic KISS fans and newer devotees with great enthusiasm. Fans of early KISS were excited to see the band playing classic-era KISS, complete with the make-up, theatrics, and pyrotechnics, while younger fans got a chance to see what made the band so special in the Seventies. This ill-fated reunion lasted just a few years, but it did produce two highly successful world tours, one pretty good but controversial new album, and a chance for millions of fans and multiple generations to see the founding members of KISS set the world on fire once again.

I was fortunate enough to see the original line-up twice on the reunion tour—once in 1996, and again in 2000. The 1996 show was interesting because I went with a couple of co-workers in their early twenties. They were casual KISS fans, and they'd never seen the band. I will never forget the look of awe on their faces when the curtain fell and the band descended from the rafters from a suspended stage, showered in fire and smoke. Their mouths were agape, their eyes wide, and stayed that way throughout most of the show. In the days after, all my colleagues wanted to talk about was KISS. They spent months collecting the band's back catalog of music. Two more soldiers for the KISS Army. This experience exemplifies KISS's impact across generations.

Kultural Impact Today

Over the last half-century, there have been just a handful of artists capable of making such a profound and lasting impact on American culture as KISS—The Beatles, The Rolling Stones, Michael Jackson—perhaps a few others. But unlike the others mentioned here, the cultural impact of KISS has never faded—in fact, it's grown stronger and entered the mainstream. For example, there are no international Beatles conventions every year, while KISS Expos are held annually in cities like Indianapolis, Atlanta, and New Jersey. (Full disclosure: there is an "international Beatleweek" festival in Liverpool, England, the birthplace of the Beatles, but this is, essentially, a local festival designed to lure fans to the city and drive tourist dollars. It's very different from the multiple KISS Conventions that are held annually in several US and European cities.

The Rolling Stones, while still a successful international touring band, don't have band-themed coffins or lunch boxes. Gene Simmons enjoyed a long-running and successful television show, while "Keith Richards: Family Jewels" will never see the light of day, mercifully. The late Michael Jackson is still newsworthy, but for all the wrong reasons.

Meanwhile, Paul Stanley is an internationally acclaimed painter, with art sales totaling over ten million dollars (by his estimation), and KISS recently appeared on *The Price Is Right*, where they gave away an all-expenses paid week on the KISS KRUISE. That's right, KISS has their own cruise, which is in its tenth year. Dedicated fans pay many thousands of dollars to see their heroes perform multiple sets over three days on board a luxury liner. All of the original band members have published autobiographies, and Gene and Paul have authored a number of titles on topics such as wealth creation and self-help. KISS comics are still going strong, and KISS merchandise has netted Gene and Paul over a half-billion dollars in profits in the last fifteen years (https://money.cnn.com/2011/10/18/news/kiss_products/index .htm). The pair even owned a short-lived arena football team franchise called, predictably enough, the L.A. KISS.

And then there is the "Vault Experience," where Gene Simmons visits your home to present you with an actual vault filled with albums, CDs, rarities, show-worn gear, and other keepsakes. Gene actually delivers it to your house, and then performs a few songs, holds a Q&A, and fraternizes with you and twenty-four of your friends and family members. The price for the vault experience: $50,000. An exorbitant price tag to be sure, but Simmons unapologetically claims that what he's selling is himself and a once-in-a-lifetime experience to have "The Demon" spend a couple hours in your kitchen! In 2018–19, Simmons traveled far and wide bringing his vault experience to his most devoted fans, and it was a success by any metric, despite what many might consider to be a prohibitive price point for said "experience."

The influence of KISS is pervasive in the US. There are nearly a dozen KISS-themed podcasts, such as "Podder than Hell," "Pod of Thunder," "Kisstory Science Theatre," "KISS-FAQ," "Podcast Rock City," and "PodKISSt: The KISS Room." Additionally, there are dozens of music-based podcasts that, while not KISS-centric per se, often delve into KISS-themed topics. My personal favorite is "Decibel Geek." Hosts AAron Camaro and Chris Czynszak are perhaps the most devoted KISS fans on the air today. Rarely do they make it through more than five minutes of discussion on any topic without KISS entering the conversation. I challenge readers to identify another band that enjoys this level of attention and devotion forty-five years into their career.

In 2012 Paul and Gene entered the restaurant business, opening a chain of eateries called "Rock & Brews." The chain is successful, with locations in many major cities across the US. What's truly unique about this venture is the pair's focus on fund-raising for and support of US military veterans. Rock & Brews sponsors many fund-raising events, with the proceeds going to Wounded Warriors and VA hospitals. On Veterans' Day, all active duty military personnel eat free at Rock & Brews. This vocal and visible support of military personnel and their families has certainly caught the attention of local and national media and military families across the nation.

Being a college educator, I choose to dress conservatively—buttoned-up dress shirt and tie is the standard uniform on campus. In my personal time, however, I often wear one of the many rock'n'roll T-shirts that I have acquired over the years. I have collected dozens of shirts from a range of artists, but none of them elicit comments from strangers like my KISS T-shirts. Without fail, if I go out in public sporting a KISS shirt, someone will come up to me and comment on how much they love the band. In the last year, KISS fans have commented on my shirts in grocery stores, the gas station, Dairy Queen, a furniture store, Target, and perhaps most inappropriately, as I was exiting an airport restroom stall. Again, this happens every single time I wear a KISS shirt. My wife noticed that on one outing, three different people commented on my KISS shirt—she recognized that this was extraordinary.

During these chance encounters, KISS fans will tell me about the first time they saw the band, where they saw them, and how old they were. I will respond by mentioning my first concert in 1979, and they will either express envy (because they saw them later), or pride (because they saw them earlier in their lives than I did). In either case, there's this fascinating bonding experience where we acknowledge the greatness of KISS, the camaraderie of being fellow soldiers in the KISS Army, and our good fortune for being long-time fans of the band.

There's usually some discussion about whether the first show they saw was with the original four members, in make-up or out of make-up, and who opened for them. Some of these exchanges last just a minute or two, but I always come away with a feeling of being part of something powerful and profound. These meetings are unlike anything I've experienced in other areas of my life. There's a special bond only KISS fans feel.

Kings of the Mountain

KISS are currently on a three-year tour of the world (even though Gene and Paul are pushing seventy). I was fortunate enough to see them twice on this particular tour, and I was impressed by the number of young fans in attendance. There were the long-time die-hards in attendance, but many older fans brought their kids and grandchildren with them. There were a number of young couples in attendance, as well as teens. These younger fans knew all the words to the songs, and their enthusiasm for the band was surprising. Further, my wife attended and it was her first KISS concert. I'll never forget the look on her face when the band descended from the rafters on shining spheres enveloped in fire and smoke, playing "Detroit Rock City." I have no doubt it was the same look of awe that I wore in 1979, when seeing KISS for the first time. I feel so fortunate that I was able to share that experience with her. She is now a Paul Stanley fan for life!

Speaking of experiences, I reciprocated my father's kindness of taking me to a KISS show in 1979 by taking him to one twenty years later. The show opened with rockers Skid Row and Ted Nugent, and both played at deafening volumes. Realizing that I had left earplugs in my vehicle (a must for any frequent concert-goer), I left my dad behind in the show and exited the arena to retrieve them. After fetching them and walking back towards the venue, I heard the voice of a young lady requesting my assistance. I stopped at her vehicle and was surprised to find a stunning young woman attempting to lace up thigh-high black leather boots, and having some trouble completing the task. She asked me to help her with her footwear. Not one to leave a lady in need, I hopped into her vehicle to assist, and we had a nice chat. She was dressed provocatively, and I was young and single. She explained that she worked for a local radio station and that she had two backstage passes to the show, offering me one of them. I won't lie, there was a split-second when I considered what Paul and Gene would do—leaving my dear old dad up in the nose-bleed seats so that I could go backstage to meet the band and spend the evening with this alluring lass. Quickly, however, I realized how important it was to share that evening with my father and the band—the real lesson of KISS. I politely explained to the young woman about my first concert in 1979, inviting my dad twenty years later, and she understood. We parted ways, and I have no regrets about that decision. My father and I saw the original four members of KISS perform, and I have another lasting memory with my dad that is all the more special since his passing in 2016.

The history of KISS is the history of each fan. KISStory can't be told without the perspective of fans. Like me, all fans have their own story about how the band shaped their youth, brought them closer to friends and loved ones, and filled their lives with meaning, providing the cultural framework that shaped their very identities. This assertion might sound absurd to non-fans, but KISS fandom is unique. No matter what our daytime responsibilities or professions may be, KISS fans can transform themselves by donning the KISS T-shirt, putting on the make-up, or simply listening to any one of the hundreds of fun and inspiring tunes performed by the band. KISS fans can live their best life, "Rock and Roll All Nite," and always find a "Reason to Live."

KISS unites fathers and sons, friends and fans, and even complete strangers based on a shared enjoyment of the band. We are KISS, KISS is our history, and together we've shaped all of history and culture.

3
Paul's Lick It Up Philosophy

COURTLAND LEWIS

I love Paul Stanley! If you don't believe me, listen to the 5:18-minute mark, just before "Rock and Roll All Nite," from Nashville, Tennessee, 2009—you'll hear me scream it. If they ever release the Louisville, Kentucky, "End of the Road Tour" on 3-12-19, you'll also hear me say, "Paul, you're my father!"

Did my love with KISS begin with Paul? No. It actually began with Peter Criss, when I was in seventh grade. I was a fan of drums, and the Topps KISS 1978 cards had some incredible images of Peter's 1977–78 drum kit. By the eighth grade, I was in love with Eric Carr. His Ludwig drum adverts convinced me he was the best. Of course, since I was tall, often considered evil by my friends' parents, and decided to play the bass, Gene became the main focus of my KISS insanity for most of my early years.

As I reached my early twenties, Ace became my focus—mainly because he was a good muse for a wild party. Finally, I matured into my Paul Stanley phase, which has lasted over twenty years. (I should note that I have a major Bruce Kulick guitar-god-crush too!) What does this all mean? Well, I believe Paul has the best, most complete, and inspiring philosophy of life, and even though there's a lot of Gene in these bass-playing fingers, I most identify with the philosophy of life that Paul has developed throughout his lifetime.

If you don't know, Paul's lyrics, songs, and life illustrate a motivation and meaning of life that is illustrated nicely in some major philosophers. He teaches us about how we need

25

a "Reason to Live," and that no matter how life tries to beat us down, we've got to "Lick It Up." With anthems like "Uh! All Night" and "Let's Put the X in Sex," some try to put him down, but I'm here to explain why the Starchild is the wisest member of KISS when it comes to how we should live our lives.

Look Inside Starchild

Stanley Bert Eisen was born on January 20, 1952, and as detailed in *Face the Music*, before changing his name to Paul Stanley, he struggled to find his place in the world. He spent much of his early life chasing approval from his parents, schoolmates, women, and eventually fans. It took years for him to look inside and actually seek approval from himself. This internal journey freed him from the "slavery" of others and set him on a path to happiness and flourishing.

Paul's realization is the hallmark of philosophy. Philosophy calls on each of us to slow down, self-reflect, ask questions, and seek a deeper understanding of ourselves and the world we inhabit. As the great Greek philosopher Socrates is quoted saying in Plato's dialogue *Apology*, "The unexamined life is not worth living." We are to examine our lives, even those dark uncomfortable thoughts that scare us, for it's only through this examination that we truly come to understand ourselves and make decisions that lead to true and lasting happiness.

As Paul tells us, in *Face the Music*, no matter how much he tried to blame others or find solutions in external thrills, his problems were inside, and it was only through confronting the truth of his internal pain that he was able to be free. He had to first get in touch with his emotions, which required accepting that people who show their emotions aren't weak—it's the ones who "Hide Your Heart" who are weak. As he says on page eight, "Being a 'real man' meant being strong, yes; strong enough to cry, strong enough to be kind and compassionate, strong enough to put others first, strong enough to be afraid and still find your way, strong enough to forgive, and strong enough to ask for forgiveness."

The sort of internal struggle Paul describes is the struggle that we all must face at some point in our own lives. It's the struggle of wrestling with our existence—the realization that we are finite beings who are constantly vulnerable to physical, emotional, and mental pains. Much of contemporary life, often dominated by consumerist desires that tell us all our ills can be solved by consuming some good or service (like a KISS Kasket!), helps us ignore our shortcomings and vulnerabilities. Philosophy, like Paul, tells us that ignoring something doesn't make it go away. Instead, we must find ways of accepting the truth, no matter how depressing or absurd. Take, for example, the existentialist philosopher Albert Camus. In *The Myth of Sisyphus*, Camus presents the Ancient Greek myth of Sisyphus as an analogy for human existence. Sisyphus was punished to push a rock up a hill, only to have it roll back down, repeatedly for all eternity. Camus suggests the absurdity of human existence is that all the time and energy we put into our projects, relationships, and even life itself are meaningless, for just like the rock, when we die, all of our efforts will have been for naught. In the face of the absurdity of this existence, Camus tells us we have two options. We can ignore our plight, filling it with distractions, or we can embrace the absurdity. The former option leads to a hollow existence where our "Reason to Live" is based on a fragile and hollow lie, whereas the latter grounds us in the truth, puts us in charge of the meaning of life, and teaches us how to be strong inside.

Speaking of a "Reason to Live," this song of Paul's captures perfectly Camus's lesson on life. If we base our reason to live on something finite and destructible, like love, then when that love comes to an end and we've been burned, we'll have no reason to live. All we'll "hear is the sound of a broken heart," and the "feelin' so strong comin' over" us will be one of despair.

On the other hand, if we base our reason to live on something that is indestructible, our reason to live will never be shattered. What can't be destroyed? For some, it's the belief in an infinite God, while for others, it's a belief in some sort of ultimate truth. For Paul and Camus, the answer is something along the lines of taking control of your life, filling it with what you take to be meaningful, or as Paul says in *Backstage Pass*, being the best YOU.

When we take control of our lives, no matter how absurd they seem, we feel as Paul sings in "Reason to Live": "Now

27

the hurtin' is through, and a new day starts, I feel a change in my life, I sailed into dark and endless nights, and made it alive . . . I'm not alone when I'm strong inside, and I realize, Everybody's got a reason to live, Everybody's got a dream and a hunger inside."

It's this hunger inside that calls us to push our own rock-of-life up the hill, and when Paul's singing about our reason to live and how we should "Lick It Up," he's calling us to embrace our life and make it meaningful and great.

We Don't Preach, We Inspire!

Have you ever wondered why—and how—the great song-writers of the past fifty years put together their master-pieces? Paul's no Beethoven, but he's written some of the most iconic and straightforward rock songs of the past fifty years. Sure, he wrote hits like "Rock and Roll All Nite," "Detroit Rock City," "Love Gun," "I Was Made for Lovin' You," "Lick It Up," "Heavens on Fire," and "Forever." These alone are more hits than most bands write. Now, consider that he also wrote "Black Diamond," "Strutter," "C'mon and Love Me," "God of Thunder," "Hard Luck Woman," "A World Without Heroes," "I Still Love You," "Hide Your Heart," "Jungle," "Freak," and so many more.

In his "The Definitive, One-Size-Fits-All, Accept-No Substitutes, Massively Comprehensive Guide to the Life and Times of Kiss," Chuck Klosterman calls "Strutter" the "clearest, classiest rock song KISS ever produced," and even though he chides Paul for spending a cross-country flight musing about his manly prowess when writing "Love Gun," he maintains that KISS's early work was a forerunner of punk and catchier than other critically acclaimed bands. Why is Paul so creative? The answer is more complex than you probably think.

There are two aspects to writing a song, especially a KISS song. First, you need a good riff or catchy group of chord changes. Second, you need some poetic lyrics. When these two aspects come together in the right way, you have a masterpiece like "Shout it Out Loud," and when they don't, you have Peter Criss's solo record. We shouldn't be too hard on Peter, because writing good songs (and he wrote a few) is a difficult process, one that involves the rational composition of music and another that involves an irrational bout of inspiration. Paul's songwriting credits show he's especially talented in both areas.

Plato's *Ion* shows us how we might understand Paul's abilities. In the dialogue, Socrates is interested in Ion's craft as a poet, wondering if poetry is a skill like painting, sculpting, or music, or something completely different. By 'skill', Socrates means an art that has defined attributes and rules that structure and create an understanding of what is good and bad. For instance, pyrotechnics is an art governed by several rules relating to the mixture of explosives. When these rules are followed, a brilliant display of explosions occurs and we say the pyro-technician is a good pyromaniac. When the rules aren't followed, explosions still occur, but there's a risk that they won't work and that people might get hurt. We would say such a technician is a bad pyromaniac.

As for music, most people think of good and bad music as something wholly subjective, but because the creation of music follows certain rules, music is more of a skill. There are only twelve notes, and for them to sound proper, instruments must be tuned properly and the notes must be composed in certain ways. Knowing how to tune and properly compose is a skill that is practiced and crafted over years. Paul wasn't born with the ability to write "Black Diamond." He had to work at it, setting his mind to being the best and working long hours to achieve his goals. Though not the main point of Plato's dialogue, when understood in relation to a rock star like Paul Stanley, we gain the lesson that if you want to be a musician you're going to have to spend time working hard, and not just fantasizing. It's never too late to work nine to five, so you better be willing to sweat. To quote Paul from *Backstage Pass*, "We must give ourselves permission to do things others are skeptical about. Do it! You have more to gain by doing it than by not doing it."

As for poetry, according to Socrates, it's not a skill. Poetry is a matter of divine inspiration, similar to a magnet that moves a piece of iron towards itself, and in time, infuses the iron with its own magnetic power. Socrates suggests that the gods strip the poet of intellect, then enter the poet (hence, the word inspiration—"in-spirit"), and finally, possess the poet in order to possess others in fits of inspiration.

As an irrational force, poetry scared Plato and Socrates because they both valued rational thought over all other things. Why would they be scared? Just think about a KISS concert. When Paul sings a song, shakes his booty, and yells at the audience, we all go hysterical. He knows what he's doing. As he notes in *Face the Music*, "I see the part I play in making them [the fans] happy and find that very fulfilling." At those moments, he could command the KISS Army to tear down the building and we would. Thankfully, he's not there to preach destruction. He just wants to inspire us to "Stand up for what you believe in!" Refuse to be a victim. Roll up your sleeves, fix your issues, change into who you want to be, make things work, and transform the world into the one you like. Roll up you sleeves and give yourself "Tough Love!"

Roll Up Your Existential Sleeves

When most people think of philosophy, they think about un-interesting lectures on topics that no one cares about, with big words. Sadly, some philosophy courses live up to this low standard, but just as KISS showed that a rock show needn't be boring, philosophy has the potential to "Rise to It." When related to KISS and Paul Stanley, the lessons of Camus and Socrates become alive and relevant, and before long we find that Paul's life and music show us a way to live our lives to the fullest.

Philosophy is ultimately about taking control of your life. It starts with self-reflection and a desire for a deeper knowledge and understanding of truth. These pursuits help you make better decisions about who you want to be and to what you want to dedicate your life. Aristotle suggested that all humans strive for flourishing (*eudiamonia*), and that the best way to achieve flourishing is to live a life of virtuous moderation.

As most KISS fans know, moderation is difficult when it comes to KISS. We want everything, even if it's another greatest hits with fifteen versions of "Rock and Roll All Nite!" The problem is that by listening to "Rock and Roll All Nite" too often, we end up ruining the song. Sure, we might still love to hear it at a concert, but other than that it's worn out. While listening recently to the *KissFAQ Podcast*, I was shocked when all but one of the participants ranked "Rock and Roll All Nite" quite low on their list of best songs on *Dressed to Kill*. How can one of the greatest rock anthems of all time not be ranked Number One, especially on *Dressed to Kill*?

The simple answer is we've heard it too often. If we had listened to it in moderation, we'd still love it like it were new. Life is the same way. For Aristotle, life is a series of choices where we must decide how much or little we do something, and the better we are at performing tasks in moderation, the more likely we will be to flourish. So, I collect KISS tour books and first pressings of their LPs, but refuse to buy a Kasket or $300 signed setlists, even though I've seriously considered buying both; and as a result, I get to enjoy KISS and still pay my mortgage. In other words, I flourish.

Of course, flourishing is not the only possible approach to how we should live our life. I argue in my book *Repentance and the Right to Forgiveness* that we should strive for peaceful flourishing, what I call eirenéism (or peace-ethic). Eirenéism is similar to Aristotle's approach, but it incorporates more of the communal nature of life and flourishing. To peacefully flourish you need the goods that make you flourish, but you also need to work towards helping others flourish. When everyone strives for both, we all flourish as a community.

I was lucky enough to get several Paul Stanley guitar picks at the "End of the Road Tour" in Nashville, and instead of hoarding or trying to sell them online, I went around and gave them out to young kids who were not fortunate enough to be up front. In this way, I flourished and helped others flourish too. Paul's throwing them out works on the same principle—he could keep them all, but he chooses to share.

Paul's approach to life is interestingly similar. As he says in *Face the Music*, "It's easy to live your life with your hand closed. But you get nothing with a fist that you can't get in multitudes with your hand open." In other words, you have to make yourself vulnerable, and be willing to give to others, if you want to find inner peace. To harken back to Camus, you can't push a rock up a hill with your hands closed. If you try, you'll be miserable. You have to open your hands, take care of who you are on the inside, and use your hands to create a better you and world.

When talking about his Jewishness, Paul notes how being good is not about following some set of rules that promise punishment if violated. Instead, you're to be good because good is its own reward. He doesn't mean you will be rewarded with a "meet and greet" pass to the final KISS show. Instead, the reward is that you live a better life, one of peaceful flourishing. To do this, however, you need to know yourself and fill your life with wisdom. You need wisdom to make good decisions. KISStory is full of individuals who made bad decisions. They did things that made themselves feel good, but in reality what they did was destructive. Their lives, friends, family, and fans all suffered because of ignorant decisions about what they thought was "good." In such cases, their ability to flourish was inhibited, but over the years some of them—Ace is a great example—have gotten their lives on track and have begun to truly flourish. Paul suffered from feelings of dissatisfaction, inadequacy, and profound loneliness, and it wasn't until he gained true wisdom that he created a system of boundaries and limitations that set him free and allowed him to flourish.

Wait, how can boundaries and limitations set you free? We typically think of freedom as a complete lack of impediments, but to do so is a mistake. Such complete freedom would be a nightmare. We could set you in a desert, completely free from any restrictions, and more than likely you're going to suffer and die. The same could be said if you lived in a society that was completely free, yet you were completely brainwashed—you're physically free, but mentally enslaved. Political philosophers such as John Locke and Jean-Jacques Rousseau tackled such issues in the 1600s and 1700s. Locke showed how giving up complete freedom, by instituting laws, creates and enhances freedom in ways that are much more desirable.

Think how difficult it would be getting to or leaving a KISS concert if there were no stop signs, crosswalks, and stoplights. It would be an all-out war getting to-and-fro. Traffic laws, though sometimes annoying, allow for greater freedom of movement than we would have without them. As for Rousseau, he was deeply concerned with how people are mentally in chains, and argued that education was necessary for freedom. Though Paul, to my knowledge, has never written a song explicitly about becoming educated, it's implied in several. Before you can "Uh! All Night," you gotta work hard. "Move On" is a theme about experiencing and learning about the world, and his solo album *Live to Win* is full of songs that inspire knowledge and wisdom. I'm not suggesting Paul is subliminally telling us to study hard, but what he's saying is that whatever it is that fills our lives with meaning, we're going to have to work hard to achieve it.

His two books offer some of the best examples of what his music inspires. In *Face the Music*, he maintains that the path to happiness and satisfaction "may not be an easy road, but sticking to that road and pushing forward is the most worthwhile thing you'll ever do." In *Backstage Pass*, he argues that life continually tells us the "*why* of life"—the reason and purpose of life—through a continuous, changing process. There's not just one "why" for everyone. Instead, each one of us must figure out our own "why," being careful to recognize that the "why" is always changing, so we must change with it.

We can't be weak, we must be "Rock Hard." We must learn to be tough on ourselves with rules based on the reality of our own experiences. Our goals should be tailored for our own unique selves, not mirrors of someone else's goals. To survive this world, we must have a fighting optimism—an optimism of agency, as opposed to just waiting for stuff to happen—"The point is what we do in our lives and what we leave behind" (*Backstage Pass*, 84).

That's What Rock'n'Roll Is All About

Let me close with a quick story of Socrates from the *Apology* that includes what I take to be one of the greatest lessons of philosophy. If someone told you, "You're the wisest person alive," how would you respond? I think most would respond with a sense of pride, even if we humbly said, "Oh no, not me." We would then move on to some other topic. Not Socrates! He was once told he was the wisest man alive. How could he be wise, when all he did was ask questions? A wise person knows things and doesn't need to ask questions. Socrates proudly proclaimed his ignorance, so he couldn't be the wisest person alive. To prove his point, he went out and found people who claimed to be experts on topics such as courage, piety, beauty, and poetry, and asked them to show their wisdom by explaining their knowledge. He discovered the people who claimed to know things couldn't explain the things they claimed to know. In other words, he discovered that everyone else was just as ignorant as himself. So, he concluded that he was, in fact, the wisest man alive. Why? Because he was the only one willing to admit his own ignorance.

Philosophy is about gaining truth and understanding, in order to live a better life. It's full of abstract theories and terms, but at its heart, philosophy is a willingness to admit that "we don't know." Admitting one's ignorance is the first step to becoming a true philosopher, and so I will leave you with words from the philosopher who is the topic of this chapter, Paul Stanley:

> Questioning ourselves is not a weakness. It's a source of strength. There's great freedom in being able to acknowledge how little we know. (*Backstage Pass*, p. 27)[1]

---

[1] I feel the need to thank Paul Stanley and all members of KISS, past, present, and future who gave me the attitude and confidence to stand up to the religious zealots of my small town, who hated and taunted me for being a KISS fan. I should also thank Matt Edmondson for being a great friend and giving me his copy of *Dressed to Kill*, which started it all, my mom who fueled my love of KISS by banning it from the house, and John Bremseth who helped me sing *Alive!* every Sunday night at Ruby Tuesday's restaurant. Finally, I should apologize to Gene Simmons. I wasn't stalking you at the Tupelo, Mississippi, concert and didn't deserve to be thrown out; but I was wrong in my zeal to deliver my letter. The KISS gods were not on my side that evening.

4
Knights in Satan's Service?

Donald Presley

We all know the excitement that comes from listening to and seeing KISS. A sense of the unknown, the anticipation of profound joy, a feeling of sacredness: these are times that are cherished memories that journey with us throughout our (hopefully) long lives.

My sacred journey with KISS began in the seventh grade, when my best friend found a copy of *Dressed to Kill* in his yard. It was an old beat-up cassette with several pictures of KISS and their women stuffed inside. My friend liked the pictures but wasn't interested in the tape, so he gave it to me. From the opening seconds of "Room Service" I was hooked, and my life was forever changed. Added to this excitement was the knowledge I was doing something profoundly evil—I was listening to the Knights in Satan's Service!

Growing up in a small, religiously conservative town during the 1980s, when all "good" religious people were concerned with heavy metal, backwards messages, and the eventual murder sprees such things were supposed to cause, listening to KISS was one of the most subversive things possible. The only thing more subversive was either trying to buy a copy of Karl Marx's *Communist Manifesto*, which most bookstore employees confused with Richard Marx and sent you to the entertainment section, or trying to buy a copy of Anton Szandor LaVey's *The Satanic Bible*, which could get you kicked out of a store. As a curious and adventurous young man, I was naturally drawn towards the unknown, and if you told me not to do something, that guaranteed I would try it at least once. So, in the late-1980s I found myself soul-deep in experimenting with KISS and their supposed Satanic messages.

Growing up, however, I never considered them Satanic, and I often defended them against being Knights in Satan's Service to teachers, youth ministers, and fellow classmates. Yeah, one of their members was the Demon, but they didn't practice human sacrifice or do any of the other evil things typically associated with Satanism. It wasn't until I got older, and was able to actually get a copy of *The Satanic Bible* that I began to understand what I took to be Satanism wasn't in fact Satanism. After coming to a better-understanding of Satanism, I began to realize that a case could be made for thinking KISS are Knights in Satan's Service, and that if true, should not be seen as the mark of shame and evil often associated with Satanism. Let me offer a few arguments to show you how I came to such an understanding.

Will the Real Satan Arise?

The word 'Satan' often evokes images of a red-horned, hooved demon with a pitchfork intent on corrupting humans through trickery, in order to feast on their souls during an eternal afterlife of torment. Yet, the original Satan (more precisely, the Adversary or Accuser) bears no resemblance to the fanciful images developed over the past centuries. In the Hebrew book Genesis, Satan is associated with the serpent who tempts Eve into eating from the Tree of Knowledge.

Though there's no direct mention that Satan is the serpent, religions like Christianity often point to Genesis as introducing Satan and showing his nature as an evil deceiver. The first official mention of Satan is in the Book of Job, when God allows Satan to test Job's faith. Unlike the story often told about Satan being a rogue angel, in Job, Satan works for and with God to test the faith of individuals and nations.

Scholars theorize that Satan's appearance in Job is the result of the influence of Zoroastrianism—a Persian religion from the sixth century B.C.E. Zoroastrianism maintains there are two waring deities, one good and the other evil. Since

God is good, Satan must be evil, and so from the time of Job to the beginnings of Christianity, Satan becomes an evil demon, bent on destroying all things good. A similar transformation occurs in the Christian New Testament, from when Satan tests Jesus in the Gospels, to the Book of Revelation, when Satan is referred to as a Red Dragon. Satan remained fairly insignificant, until the end of the Middle-Ages, when he becomes the scapegoat of mysticism, witchcraft, and a whole host of other events and actions. Aided by stories from Dante's *Inferno* and Milton's *Paradise Lost*, Satan slowly became a central figure for Christians in Europe and America, and though the stereotypical image of Satan that appears in these sorts of writings never appears in Hebrew or Christian scriptures, it's this image that is the focus of contemporary understandings of Satan.

Fast forward to the early 1970s, as the pendulum of history swings from the peace, love, and happiness of the Sixties Woodstock culture to the drugs and violence of a post-Altamont world, and you set the stage for the Hottest Band in the Land, KISS. Inspired by the antics of the New York Dolls, the camaraderie of the Beatles, and the shock rock of Alice Cooper, some religious folks believed that not only were Paul, Gene, Ace, and Peter inspired by Satan, but they were religious zealots looking to usher in Satan's Armageddon. KISS was destined to offend and incite claims of Satanism. They were from New York City, the "capital" of evil, corruption, sin, and Satan. They deceived fans by covering their faces with make-up. They wore leather and studs, their lead singer dressed as a demon, spit blood and fire, and they played heavy metal music. They glamorized sin and debauchery, in order to tempt young people into sex, drugs, and who knows what else—sacrifice, demonic worship, murder?

Of course, if you actually listened to KISS, you'd scratch your head wondering how people could come up with such fanciful claims. Sure, the lead singer and bass player spit blood and fire, and stuck out his tongue like some sort of lizard-demon, but nothing else resembled the evil associated with the band. Sure, one of their songs praises the effects of cold gin, but the rest of them simply talk about having good times with women.

Their second album was called *Hotter than Hell*, but oddly enough, the song "Hotter than Hell" is about a good lookin' woman who turns Paul down because she's married. So instead of being about a sinful extra-marital affair, it's about a committed monogamous relationship. The only songs that come anywhere close to the evil suggested by religious groups scared of KISS's Satanism is "God of Thunder" (*Destroyer*, 1976) and "Unholy" (*Revenge*, 1992). In the 1980s, some religious groups tried to say "Heavens on Fire" was a celebration of Satan's burning of Heaven, but they obviously never actually listened to the song, which is clearly about a woman and Paul's heavy breathing—hah, hah, hah.

Missing the Point

"Missing the point" is an error in reasoning, where someone's argument simply fails to be relevant to the topic under consideration. It would be like one of your friends arguing why KISS-in-make-up is the best, and another friend responding with, "L'Oréal is my favorite make-up." Huh? What are you talking about? We're talking about KISS, not make-up brands!

When people talk about the evil of KISS and the evil of Satanism they are missing the point. Either as a result of ignorance or misinformation, they have applied fictional stereotypes to things they think fit those stereotypes. For instance, as we saw, Hebrew and Christian scriptures don't contain the image of Satan commonly portrayed in popular culture and within some religious organizations. The image of the pitchfork-wielding tormentor mostly comes from literature, secondary sources, and popular culture. Books, movies, pastors, churches, and musicians have made billions portraying Satan and Satanists in certain ways. From old black-and-white horror movies to Seventies classics, such as *Race with the Devil*, producers know that if people think there are secret societies of Satanists bent on sacrificing your soul in elaborate rituals, especially if you think they're your neighbors or children listening to KISS, you'll keep buying movies and albums—even if you only plan on burning them.

The band Black Sabbath saw great potential for making money in being evil, as did Slayer, and they both benefited greatly from their association with "Satanism." Some preachers saw the same potential for money and fame, and so began speaking out against their "sins." Nevertheless, the image of Satan in popular culture is based more in marketing than scripture.

The same is true for KISS. To saddle KISS with accusations of Satanism is to show a complete ignorance of both KISS and Satanism. Sure, bands like Slayer excel in speed and lyrics about hell, Satan, and demons, but KISS is about as far from being Slayer as Peter Criss's Eighties solo albums are from being heavy metal. The only evidence one might have for applying the stereotypical image of Satanism to KISS is Gene Simmons's demon persona. Let's see if this evidence withstands cross-examination.

In a famous early interview from *The Mike Douglas Show*, Gene calls himself "evil incarnate." This was early KISS, when Gene and KISS were mostly interested in shocking and enticing people to buy albums and attend concerts. With demon make-up and a skull-and-crossbones shirt, sitting beside an elderly Totie Fields, what could be more shocking than claiming to be "evil incarnate." Only the gullible masses believed that Gene actually thought he was an evil demon, whereas Totie Fields saw right through his mask— under all that make-up was simply a nice Jewish boy, whose mom survived the Holocaust, and who spent time as a teacher and editor before becoming "the Demon." With the hindsight of Gene's autobiography, movie career, and *Gene Simmons Family Jewels*, we see that the Demon is obviously a persona, one that he uses to explore certain primal urges and, of course, to make money.

So, there doesn't seem to be any evidence that Gene is actually an evil demon, but what about his songs? If he's the Demon, then he should have some demonic songs that praise the sick and demented evil of stereotypical Satanism. Matthew Wilkening's article for Ultimate Classic Rock, "10 Most Demonic Gene Simmons KISS Songs," suggests the following top-ten list of Gene's demonic songs, of which I've added some commentary:

10. **"Not for the Innocent"**: With lyrics like, "I spit the hangman in his face" and "Gonna . . . rip the flesh off your bones," this one

sounds pretty evil. Yet, from looking at the lyrics in context, Gene is presenting himself as a tough, experienced man whose real interests lie in your daughter. So, it's a sex song with lots of machismo.

9. **"Mr. Blackwell"**: It's a song about a fictional bad guy.

8. **"Rock and Roll Hell"**: A young man ready to make his break from the "hell" of obscurity into stardom.

7. **"Goin' Blind"**: Strange story of an old man, who I always imagined was Gandalf hitting on a young elven girl.

6. **"I Love It Loud"**: Kids love rock'n'roll and love it loud.

5. **"Almost Human"**: A woman has turned him into an animal—rarrrrr!

4. **"War Machine"**: Pretty dark stuff, but mostly reminiscent of Milton's *Paradise Lost*. We don't call Milton Satanic, so calling Gene Satanic seems disingenuous.

3. **"Unholy"**: Gene claims to be the unholy one, which sounds like good evidence for those wanting to show he is evil. Sadly for them, however, we've already shown that he's not actually evil. It's a persona, one that works great when he sings songs like "Unholy."

2. **"Watchin' You"**: Not sure how this is evil. It's a story about a good lookin' woman at a KISS concert, which sounds pretty darn good to me.

1. **"God of Thunder"**: Could be about Satan, but Paul Stanley wrote the song, so it's best interpreted as a song about Paul being a sex god, which is kind of funny to think about Gene singing it as an ode to Paul's sexuality.

Here are a few more possibilities from a KISS FAQ poll:

1. **"Within"**: I don't see anything evil. Seems like someone seeking truth.

2. **"Seduction of the Innocent"**: Religious hypocrites and charlatans are bad.

3. **"Hate"**: A human emotion, but it's not evil.

4. **"The Devil Is Me"**: Quite a powerful song about how the "tempter" is oneself. We can't blame some demon for our short-comings and failures, because the Devil is "me."

What did we learn from looking at some of Gene's most "demonic" songs? Well, most aren't demonic, in the sense that they support evil acts of cruelty, sacrifice, and the occult. The closest one gets to pure evil is "Unholy," but one song out of around 219 total KISS songs is not enough to make the band Knights in Satan's Service. More than likely, "Unholy" is simply Gene setting the tone for KISS's harder sound on *Revenge*, which he achieves masterfully. After examining the evidence, for someone to draw the conclusion that KISS are Knights in Satan's Service is truly missing the point.

Let's Put the S in Satan

So far, the only evidence that KISS is a demonic band dedicated to Satanic evil is one of the members wears the make-up of a demon, spits blood and fire, and has one song that is about evil. Yet, this is where it gets interesting, because the Satanic evil seen in popular culture and espoused by fundamentalist political and religious groups, as being part of Satanism, is not actually part of Satanism, at least not that of *The Satanic Bible*. Let's see what it actually says.

First, Ashley Palmer notes in an article for the *Independent* how LaVey's Satanism is based in science. Instead of idealizing humanity, Satanism "recognizes that the natural world is stratified, exceptional talent and genius is rare, and the universe doesn't care." In other words, just like KISS, you can't just sit around waiting to become great. You have to work hard, bite, claw, and sacrifice for any greatness you hope to achieve.

Second, Clarie Lower's article "Surprisingly Good Life Lessons from the Satanic Bible" suggests that LaVey's main lessons are life-affirming and focused on individual freedom, two of KISS's main lessons. According to Lower, besides LaVey's emphasis on sex, Satanism promotes youthful vigor, self-acceptance, self-indulgence, and self-respect. Satan is a force to be harnessed to live an enjoyable, successful life, one that promotes freedom over the following of religious dogma designed to get you to ignore your natural desires for sex, power, and money. It's okay to want to feel good, and you shouldn't let others prevent your enjoyment of life, as long as you don't harm anyone in the process.

Satanism sees envy as the great motivator for bettering ourselves and accomplishing our goals. Indulgence in food and pride make us productive members of society, and though some claim Satanism promotes selfishness, Satanism is designed *not* to force any dogma on its followers. It's up to each person to decide if they will be selfish or dedicated to helping others. Finally, as Lower makes clear, *The Satanic Bible* is pro sex and sexual freedom, but it must always be consensual and respect the agreements made with one's partner or partners—straight, gay, self, group, and even no sex.

Third, if we go straight to the source, we find that *The Satanic Bible*'s most important lesson for us to learn is to *live*. We must indulge our animalistic desires, seek wisdom, be kind to those who deserve it, and make the most of life by embracing material success. Blessed are the free, strong, bold, powerful, victorious, and destroyers of false hope. In a world that often teaches us the opposite, that living is evil, we shouldn't be surprised that 'evil' is simply 'live' backwards.

With these three bits of information in mind, we have enough evidence for showing that KISS does stand for Knights in Satan's Service. They aren't Knights because they're evil, but because KISS promotes freedom, self-empowerment, and achieving our deepest desires. As other authors, like R. Alan Siler and Courtland Lewis, have deftly shown in this volume, KISS's main lesson is for you to take control of your life, quit following the rules of "normal" society, and to work as hard as you can to achieve your dreams in life.

Hold on, just as it's wrong to saddle KISS with the stereotypical Satanism of being demonic, blood-thirsty murderers, it would be wrong to simply label them as followers of LaVey's self-centric Satanism. We need proof, and there isn't any direct evidence that KISS are Satanists. Yet, there's tons of proof to say there's a substantial overlap between Satanism's and KISS's values.

KISS has consistently promoted a philosophy that calls on fans to follow their dreams, take daring actions, and do whatever it takes to indulge their desires, whether it be musical, sexual, and/or monetarily. KISS's most prominent theme has always been about celebrating women and the pleasurable activities that occurs between men and women. KISS is a rock'n'roll band, and since rock'n'roll started as a euphemism for sex, it should be no surprise that KISS loves and promotes all things rock'n'roll. Lewis's chapter "KISS Was Made For Lovin' You," in this book, categorizes each KISS song, and shows that only a few fail to be about love. Of course, you can look for yourself. There's a compendium at the end of the book. Look at each album, ponder their overall theme, and look for songs that don't deal with women or sex in some way.

Here are a few I noticed. Their eponymous first album celebrates nothing but women. From the opening lines of "Strutter" to the closing notes of "Black Diamond," it's all about women. The already discussed *Hotter than Hell*, even with its message of monogamy, is all about women, as is *Dressed to Kill*. *Destroyer* offers some variety in song meanings, including tracks like "Detroit Rock City," "Flaming Youth," and "Shout It Out Loud," all dedicated to rebelling and partying. Their next several albums all deal with sexual exploration, women, or a rebellious party-centric lifestyle. It's not until *Music from 'The Elder'* that KISS omits sex completely from the setlist in favor of self-realization. So, even though it's different, *The Elder* still emphasizes a major KISS virtue, one that will dominate most of KISS's following albums. KISS's Eighties albums all have a mixture of sex and self-realization, with the Nineties' *Revenge* and *Carnival of Souls: The Final Sessions* offering darker songs like "Unholy" and "Hate." With their final three studio albums, *Psycho Circus*, *Sonic Boom*, and *Monster* they return to their rock'n'roll roots. Gene sings "I'm an Animal," while Paul embraces his inner "Freak."

Granted, I've only offered general reflections about each album and a few songs, but for any KISS fan who has listened to their albums will attest, KISS is only concerned with living a fulfilling life that includes most, if not all, of the Satanic values mentioned above. From Palmer, KISS is adamant that greatness and success only come to those who work hard, bite, claw, and sacrifice. Even though they didn't write it, "God Gave Rock 'n' Roll To You II," or as Siler suggests, "Little Caesar," perfectly sums up this aspect of KISS's philosophy. From Lower, we see that KISS supports the life-affirming individualism of Satanism, along with its focus on sex, youthful vigor, self-acceptance, self-indulgence, and self-respect. Embrace your natural desires for sex, power, and money, and as long as you don't wrong others during your embrace, your free to rock'n'roll however you want. Finally, from the *The Satanic Bible*, we see that KISS tells us to enjoy our animalistic desires, and that we should bask in being free, strong, bold, powerful, and victorious.

Benediction

Is KISS Satanic? Are KISS Knights in Satan's Service? The simple answer is "NO!" If KISS were Satanic, then they would openly market themselves as such. As Satanists, they would be required to live authentic lives that celebrate their love of Satanic values. No, KISS is not Satanic, but they do celebrate many of the same values, as do many other bands and philosophical movements.

Aristotle recognized how each individual has specific goods, and that by nature we all pick what we think is good, in order to help us flourish. He argued that with careful reflection we could come to understand and properly indulge our unique desires in ways that allow us to flourish. We don't have to abstain from sex and alcohol simply because someone dogmatically told us both were sins. For Aristotle, as long as they are enjoyed in proper amounts, both can lead to a more flourishing life. This seems to mirror KISS's overall message, even if some members (and fans) struggle sometimes with enjoying the proper amounts of some substances. It also seems to match LaVey's Satanic approach to self-realization.

Most readers will think Christianity the natural foe of Satanism, and of course KISS. Christianity has a long history of emphasizing Satan and blaming all of humanity's faults and mistakes on the Devil, and the people standing outside of KISS concerts viciously condemning fans to hell, all claim to be Christians. So, can Christianity, KISS, and some of the virtues of Satanism co-exist? Hell yeah, they can!

Like any belief system, Christianity is complex and allows for a diversity of beliefs and practices. Some Christians believe the Bible is the inerrant word of God, while others see the Bible as a book written and edited by many different humans over a period of several hundreds of years. Some seek to understand the original Hebrew, Aramaic, and Greek texts, while others believe the King James Version of the Bible (translated in the 1600s) is the only authoritative version of the Bible. Some hold primary a belief in the virgin birth of Jesus and his divine nature, and others reject the virgin birth (really, all miracles) and see the requirement of Jesus's divinity as a later development of the religion. You see, to say you're "Christian" can mean just about anything, even though some will argue there's only one proper meaning—usually the one they practice or came up with.

The truth is that many Christians accept normal human desires and activities as positive aspects of life. Unlike Augustine, who argued that the only acceptable performance of sex is to procreate, many Christians have accepted the value of sex as simply a pleasurable act between two people who love each other. Granted, there are many disagreements over when and with whom such pleasurable acts are appropriate, but they agree that sex is a natural part of human nature—one to be enjoyed. Many Christians also accept philosophical pursuits of self-realization, hard work, enjoyment of music, and success. There are many warnings and caveats about when such things are bad—but the same is true for KISS and Satanism.

Since all three deal with human nature, we shouldn't be surprised that they share many of the same virtues. It would be a mistake to say that because they share virtues, they are the same. We shouldn't call KISS a Satanic band, just as we shouldn't call them a Christian band. They are a band that promotes human flourishing, and most religious systems do the same.

What's interesting is that KISS fails to be the demonic force of evil stereotypically associated with Satanism. Instead, KISS's life-affirming message of rebellion, indulgence, and freedom ironically resembles the actual teachings of Satanism.

5
Greatness or Nothingness

COURTLAND LEWIS

I magine being on a plain chased by an enraged beast, and in order to escape, you climb into a dry well. To your horror, you see at the bottom of the well, a dragon that has opened its jaws to swallow you whole. To save yourself from the dragon, you grab a twig growing in a crack in the well. You hang desperately, knowing that you can't climb out of the well, yet letting go means certain death by the dragon. To make things worse, two mice—one black and one white— take turns gnawing on your limb, and the only comfort you have during this time of distress is the taste of sweet honey found on some of the leaves of your twig. What do you do?

In *A Confession*, Leo Tolstoy imagines such an allegory for life, and says, "So I too clung to the twig of life, knowing that the dragon of death was inevitably awaiting me, ready to tear me to pieces; and I could not understand why I had fallen into such torment. I tried to lick the honey which formerly consoled me, but the honey no longer gave me pleasure, and the white and black mice of day and night gnawed at the branch by which I hung. I saw the dragon clearly and the honey no longer tasted sweet. I only saw the unescapable dragon and the mice, and I could not tear my gaze from them." Again, what do you do?

Many simply try to ignore the dragon and focus on the honey. Honey is good and pleasurable, so we're typically drawn to the honey. I mean, who would prefer pondering death? Well, philosophers tend to be enamored with death.

47

Existentialists suggest that human freedom and meaning begin with the recognition we're all going to die. Socrates maintained that philosophy's main purpose was to prepare us for death. Similarly, Aristotle argues that each day we must have the courage to live our lives in the ever-present face of death. So, whether we're enamored with death or trying to avoid thinking of it at all costs, we're hanging from a twig in a well. If you still don't know what you would do, let me ask this: what would KISS do?!

You see, KISS does more than provide us with "honey," in order to ignore the troubles of life. KISS also provides answers to the above riddle. No, KISS doesn't teach us how to slay the dragon, but KISS does tell us how we should face everyday life. As R. Alan Siler notes in "The Message of KISS," found in this book, KISS's message of self-realization and achievement is the central theme of Eighties and early Nineties KISS, but it's been a part of KISS from the beginning. In fact, without "The Message," KISS would've never existed. Paul, Gene, Ace, and Peter found themselves hanging on to a twig in the early Seventies, but thanks to the creative vision and conviction of Paul and Gene (and of course, the super-talented Ace, Peter, Eric Carr, Vinnie Vincent, Mark St. John, Bruce Kulick, Eric Singer, Tommy Thayer, and everyone in between), KISS would become the "hottest band in the world." From studying KISS we too will find a way to approach life, enjoy some "honey," and face death with the dignity of a fire-breathing demon.

Alive!

KISS fans love the story of KISS. Gene's family survives the Holocaust, emigrates to America, and raises a son who becomes a teacher, magazine editor and aspiring rock star. Paul grew up in New York, was fascinated by all things rock, and spent his teens playing in several bands, until joining up with Gene in the band Wicked Lester. When Wicked Lester fell apart, Gene and Paul recruited Peter Criss from an ad in *Rolling Stone* magazine. The final piece was Ace Frehley, who joined the band after an audition advertised in *Village Voice*. Supposedly, wearing two different colored shoes and tuning his guitar during another player's audition, Ace would complete the original KISS line-up and help design the original KISS logo.

During a time of non-stop rehearsing and writing songs, the band began experimenting with make-up, and by the spring of 1973, they performed clubs in New York and eventually signed a contract with a new record company named Casablanca. KISS would spend the next few years recording three records, touring the country, experimenting with pyro-techniques, enjoying a fast life of sex and drugs, especially for Ace and Peter, and for the most part failing as a hit rock band.

The early story of KISS is really about recording three albums in two years, car wrecks and in-fighting, sexual overindulgence, and an almost bankrupt record company. Nothing they did seemed to work, yet to listen to their albums, one would think they were at the height of their success. Each song, each lyric, and each lick exudes confidence. Songs are tight, clever, and give listeners the impression of success, yet KISStory shows they were barely hanging on to the twig of life. With the death of KISS lurking in all directions, they had to make a choice about how to die or be *alive*.

Life is merely a set of choices, and each one has the potential for great harm or good. With this in mind, William Kingdom Clifford presents a thought experiment where we're to imagine ourselves as a ship owner. Though his ship is apparently still seaworthy, the ship owner knows it is badly in need of repair. Instead of fixing the ship, however, he convinces himself it will make one more trip, and so rents it to a group of emigrants who subsequently drown at sea. Was the ship owner innocent of any wrongdoing? Was he responsible for fixing the ship? If he were ignorant, then maybe we could defend his actions, but he knew it was dangerous, yet convinced himself of a lie that the ship was seaworthy. Clifford argues that the ship owner was guilty of acting without sufficient evidence, and that because we're all culpable for our actions, we should never act without sufficient evidence.

So, if Clifford were part of KISS, he would require the band make a decision based on sufficient evidence. Of course, this is exactly what KISS tried to do with "Rock and Roll All Nite." What better way to increase sales than to have a hit rock'n'roll anthem, and against all odds, Gene and Paul wrote one. The only problem was that it was a flop. It got some air play, but was mostly ignored. Instead of choosing a path based on sufficient evidence, KISS chose to record a live album, which at the time was considerably risky—like trying to sail a broken ship across the ocean.

Live albums sold poorly and were definitely not a means to becoming a hit band. Nevertheless, KISS recorded and produced *Alive!*, which would become the greatest live album of all time, making KISS famous beyond anyone's imagination. If they'd listened to Clifford, then they would've simply hung on to the "twig" until the band went their separate ways, because they lacked sufficient evidence for how to move forward. Instead, they made a risky choice that led to success and the continuation of KISStory.

Goin' Blind

We make risky choices all of the time. You don't have to be the main character in "Detroit Rock City" to be in danger of dying in a car crash. Driving is the most dangerous activity people do every day, and the truth is most probably never even consider the dangers of driving. The danger KISS faced was not the zero-sum choice of dying while driving, but instead, there choice was a partial-sum choice of being a success, remaining underappreciated, or being a failure.

Blaise Pascal's wager offers a way to make choices in a partial-sum decision. Pascal wanted to show that belief in God was rational, and developed a decision-making procedure to show how it's not only rational but also leads to the best possible outcome. Pascal's wager suggests: Either God exists or doesn't exist, and either we believe or don't believe (see Figure 1).

FIGURE 1

Pascal's Wager	God Exists	God Doesn't Exist
Believe in God	Eternal reward	Nothing
Don't Believe in God	Eternal punishment	Nothing

Of course, this is a simplified version of the wager. If we were to add detail, we'd include Pascal's assumptions that belief in God creates certain advantages to life, even if God doesn't exist; while not believing in God allows for certain pleasures in this life that will be negated by the pain suffered during eternal punishment. Regardless of your religious leanings, Pascal's wager provides a decision-making procedure for how to make decisions about unknown future events, like God and the afterlife, and like how to proceed as a rock band.

KISS's wager was slightly different. After the disappointing sales of *Dressed to Kill*, KISS could've tried to record another studio album. Sure, it might have been the raging success for which they dreamed, but past efforts suggest it would've been another flop. With Casablanca's financial woes and tensions already mounting in the band, the most likely outcome is that KISS would've disbanded. On the other hand, a live album was something they'd never tried. History suggested a live album would flop, but due to the popularity of KISS's live show, there was the chance they would be the exception to the rule. Though reason suggests it wouldn't lead to success, a live album is cheaper to produce; and since it was something they'd yet to try, due to KISS's live success, it was possible a live album could generate enough revenue to keep Casablanca afloat, while also allowing KISS to keep recording (see Figure 2).

FIGURE 2

KISS's Wager	Studio Album	Live Album
Success	Stardom	Stardom unlikely, but could provide the cash flow needed
Failure	KISS disbands	Maybe record a new studio album, or disband

According to Pascal's approach, KISS made a calculated decision, one that could've led to their dissolution, continued recording, or success. With these options, the only logical answer was to record a live album. Spock would be impressed, but the different accounts offered about *Alive!*'s recording don't imply such a logical response. There was logic involved, but there was a lot more faith and hope involved—what might be called gut-intuition.

Pascal's approach can be helpful, but it omits the gut-intuition that goes into many of our decisions. It takes the particularities of each individual and replaces them with cold dogmatic logic. Hence, the reason Spock would be proud. There are times when cold dogmatic logic is helpful, but when writing music, betting everything by doing something risky, like recording a live album, or believing in God, one's gut-intuitions are often the best determiner of how to decide.

Don't get me wrong, KISS sometimes used an approach similar to Pascal: if KISS albums like *Destroyer*, *Rock And Roll Over*, and *Love Gun* are best sellers, then four solo albums by each member of KISS will all be best sellers. Wrong! One of the things we see in Pascal's Wager, especially when applied to the Prisoner's Dilemma is that greed and mistrust lead to devastating decisions. The Prisoner's Dilemma, it's the same sort of decision seen in Figure 1, except your choice is made in relation to someone else's decision. If you and a cohort are arrested for a crime, then both of you need only to remain quiet to be released. The worry is that your cohort will squeal on you, which means you go to jail and she is released. Greed and mistrust, then, lead you to the decision to squeal, and the same is true for your cohort. So, you both stay in jail. In the KISS solo albums case, everyone overlooked the signs that such an idea was a mistake, though it should've been obvious, especially since each album contained studio and guest musicians and not the original members of KISS who were part of the successful albums.

Nothing to Lose

The real issue with Pascal's approach is when applied to KISS it ignores the emotional, gut-intuitions of the band. From their initial choice to put on make-up, to their choice to release a live album, KISS relied on something deeper than Pascal's emotion-absent decision-making wager. William James noticed the same problem with Pascal's Wager. For James, both Clifford and Pascal get it wrong. Clifford's approach tells us to do nothing, since we can never have sufficient evidence for what is the right decision, while Pascal teaches us to have a dogmatic devotion to reason, which can lead us blindly down the wrong path. James, on the other hand, suggests a middle road, one where you spend time figuring out who you are and what you believe; and once you figure this out, you live as if you believe it!

James was one of the early developers of the philosophy known as pragmatism. James's approach was to see life as a narrative. Each of us has a narrative that begins when we're children and develops with every new experience. As we get older, we gain a clearer picture of our identity, and as we continue to live, everyday events sometimes support and sometimes challenge our identity.

KISS, with their emphasis on KISStory, illustrates this narrative approach much more than other bands. Think back to when they started experimenting with make-up, and if you believe Gene and Paul, began their journey to rock-'n'roll stardom. They had fun portraying different characters, it set them apart and they liked it, and it caught the attention of others. So, they made make-up part of their identity—their life-orienting story. They then added pyro-techniques and other gimmicks to their narrative and became the KISS we know and love.

Each time one of their decisions worked, it supported the narrative they wanted to create. They saw themselves as the "hottest band in the land," and eventually "the world," so they created a narrative that supported this vision. Not only did they create a vision, but KISS oriented their lives around these decisions. From the non-stop rehearing to releasing three albums in two years, they made stardom their meaning of life. They didn't sit around doing nothing or pondering the best possible choice for how to proceed, they acted with passion and conviction. So, when we think about the decision to produce *Alive!*, it seems like the natural progression of their narrative. They thrived in a live atmosphere, fans loved the show, and so the only logical thing to do according to their narrative was to roll the dice on a live album. It worked and continued to support the narrative that KISS is "the best."

James's pragmatism isn't all pie-in-sky, self-realization nonsense. He recognizes that philosophy is at once the most sublime and the most trivial of all pursuits. Philosophy "bakes no bread," but when applied to the concreate world of everyday life, it inspires and challenges us to flourish. For James, we should never ignore the "concrete reality" of our existence, which is tangled, muddy, painful, and perplexed; but we should also never forget the power we have over how we judge and feel the universe. In other words, three albums with disappointing sales might be our reality, but we must choose whether we quit or do something risky, like record the greatest live album ever. Of course, the same is true in the negative. Three best-selling albums might be our reality, but it doesn't mean we record four solo albums with all studio and guest musicians.

Several authors in this book have raised questions about the authenticity of several of KISS's decisions: did KISS sell out when they went "disco," recorded *Unmasked*, attempted a concept album, went hair-glam, went grunge, reunited, marketed a Kasket, and so on? Such theoretical questions remind me of the medieval theologians who pondered, "How many angels can dance on the head of a pin?" We could spend the rest of our lives debating whether and in what ways KISS sold out, but to do so misses The Message of KISS and of William James.

We each have a narrative—our life-orienting story—that tells us what is true and what is false. Yes, there are truths independent of our existence, like the number of studio KISS albums, but much of our life is simply us deciding what is true and false. If I believe God exists, then absent empirical evidence, I decide whether such a belief is true or false. The same would be true, if I were an atheist. I decide whether the existence of evil undermines a belief in God. I decide whether a horrible disease is consistent with an all-knowing, all-powerful, all-good God. I decide whether to accept orthodox teachings of the virgin birth, the trinity, and the resurrection are true or false. Of course, our beliefs should have some level of consistency, or we would be guilty of being poor critical thinkers or something worse, like immoral hypocrites.

According to William James, then, our beliefs are rules of action. If belief in God, or that KISS is the greatest rock band, ever, makes no difference in how I act, then the truth of such claims doesn't matter. The amount of angels capable of dancing on the head of a pin has no bearing in my life, and so, I should ignore debates that attempt to settle the issue. James wants us to consider the consequences for holding beliefs, and if no practical difference exists in regard to how we live our lives, then we shouldn't care about such beliefs. What if the belief means a great deal to your life-orienting story?

If you're reading this book, I assume KISS has some bearing on your life. Let's assume, as they do before every show, "You wanted the best, you got the best." To use James's terminology, your belief that KISS is the best is a living belief: it has practical implications for your life. Next, you must consider whether your belief that KISS is the best is forced or avoidable. If forced, then there's no way you can avoid making a choice, and if avoidable, then you can remain indifferent to the choice.

I guess for some, a belief in KISS being the best is avoidable; but for KISS fans, I see no way around deciding whether KISS is the best—however you want to define 'best'. This is especially true when we consider the last of James's considerations. Is belief in KISS being the best momentous or trivial? In other words, does it have great impact on your life or is it insignificant? Any KISS fan worth their weight in rock'n'roll will tell you a belief that KISS is the best is momentous, which also explains why such a belief is forced. Belief in KISS being the best is living, forced, and momentous and, therefore, a genuine option for how we live and orient our lives.

Now, back to the band. KISS has its own narrative about itself, which is one reason it makes sense to talk of KISS outliving its members. This narrative was something the band had early on, and it influenced fans and future members of the band. So, even though we might have different narratives about the actual events surrounding KISStory, the underlying theme is the greatness of KISS. As long as Gene and Paul—and anyone else involved in making big decisions for

KISS's future—were attempting to decide KISS's future in terms of the living, forced, and momentous belief that KISS is the best, then their decisions were authentic. No matter how strange, off-putting, ludicrous, risky, insensitive, or cheesy, as long as the belief in KISS being the best was the gut-intuition driving force, then they were following KISS's authentic identity.

The Greatest Band in the World

I've tried to show that William James offers a more complete explanation of how we as individuals live and make decisions, while also showing how pragmatism explains KISS's often risky career choices that have led to their greatness. However, I don't think James's pragmatism explains all aspects of KISS's identity and decision-making. For such an explanation, we need someone as over-the-top as some of KISS's antics. We need someone who would accept James's overarching principles of self-reflection and the living out of one's beliefs. We need the existentialist Friedrich Nietzsche.

Sometimes we simply don't know how to move forward when making life's big decisions. Clifford suggests gathering evidence, Pascal suggests dogmatic reason, and James attempts a middle road, where we choose based on the beliefs central to our life story. Sometimes, however, we find ourselves stuck. Should I leave my reliable job? Should I leave my partner? Should I follow my dream of being an actor, Broadway dancer, member of a KISS cover band? You can use every tactic in the world, every bit of reason and self-reflection, and yet, find yourself hanging from the twig of life— pondering the eternal death that awaits below or licking honey in a sad attempt to ignore your "fate." What do you do in these situations?

Nietzsche tells us to jump! For him, to be human is to be unspectacular, part of the herd, a slave ruled by other slaves. In light of this existence, Nietzsche argues that humans are a tightrope to greatness, and to achieve greatness we must be willing to risk it all in the face of death—and possibly, an eternal punishment of re-living our lives. To achieve greatness we are to live dangerously, walking the tightrope that leads to our own self-defined success, as though we're jumping from mountaintop to mountaintop. Yes, we risk much, but such a risk is more likely to lead to greatness than living as a timid deer in the woods.

So, when life gives you three bad records, do the unexpected and produce the greatest live album, ever. When life gives you success, do something crazy, like recording four solo albums without the band members that made the other albums successful. When you're struggling through the uncertainties of life, make a pop album, then a concept album, then a rock one, some hair metal ones, a come-back album, a grunge one, a couple more solo albums, and whatever else you want to do. Screw what everyone else thinks or wants. It's your life and it's your story. Only you can live it, so only you should decide the beliefs and actions that comprise your story. That's The Message and KISStory of the greatest band in the world.

Let's close with James's beautiful illustration from *The Will to Believe*, which might go well with a tune from one of your favorite KISS songs:

> Each must act as he thinks best; and if he is wrong, so much the worse for him. We stand on a mountain pass in the midst of whirling snow and blinding mist, through which we get glimpses now and then of paths which may be deceptive. If we stand still we shall be frozen to death. If we take the wrong road we shall be dashed to pieces. We do not certainly know whether there is any right one. What must we do? Be strong and of good courage. Act for the best, hope for the best, and take what comes . . . If death ends all, we cannot meet death better.

II

The Space Ace

6
The KISS Franchise

PETER FINOCCHIARO

I was driving down the highway, listening to a radio DJ interview Gene Simmons. At a certain point, the conversation turned to retirement. That's nothing new—Simmons has talked about retirement for years. But then he said something that shocked me. He said the band could go on without him. In fact, he said, the band could become a franchise. He then described a possible future where he managed an entirely new crop of musicians who would perform as the hard-rocking, fire-breathing, made-up characters we all know: the Demon, the Starchild, the Spaceman, and the Catman.

Sure enough, he's not the only one who has said this. Paul Stanley, the only other constant in KISS's history, has also said that the band could go on without him. He once compared KISS to a sports team, wondering why the band would need to stop when its original members leave. And back in 2005, KISS manager Doc McGhee compared KISS to Doritos and Pepsi. In a 2018 interview, he reiterated that point, though he changed the comparison from food to superheroes: "Is there a next generation of Superman? No, there's just fucking Superman."

I have to admit—I had a hard time understanding what Simmons, Stanley, and McGhee were talking about. The idea seemed ridiculous. KISS has never been shy about doing things that bands do not traditionally do. But never before in the entire history of rock has a band done anything even remotely like that. How could KISS be a franchise?

Let's find out.

Wooden Ships and Hard Rock Bands

There's an old philosophical puzzle involving a man named Theseus. Theseus (he's the guy who killed the minotaur) was revered by the people of Athens. According to legend, the Athenians preserved his ship as a memorial for hundreds of years. But the ship was made of wood, and one thing that wood does is rot. So, when a plank of the ship succumbed to rot, the Athenians had to replace it with a new, fresh, plank of wood. As time passed, the memorialized ship came to have fewer and fewer of the original planks and more and more of the new ones, until eventually it was made entirely of new planks. This caused some old Greek philosophers to worry. If the memorial ship was made entirely of new planks, was it really the ship that Theseus rode? If not, then just how many planks of wood could be replaced before the ship was no longer "the same" ship?

We can ask the same sorts of questions about rock bands. In this case, we're not replacing rotten planks of wood but rather members of the band. Bands do this all the time. KISS, in fact, has done it no less than ten times. The first time was in 1980, when KISS replaced Peter Criss with Eric Carr. Then, in 1982, KISS replaced Ace Frehley with Vinnie Vincet. Though these replacements were controversial, KISS seems to have survived. So, it seems, some bands can still be "the same" band after a single member is replaced. But how far into this process would that remain true? Could individual members of the band be replaced one by one until none of its original members remained? How long could that go on for? Could a band like KISS be like the Supreme Court of the United States, perpetually replacing its aging members for hundreds of years?

For that matter, what happens when the original band members get together? In 1996, Frehley and Criss officially re-joined the band (effectively replacing the new planks of wood with the originals). KISS then embarked on the 1996 reunion tour, recorded *Psycho Circus*, completed the original Farewell tour, and once again replaced Criss and then Frehley. KISS was reunited, and then it was not. No new philosophical puzzles there. But imagine if things had gone differently. Imagine if, by 1996, every original member of the band had been replaced, including Gene Simmons and Paul

Stanley. And now imagine that the original members had gotten back together and went on a reunion tour. In this imaginary scenario, there are two bands: one that lacks any of the original members but has a clear continuity of performing as KISS, and one that lacks any such continuity but does have the original KISS members. Which band is the *real* KISS?

When we ask which of the two bands is the *real* KISS, we are asking a question about the band's *identity*. But, as we've already seen, identity is a complex philosophical phenomenon. We should distinguish between *qualitative identity* and *numerical identity*. In a perfectly ordinary conversation, I might say that the shirt my friend wore to the concert was the same shirt I wore to the concert. What I mean when I say this is that they have the same features: they are both black, they are both made of cotton, they both list the dates and venues of the 1976 Destroyer Tour, and so on. My friend's shirt is *qualitatively identical* to my shirt. In another perfectly ordinary conversation, I might say that the shirt I wore to the concert is the same shirt my father wore to his last concert. What I mean when I say this is that, despite the decades-long wear-and-tear, the shirt I wore is the very same item my dad wore. The number of shirts worn by me and my dad is one; my shirt is *numerically identical* to my dad's shirt. These two senses of identity are importantly different. If I were to see you wearing a shirt qualitatively identical to my own, I would probably strike up a conversation about the coincidence—did your father also see KISS back in 1976? But if I were to see you wearing a shirt numerically identical to my own, I would demand that you give me back my shirt— my father gave me that shirt!

Sometimes, all we care about is qualitative identity. If I taste your French fries and decide I want some, I order my own. What I care about is the flavor, and the flavor of the new fries will (hopefully) be the same as the flavor of the ones I tasted.

But, more often than not, we care about numerical identity. If I order some fries and then eat the ones in front of you, I've done something wrong. You'd rightly be mad at me for eating *your* fries. What you own depends on numerical identity.

Similarly, *who* owns something depends on numerical identity. Only you own the fries that you ordered. Your identical twin does not own them. Consequently, only you can be mad about someone eating your fries. Your identical twin can at most be mad on your behalf. The same is true of rock bands. When KISS plays their last show, they will be playing *their* songs. When a tribute band (like Mr. Speed) plays those same songs, they are playing someone else's songs.

Let's return to our imaginary two-band scenario. In theory, the two bands can play qualitatively identical songs in qualitatively identical costumes with qualitatively identical pyrotechnics. In this way, the two bands can both be qualitatively identical to KISS. But the two bands cannot both be numerically identical to KISS. Imagine if both bands went on tour. Which band would be allowed to use the trademarked make-up and which band would be in legal trouble? More importantly, which concert should a KISS fan attend? The easy answer is: whichever band is numerically identical to KISS. But how do we determine which band that is?

All I've done so far is ask questions. Now let's try to answer them.

The Powers of Rock

Of course, rock bands are in some ways unlike wooden ships, concert shirts, and French fries.

Most importantly, bands do things: they write music, they go on tour, they break-up, re-unite, and retire. Bands do these things with purpose. When KISS performs a live set, they are not just mindlessly playing on their instruments. What KISS plays and how they play it is directed by what they are hoping to accomplish. To be more philosophical about it, we can say that bands perform *intentional actions*.

But, when you think about it, that sounds kind of weird. It seems like what makes an intentional action intentional is what the actor intends to be doing. From the outside, my purposeful practicing on my bass may seem indistinguishable from mindless noodling. (I'm not very talented, after all.) What makes these two actions different is a matter of what I intend to be doing. Yet "what I intend to be doing" is a matter of what is going on in my mind. It doesn't seem like we can say the same thing about the intentional actions of bands. What makes KISS's live performance of "Detroit Rock City" a *performance* rather than a massively coincidental sequence of noodling is what KISS intends to be doing in that moment. But what KISS intends to be doing cannot be a matter of what is going on in KISS's mind—KISS is a band; it doesn't have a mind!

Thankfully, we needn't say anything so weird to make sense of the intentional actions of a band. KISS does not have a mind, but it does have members who have minds. So, what is going on in KISS's metaphorical "mind" is determined by what's going on in the literal minds of its members, taken collectively. In philosophy, we call this "coming together" of individual minds *collective intentionality*. KISS's performance of the song is an intentional action because of what the members of KISS collectively intend to do.

Collective intentionality is a huge part of our lives. It lies at the foundations of music, sports, politics, and voting, and nearly every other social activity. And it seems to give us some straightforward answers to our philosophical questions about the identity of KISS. What a band does depends on what the members of that band collectively intend. So, if KISS retires, it will be because its members collectively intend to retire—as they have said they will do when the End of the Road tour finishes. Similarly, if KISS instead becomes a franchise, it will be because the members of the band intend to turn it into a franchise.

Unfortunately, these answers aren't good enough. In my imaginary two-band scenario, both groups of musicians intend to tour as KISS. But their collective intentions conflict. Each thinks that *they* are KISS and the other is not. They can't both be right! So, while the collective intentions of a band's members play an essential role in the story about what that band does, they do not fully explain what the band can and cannot do.

What Makes Gene Simmons Gene Simmons?

I promise I'm going to talk about the KISS franchise soon. But I want to talk about my imaginary two-band scenario a bit more. Trust me, this is going somewhere.

Let's take a more careful look at the two groups of musicians. They both have a historical connection to KISS's creation. But those connections are really different. Take the group consisting of Simmons, Stanley, Criss, and Frehley. The connection there is pretty straightforward. The members of this group are the original members of KISS—they are numerically identical to the four people that gigged in New York City, they are numerically identical to the four people that signed with Casablanca Records, and so on. To give this connection a name, let's call it the *originality* connection. The other group's historical connection is a bit more complicated. Because it has entirely new musicians, it doesn't have any direct connection to the original creation of KISS. But it does have an indirect connection because of its much smaller, direct connections over time. Take all of the days between KISS's first 1973 gig and the start of my imaginary 1996 two-band scenario. For each day, the band that calls itself KISS on that day has a direct connection to the band that calls itself KISS on the day before. Let's say that a band has a *continuity* connection to KISS's creation when these direct connections can be chained together to connect it to the creation of KISS.

So we have two kinds of connections: the originality connection and the continuity connection. Either seems like it would be, on its own, enough to prove that the band calling itself KISS is numerically identical to the band created in 1976. Conveniently, in real life they have never come into conflict. (That's exactly why I had to introduce an imaginary scenario.) But what would happen if the two connections *did* come into conflict? What's more important to KISS's identity: continuity or originality?

Philosophers fight about a similar sort of puzzle when it comes to people like you, me, and Gene Simmons. It seems like two things connect us to our respective creations: 1. our bodies, and 2. our psychologies—our personalities, memories, and beliefs. Ordinarily, these two connections go together. While Simmons's body has definitely changed over time, it's always been the same body. So, too, for his psychology. And his psychology has always been located, so to speak, where his body is located.

But they can come apart. There's no shortage of books, TV shows, and movies that describe how that might happen.

What should we say about these kinds of situations? What's more important to Simmons's personal identity: his bodily connections, or his psychological connections?

It's a really tough question! But it's also a really important question to answer correctly. The consequences of answering incorrectly are pretty bad. As we saw before, numerical identity determines a lot of the things we care about. If we make a mistake about Simmons's personal identity, then we might also make mistakes about his property, about his personal commitments, and about the ways in which he is or is not responsible for his actions.

I want you to notice something, though. The way that we tend to think about personal identity suggests that there is something there for us to *discover*. Reality has its rules. It might be hard for us to discover what they are—maybe it's even impossible for us to discover all of them. But the rules are there, regardless of whether we find them, and regardless of whether we care about them. So, when it comes to personal identity, there is some fact of the matter as to what the correct answer is. (Even when a medical commission offers a new definition of death, what they are trying to do is offer a more accurate description of when people actually die.) We do not get to "decide" when someone survives. We don't have that kind of power.

Perhaps that's true for people. But it's not true for bands.

The Creation of Social Rules

It seems as if the rules that scientists discover are unchanging and beyond our control. We don't get to decide how fast something falls. We can change how it falls by, for example, changing its shape. But all we have done there is change the conditions to which the rules are applied. The rules themselves remain the same.

Some rules, however, we create and have the power to change. When a professional NBA basketball team gains possession of the ball, they need to take a shot at the basket before the twenty-four-second shot clock expires. But basketball didn't always have a shot clock. Before its creation in 1954, teams could hold onto the ball indefinitely. That made for a really boring game where leading teams held onto the ball for far too long. So, to make the game better, we changed the rules of basketball.

We also create the rules of music. In the Western musical tradition, we divide the octave into twelve tones. We set our guitars to this standard, and as a consequence my friend yells at me when the sounds I produce do not fall within the acceptable limits set by this standard—in other words, my friend yells at me when I'm out of tune. But this musical standard is unlike the standards discovered by scientists. While there is a scientific foundation for music, the standards for what's acceptable are something we create. Just think about other musical standards. Arabic music divides the octave into twenty-four tones. What sounds good in the Arabic tradition may sound out of tune in the Western. Yet there is no scientific rule we can point to that would explain why one standard is better than another. They're just different sets of rules that we created that operate in different situations.

The rules that govern social activities determine what counts as doing that activity well. But they don't only do that. They also determine what counts as doing that activity at all. Basketball is a game of dribbling. As it stands today, any game where players run down the court with the ball in their hands simply isn't a game of basketball. Similarly, any music that does not predominantly follow the twelve-tone division of the octave simply isn't music that follows the Western tradition.

What Makes a Genre a Genre

We also create the rules that govern genres of music. The sound of rock is typically defined by its focus on electric guitars, electric basses, and drum kits. Not every rock song includes each instrument, of course. But a song that abandons all of three of them simply isn't a rock song. (Go ahead and try to find one that does—I'll wait.)

I believe that the rules that govern genres aren't restricted to just the genre's musical elements. Think about punk. Punk definitely has a distinctive sound. But punk is so much more than a sound. Arguably, for a punk band to be a punk band, it has to adopt a certain kind of anti-establishment attitude. So, even if the music KISS played sounded like punk songs, KISS would not be a punk band. Their brand is way too commercially successful. KISS coffee mugs and Christmas ornaments aren't punk. The KISS Kruise is about as antithetical to punk as it gets!

In general, social rules are set by the collective intentions of society. But philosophers disagree as to how those collective intentions are determined. Some social rules seem to be set through highly structured processes. The rules of basketball, for example, seem to be largely determined by the decisions made by members of official organizations like the NBA. But other social rules seem to be set through much less structured means. There are rules to fashion that determine what counts as "business casual" attire. But, even though it would be nice if we could settle the issue once and for all, no organization has the authority to set or change these rules.

I think musical genres have rules that are similar to those of fashion. But, unlike the rules of fashion, the rules of genre are set by a much more intimate process. Society as a whole does not have much to say about what genres of music there are and what they are like. (Just think about how many genres of metal most of the world has never even heard of.) Rather, the rules for genres of music are set by participants of that genre, including bands *and* their fans.

What Makes a KISS Franchise a Franchise?

Let's return, at long last, to the idea of KISS as a franchise. First things first: what does it even mean to say that KISS could be a franchise? It seems to me that there are two possibilities. Each possibility turns on a distinct way of understanding the relationship between the characters of KISS and the musicians that perform as those characters.

According to the first possibility, KISS is a band that consists of four characters, but those characters can be played by more than one musician over time. KISS has the Demon, the Starchild, the Spaceman, and the Catman (though, as the 1980s showed, there can be others). These characters are immortal. But the musicians who perform as them are not. So, according to this first possibility, KISS is a franchise in the sense that its identity depends on the identity of its characters, rather than the identity of its musicians. So, when

Gene Simmons ages and retires, he can be replaced by a new musician who will perform as the Demon.

According to the second possibility, KISS is a brand. That brand is currently represented by the band consisting of Simmons, Stanley, Eric Carr, and Tommy Thayer. The band "is" KISS in a way similar to the way that a bag of chips "is" Doritos. But there's nothing stopping KISS from expanding the brand to include another band that adopted the same characters. The newly franchised band could act as a replacement for the current band when it decides to retire. Alternatively, the new band could continue alongside the current band, touring elsewhere in the world in order to create a better, more KISS-filled world.

Both possibilities deviate from our normal understanding of KISS as a group of musicians. Nevertheless, I think that both could fit within the social rules that govern the identity of a rock band.

It's Up to the Fans

I've suggested that fans play a crucial role in establishing the rules that govern a genre of music. These rules include musical standards as well as standards of presentation. These standards determine whether a group of musicians is a good band or a bad band. These standards also determine whether that group even succeeds at being a band. In other words, fans help set the rules that determine facts about the identity of the bands they listen to.

Come back, one last time, to my imaginary two-band scenario. How do we determine which band is the real KISS? If the identity of a band were like the identity of people, then we would have to try to discover some deep, mysterious, philosophical truth. But bands are social objects governed by social rules that we create. We get to decide which band is the real KISS. There seems to be no fact of the matter right now as to which band would be the real KISS. But why would there be? Such a bizarre scenario has never actually occurred. If it were to occur, though, then we would need to decide. Given that both bands have an equal claim and nothing about what they do makes one of them a better candidate than the other, it is ultimately up to the fan base to decide who the real KISS is.

I think we should say something similar about the potential KISS franchise. Never before in the history of rock has a band changed its entire performing line-up. It's no surprise, then, if we don't know what to think about it right now. But it doesn't seem as if there is anything inherent to the rules of the rock genre that precludes its possibility.

Similarly, there doesn't seem to be anything stopping us from identifying a band with a group of characters rather than a group of musicians. (In fact, this possibility has potential precedents, including the virtual band Gorillaz as well as helmet-wearing electronic music artists.) The second franchise possibility would be harder to realize. There doesn't seem to be anything in the rules of rock that preclude there being multiple qualitatively identical bands. But we would have to create a new rule that groups these bands together under a common KISS brand. That's not impossible, but it does seem somewhat antithetical to the creative independence we typically expect of rock bands.

Rock is a popular and commercially successful genre. KISS has done a remarkable job capitalizing on its own success. Simmons's suggestion of updating the band with fresher (younger) talent seems to be the next logical step. Yet KISS does not set the rules on its own.

If—when—the time comes, its fans will need to decide: will they accept a KISS franchise?

7
Destroyer Unmasked

L.A. RECODER

Who would not like a philosophy whose germ is a first kiss?

—NOVALIS

KISS was a philosophical toy I picked up as a kid growing up in the late 1970s. Prior to welcoming KISS into my expanding universe of metaphysical playthings, Lego reigned supreme. If Lego awakened my powers of creativity through construction then KISS was the spectacular occasion whereby this nascent aesthetic detonated to blow up and thus radically expand my powers of creativity through destruction.

The pedagogical value of creative destruction immanent in playing with KISS between the ages of seven and ten (circa 1977–1980) was only possible for me on the precondition that the dialectical stage set ablaze by their pyrotechnics was already dormant though not recognized as such while contemplating the ruins of my Lego constructions deconstructed before putting the rubble back in the toy box. KISS provided the decisive plasticity.

But like all philosophical toys in the service of early mental development the discipline of enlightenment facilitated therein expires once mastered. At some point I stopped playing with my Lego set and KISS dolls. In short, the pole of creativity through destruction gained the upper hand to such a degree that it miraculously turned-round-upon-itself to destroy the toy of toys which introduced the agency of the destroyer in the first place.

Through the dialectical play of KISS I became not only a KISS Destroyer *but also a* Destroyer *of KISS.*

KISS! KISS! KISS!

In dusting off the old philosophical toy after nearly four decades in order to think, or rather rethink, through "KISS and Philosophy," I caught up on a sampling of the burgeoning KISS bibliomania and came across Ken Sharp's essential title *Nothin' to Lose: The Making of KISS (1972–1975)*. Essential for me first and foremost because the book's climax is the object *par excellence* of my first KISS, namely, the release of their 1975 double LP *Alive!* album.

Among the litany of oral histories featured I was particularly drawn to the more sensational recollections of being "blown away" by KISS during some of their earliest live performances. Blown away by KISS during this early phase becomes an absolute along the royal road to transcendental rock stardom the moment they begin to consistently upstage and ultimately destroy the headlining act. The monument of KISS as destroyer before the *Destroyer*, so to speak, is thus already set in stone in what founding band member Paul Stanley unveils as the "sonic souvenir" engraved in the grooves of *Alive!*

The highpoint for the destroyer is without a doubt the decisive battle over the title of heavy metal masters, dramatically captured by KISS's road manager J.R. Smalling—whose famous intro on the "hottest band in the land" kicks off *Alive!*—as follows:

> A half an hour after KISS left the stage, Black Sabbath's crowd is still chanting, "KISS! KISS! KISS!" They threw us off the tour. Ozzy [Osbourne] was man enough to come backstage and shake everybody's hand and say, "Man, any time the headline act can't hold their crowd that opening act must be a motherfucker. You guys are great."

So great was the destructive force of the "KISS! KISS! KISS!" incantation in the face of Black Sabbath that

Osbourne, according to Gene Simmons, was "spooked" by the experience and therefore took flight from his own spooky group. Whether we believe this haunted tale from the KISS crypts or not is beside the point. For spooky is indeed what is at stake in Sabbath bass player Geezer Butler's sublime KISS of death requiem as he describes the bloody procession and dance around the fire of the opening act, not to mention the terror of having to approach the altar to deliver the sermon of doom classics as headliners.

His shocking confessional that KISS "completely blew me away" is scandalous *in extremis* if we pause for a moment to reflect on the concept title for the 1975 album that Sabbath has just released and is touring at this fatal hour in the cataclysmic changeover of heavy metal masters: *Sabotage*.

Sabotaged by the KISS saboteur, Butler nonetheless survives his Sabbath bloody Sabbath. In fleeing from the gallows the following day, he runs into his executioner who initiates the first move in a curious game of seduction that gives us a glimpse into the ruling passions behind the transcendental make-up of the KISS destroyer. A surprising display of mutual admiration is exchanged in Butler's report where he learns that the bass player Simmons is an "admirer" of Butler's bass playing, which in turn prompts a reciprocal show of affection by revealing just how much he "loved" KISS's act. Exactly how much is not divulged. We can only speculate on the extent of the hyperbolic innervation among spooks as Butler's admirer reciprocates once more by flashing his notorious collection of "Plaster Caster" exposures.

The Making of KISSosophy

The KISS destroyer destroys not out of animosity but out of veneration, reverence even, for the object of destruction. A dialectical undercurrent informs Paul Stanley's exquisite formula for love which masquerades like a time bomb exploding onstage to unmask itself as the Janus-faced formula for destruction: "We had camaraderie with the other bands we played with, but it ended once we went onstage. We loved you until we strapped on our guitars, and then we were there to destroy you." (Final interview entry in the chapter "On the Radio" in *Nothin' to Lose*.) Here we have the key to the metaphysical mysteries of what will become the *Love Gun* masquerade unmasked as the legendary *Destroyer*, or, and as our title formulates it, the *Destroyer Unmasked*.

The encounter with members of Black Sabbath certainly puts both sides of this fundamental antinomy at the heart of KISS through the rigor. What we are left with is by no means destruction for destruction's sake but an encore—if not a bonus track—that plays itself out among the ruins left in the wake of the KISS destroyer. The attraction that makes Butler light up in the arms of his executioner and demon lover Simmons stems from the same reservoir of innervation unleashed in the sentiment that KISS "completely blew me away." The destroyer unmasked in these loaded words returns full circle to reload, or rather overload, and therefore revitalize the tenuous bonds of love in the rock arena.

How to become a KISS destroyer via the radical *Destroyer Unmasked* philosophy salvaged in the metaphysical battlefield of heavy metal masters is a lesson perhaps nowhere more comprehensively put into practice than in the case study of a guitar-wielding maniac Ted Nugent. Unphased by the specter of a threatening incantation throughout his set as opening act for KISS, Nugent was indeed blown away and destroyed *ad infinitum* but only to bounce back as destroyer far beyond his wildest dreams:

> I thought I was the baddest motherfucker in the world but when I saw the insanity level that these guys pumped into their show I went, 'Oh yea? Well, watch this.' I was challenged by that and there's nothing more important than that. I knew I couldn't settle for what I think is intense and outrageous because these guys are showing me a whole new level of intense and outrageous and I better turn up the fuckin' heat.

How I became a KISS destroyer as a kid growing up in the late 1970s approaches Nugent's clinical picture of rock star insanity set ablaze by the very essence of his innermost combustibility before the high alter of the gods of thunder. Turning up the fuckin' heat ripped right through the decade and into the next thanks to a rising legion of metal destroyers I embraced in my early teenage years such as Slayer,

Mercyful Fate, and Possessed. The levels of intense and out-
rageous stagecraft insanity reached their peak in the late
1980s with the formation of my own straight-edge hardcore
punk band—a rather short-lived venture which I offer here
in hindsight as the logical endgame for exacerbating, ex-
hausting, and ultimately mastering the explosive vicissi-
tudes of a subterranean KISS *Asylum* implanted by the sonic
souvenir of my first KISS.

Lord of the Wastelands

With this last thought on hardcore in mind, I repeat my
opening thesis: through the dialectical play of KISS I became
not only a KISS *Destroyer* but also a *Destroyer* of KISS.
Hardcore went the furthest in putting this thesis to work,
that is, with my Gibson SG guitar in hand and the compelling battle-of-the-bands type camaraderie I lived through
and which corresponds with the creative-destructive principle of the KISS destroyer according to Paul Stanley's lead.
Although I stopped listening to KISS shortly after the release of their 1980 *Unmasked* album the brutal rehearsals
of the *Destroyer* and its dialectical discontents discovered an
exciting underground venue in the hardcore of my power
chord riffage decked in the proverbial punk artillery of dis-
tortion and feedback aimed at blowing away countless headlining acts. (Harnessing the power of punk ultimately finds
its roots in Pete Townshend's "auto-destructive" shock rock
aesthetics which core members of KISS tacitly incorporated
early on in their pyrotechnic arsenal, including guitar-
smashing and ear-splitting dB levels approaching if not ex-
ceeding the sound of thunder.) At some point I stopped
playing straight-edge hardcore and became an experimental
film-maker. Is KISS still killing me softly?

To help us think through the legacy of the *Destroyer Unmasked* underground, I turn to the late death metal pioneer
and KISS ARMY veteran Chuck Schuldiner of the legendary
band Death (1984–2001). For this true metal icon is the shining paragon of my thesis. Conditions for the possibility of becoming a KISS destroyer and a destroyer of KISS abound in
Schuldiner's *curriculum vitae metallicus*. Speculation on the
following honorable mentions alone ought to further yield a

preliminary outline for drafting the official KISStory of death metal metaphysics: 1. Schuldiner's first KISS as a young kid growing up in the 1970s is the 1976 *Destroyer* album gifted to him by St. Nick, and 2. Death records a tour de force death metal riff on "God of Thunder" from the *Destroyer* album during the studio sessions for their highly acclaimed 1991 *Human* album and released as a bonus track exclusively on the Japanese reissue of the album a few years thereafter.

The guiding thought is that within this unprecedented case study in the philosophico-KISStorical continuum of Schuldinerian death metal, the KISS of Death turns-round-upon-itself and becomes the Death of KISS. The dialectical movement from the KISS of Death to the Death of KISS exquisitely performs what the Hegelian phenomenology of spirit famously introduced as the creative-destructive principle for historical change, namely, the experience of tarrying with the negative. Death metal metaphysics in Schuldiner's ode to the *Destroyer* tarries with its innermost negative buried in the spiritual holocaust of a cunning "God of Thunder." In tarrying with the "lord of the wastelands," the Death of KISS magically reverses and shatters the eternally spellbound KISS of Death issuing from the accursed doctrine of the soul haunting the chapel: "The spell you're under / Will slowly rob you of your virgin soul."

Death's phenomenological *Spiritual Healing* (title of their 1990 album) is nowhere more rigorously executed than in the penultimate 1998 masterpiece *The Sound of Perseverance*. Title tracks such as "Scavenger of Human Sorrow," "Spirit Crusher," "Voice of the Soul," "To Forgive is to Suffer," admirably persevere in the utterly severe resounding severance of souls spirited away by the "God of Thunder." "Spirit Crusher" memorializes the desecration of souls the furthest such that it grants voice to a soul survivor. What better way than to crush the *Spirit Crusher God of Thunder* than to rehearse to death with Death and beyond the spiritual hymn that promises to deliver us from the rock steady "spell you're under"? KISS is dead, long live KISS!

It comes from the depths
Of a place unknown to the
Keeper of dreams

Destroyer Unmasked

If it could then it would steal
The sun and the moon from the sky
Beware
Human at sight, monster at heart
Don't let it inside it could
Tear you right apart

No guilt, it feeds in plain sight
Spirit crusher
Stay strong and hold on tight
Spirit crusher

Speaking in killing words

The vicious kind that crush and kill
No mercy, its pleasure to taste
The blood that it bled

When it's time to feed to fulfill
The need to consume a breath
Some will rise standing tall
Breathing out all the breath from
The voice of a soul[1]

---

[1] Chuck Schuldiner, "Spirit Crusher" (Death), *The Sound of Persever-ance* (Nuclear Blast: 1998).

8
Philosophy and the Personae

RANDALL E. AUXIER

The secret is out. Bob Dylan's decision to put on white face in the Rolling Thunder Review was inspired by the KISS make-up.

Martin Scorsese's documentary has confirmed what was rumored for decades. And now we know the link. The natural path would have been Scarlett Rivera, who was Dylan's violinist and Gene Simmons's girlfriend, but no. It was Sharon Stone? You gotta be kidding me. But there she is in living color, with her KISS T-shirt, talking KISS and Kabuki with the ragged clown behind. That particular ragged clown, and his skipping reels of rhyme has been the inspiration for what I have to say here—calling it an "insight" seems a bit vainglorious, but hey, they gave him the Nobel Prize, so maybe the fact that the Nobel laureate ripped off a lick (which carries an interesting mental image) from Gene and Paul and the boys isn't all that interesting to KISS kids. Who the hell is Bob Dylan anyway? Sure, everybody rips off Dylan. But not really quite everybody. I can't find one single moment in the entire history of KISS (and their transformations) where I was thinking, "Hey, that's similar to Dylan." Except for, perhaps, the song Dylan actually *wrote* for Gene.

And the ironies cascade. They didn't even have a "Christian period" either, which is a welcome change. Most bands rip off Dylan somewhere somewhen, but in this case it went the other way. That's worth a beer. I think I'll have one if you don't mind. I need to get settled in to do this thingy I have in mind. You might want to get a beer too, or something stronger. You don't need fortification for this, you need a free mind, so, whatever does that for you.

Money?

Let's get this out of the way. KISS, by design, is surely the most commented upon band of all time, with the possible exception of The Beatles, which Gene admits was the reason he's doing what he does. The prospect of saying something new about KISS is bleak. Part of it is that the information and misinformation has always flowed in a Niagara of availability, turning the generators of fandom, and going caching often enough to make Roger Waters the prophet of profit. Let's just say: Money? It's a hit, and without the do-goody-good bullshit. The merchandising started with the concept of the band itself, as everybody knows.

If you Google the net worth of the band, you discover a hierarchy of sorts. Simmons, 400 million, Stanley, 200 million, and Kulick and Singer are tied for third at 15 million. Tommy Thayer follows at 10 million. Yeah, yeah you wanna know about Criss and Frehley, even though you can look it up as easily as I can. Well, a disappointing 3 million and 1 million respectively, according to Google, which never lies.

Google also says that Bob Dylan is worth 200 million, so the same as Stanley and half of Simmons. To say that there have always been winners and losers in this sort of endeavor puts a rather un-KISSish soft touch on the matter. (Don't even start looking up what Robbie Robertson did to his bandmates in The Band.) When it comes to KISS, we all know about the squabbles, and we all know who won, who lost, who kissed and made up. And speaking of making up, let me get to the heart of the matter. The money hierarchy provides me with my structure.

Personae

Let me say first off, I love cats and I have nothing against NASA. The recurring characters in the long opera are cool. And the other personae that strutted and fretted for an hour here and there are fine by me too. But, following the money, and other paths yet to be revealed, it becomes clear that this show is not about those other guys. Gene says that the band was designed to be a democracy, but it just didn't work that way: "The truth was that Ace and Peter simply were not qualified to make decisions about band matters that depended on organization and structure. They were not willing to put in the time to think things through" (*KISS and Make-Up*, p. 80). It didn't end up being a democracy, but I think it wasn't unfair.

The money differential (if that website is to be trusted) would tend to confirm Gene's view. Ace and Peter certainly made a lot more money than they have now. But it looks like Gene and Paul really tried to pull them along. And there was respect for the creative moment. Even when Gene confirmed that KISS, Inc. owned the Spaceman persona, when they put on the make-up again after being unmasked for over a decade, Ace complained and Gene and Paul respected it and reached elsewhere for ideas. Everybody seems to agree that it didn't suck, but it wasn't the same.

We all know the story about how the band members chose their own personae and that each was supposed to, in some way, say something about them personally. It wasn't wholly original. The New York Dolls were wearing make-up (and Peter was a childhood friend of Jerry Nolan, their drummer). Alice Cooper was already doing his schtick. Slade had made its mark, especially in Gene's mind. Glamrock was in the offing. Led Zeppelin was choosing symbols for their fourth album at about the same time. Our boys were considering themselves, considering their big idea, and trying to graft a persona on their existing traits. It worked. Big time.

Why?

I want to say unequivocally that the supporting actors don't matter in the KISS Kabuki Opera, even if their personae did, well, support. Only the Demon and the Starchild make any final difference to the tale, as history has demonstrated. But there is something in the Catman and the Spaceman that did something.

Paul says that when the fans come out in droves, it's to see the *characters* they created, not the actors playing those characters. He says he is replaceable, and that even gives him a thrill. I think I can agree that we come to see the characters. But I think he is wrong about being replaceable. Gene isn't replaceable either. Peter, the most often and completely replaced persona, apparently said: "No matter who they get to put stuff on their face, it ain't us." But I think that only extends so far. The truth must be in the middle of replaceability and irreplaceability.

Yes, we knew their real names all along. Well, their stage names anyway. I mean, Jesus (or more precisely, Holy Moses), Chaim Witz, and Stanley Eisen? It just doesn't sing. And who can even spell Peter's real last name? But that real name stuff didn't matter either (as they learned during the unmasked period). So we have three levels. The people, the actors, and the personae. The people these guys are became the characters they portray, and that was a process. It didn't happen all at once, and in some ways they improvised, in other ways they envisioned it. It was more than luck and less than fate. Ah, yes, now there we have a couple of concepts we can work with.

So why did it work? If it wasn't fate but more than luck? There was something ancient and something new in this. What drew us in was the Demon and the Starchild. My thesis. Both personae aged gracefully, doing slightly better than the human bearers of those masks (with their maladies and hip replacements). The connection of KISS to Kabuki has been observed, then written on, then analyzed, then sliced, diced, made into Julien French fries, eaten, shat, and then re-cooked for re-digestion. The same may be said for Japanese comic books. So that's something ancient and something new.

Let's not do that, especially since my ignorance of Kabuki and Japanese comics is pretty impressive. But the thing that I observe that has been less well digested has to do with above and below, with the heavens and the hells, and with the demons and angels that populate each. Yes, you had better be careful about what comes from the airy places if you are a mere mortal dealing with those ethereal Kami. And be sure that the fiery demons aren't always bad guys. There is a delightful ambiguity in the Japanese cosmologies. I want to bow to the heavens and the hells, but I am looking for something human in it.

A Method to This Madness

Let's think about that. When Aristotle had a philosophical question, such as "Why?" he had several methods he liked to employ. Some of these methods are too fancy for us. But two are not. The method of the "wise and the many" is easy enough. You check to see what most people say, and then you check to see what the wise ones say, and you assume that each has good reasons for saying what is said. As I said, the many have been chattering ceaselessly for almost five decades. It's easy to find out what they think. The wise have been less often consulted. I'm going to consult them.

A second method Aristotle liked to use was the *"aporia."* This is a Greek word that translates as "puzzle." Now, I don't know Greek (or Latin for that matter), but I was taught to use Greek words to impress people. It's a part of my persona. Does aporia really mean puzzle? I have no idea, but I do know what a puzzle is, and I am going to approach this "Why?" question as a puzzle. This puzzle has four pieces, as you might imagine. There is a demon, a starchild, a catman, and a spaceman. In that order. They aren't all the same size. They vary by about the proportion of current wealth held by the people who have been the actors playing these characters.

Puzzle Piece Number One: The Demon

I Am a Demon and Nothing Demonic Is . . .

. . . alien to me. Terence said it. Sort of. In Latin. I have adapted it to Gene and his persona as I understand them. That continuity between the men and their personae is a pivot point, and it was always intended to be that way, but let's also not be hasty in taking one for the other. Gene is only sort of a demon. He is unconventional to the point of disturbing.

As we all grew up (to the extent we ever did), we came to understand that Gene needed to shut up sometimes, but the Demon, on the other hand, never needed our advice, and maybe that is because he sees some things we don't—ugly things. Gene, for his part, sees them in several languages, including the languages of a couple of nations that Hitler tried to exterminate. For both Paul and Gene, this part is personal. They both lost family to the Camps. But there is a difference even there. The Demon sees these things in a more universal language, one not so sympathetic to human weaknesses. Let's see if we can tease out *his* viewpoint—the Demon within Gene, I mean.

First, some differences, some irregular curves in the puzzle piece. Gene is an Israeli as much as he is an American, and his losses were closer to the bone, and the flesh and blood, than Paul's. Gene's very mind (I would say soul, but he may not have one, in his own opinion) was formed in the struggle of Israel to exist (and I am going to stay as far as possible from the politics). *But,* I have been there myself, and I have seen first-hand how complicated the struggle is in the Holy Land. I do not take sides. It just isn't my struggle. But I have also spent a lot of time abroad, both in places that were devasted by Hitler and places that were home to Hitler.

Why do I bother you with this autobiographical trivia? I had to learn something firsthand that I never would have understood if I didn't travel a lot. Anyone who travels a lot for long periods is going to recognize what I'm saying. KISS travels a lot, but for Gene, it's way beyond just traveling. With him it's a native difference. We come to see and understand America in a different way when we spend enough time outside of it—especially if we're not locked within the English language, as Gene most definitely is not. I think that a lot of the things Gene says make a lot more sense if you have *his* context. He is a cosmopolitan. And a demon. He takes a dim view of human nature. And he pities humanity.

The things Gene says that piss everybody off actually make sense to me (mostly), even when I don't agree. He loves America, but he sees it more clearly than most people who have spent their lives here, speaking only English. He sees endless opportunity, courage, creativity, freedom, and a list of other things that most Americans either take for granted or even denigrate when they are feeling guilty for our endless greed, selfishness, misuse of freedom, and hollow bravado.

For Gene there's a justification for wanting to be rich, a virtue to selfishness, a license with freedom, and the bravado, well, that's what makes him spit blood and breathe fire, and I, for one, am not going to do those things, especially the second one. Most Americans just aren't like Gene. I feel ambivalent about our American sins in a way he clearly doesn't. I want us to use the opportunity, the freedom, blah, blah, blah, only for good. And that brings us to where Gene overlaps with the Demon.

The Demon in Gene says "Fuck you, Chaim, I'm about power, sex, money, and everything the depraved humans really want, and you give me permission to be what I truly am every time you put on the make-up." Chaim says, "You don't know shit; I've seen it all, and you're my bitch." Gene says, "fellas, fellas, let's play some music, make lots of money, have sex with five thousand women, and live this life by our own lights." Frankly, the Demon is just as capable of ordering the Holocaust as of playing the bass. It is not Chaim Witz, or even Gene Simmons, who bedded five thousand women, it is the Demon. The Demon is quite beyond good and evil.

Sex and the Family Man

I think Shannon Tweed is probably married to Gene, not to Chaim or the Demon. Ask her for me, if you see her. She has the Succubus for an alter-ego after all. (Man I used to drool over those movies.) Heaven knows how many men that Demoness has bedded. More than a few, I'd wager. And why would that bother Gene? *Shannon Lee* (the person) probably sleeps only (or mainly) with him and *Gene Chaim* sleeps only (or mainly) with her, and they have real kids and a house, in addition to the kids and house depicted in their television series, but Gene and Shannon (*sans* Lee and Chaim) have another side that understands (and sometimes does) what the humans really want.

I am reminded of the question Billy Joel asked: "Did you ever let your lover see The Stranger in yourself?" Billy, with his standard New York, American Jewish guilt assumes the answer is "No." Gene says? Well, I'm imagining: "Of course! Shannon loves that shit. If you had been a little bit braver, Billy, a little less guilt-ridden, you might still be with Christy. I had a Jewish mother too, you know." (Gene has been known to be an asshole.) But here is the point. A great part of what made Gene the rich and famous man he is comes down to not being inhibited in the way most people are—even Paul looks pretty Vanilla by comparison.

Progress!

And there we have the first piece of the puzzle. Gene Simmons is an uninhibited cosmopolitan. These are not so common in American Rock Music. The uninhibited is more common than the cosmopolitan, but seeing the American Rock fan *as we are* is a big part of the trick. Gene knows what we want to see but don't really want to do, where that line is when everyone becomes a voyeur. We want to live in the light but watch what they do in the shadows. He also sees what we don't see about ourselves. He pities us, but not enough to indulge our over-weaning guilt. I note that Shannon is not an American either. Holy cod, Newfoundland? How did she ever get rid of the accent? And then Saskatoon? It's like Bismarck, only much colder and quieter; but, well, uninhibited, somehow. Met Gene at the Playboy Mansion. *Cosmopolitan* probably came during her long residence there.

Kami to Kabuki to Comics to KISS

We're almost done with the biggest piece of this puzzle. But something more about Japan has to go here. Paul remarks that when KISS got to Japan, it was like their comic-book heroes had come to life. There is a direct line traceable from Japanese traditional religion, to Kabuki, to Japanese comics, to KISS. Even though none of the personae was directly based on any particular comic book or Kabuki character, or any of the Kami, these personae really resonated with Japanese audiences, especially kids.

And here we come to the sticky part. Kids. KISS has always been fascinating to kids of all kinds. I don't think anyone in the band ever planned this, but they recognized it and embraced it. This kid-appeal has regenerated the band's audiences in ways that have to be the envy of other stars with their aging followers. Kids still just love KISS, no matter how old the fellows get.

Now, the Japanese are bad about sexualizing kids. I mean, it happens everywhere, but for the Japanese there is this creepy thing connecting it with their folk religious history, their weird fascination for the West, and their issues with power and suffering and torture. Gene says some things I wish he hadn't said about this. I am too squeamish to describe it, so I'll let him speak for himself.

> The girls in Japan were also wonderful, very willing, and very available. The interesting thing about Japanese women, in my experience, is that they have a little girl quality, a certain innocence about their sexuality. *Coquette* is a French word, and that concept just doesn't exist in Japan, at least as far as I saw. For instance, when Japanese girls orgasm, a peculiar sound emanates from them that sounds almost like a baby crying. (*KISS and Make-Up*, pp. 133–34)

I'm sorry, but ewwww. Not the facts. I think most grown men (and many teenage boys, and a lot of women) are aware of what Gene is describing. This is the age of the Internet. It's the *way* he describes it. He makes a comparison to babies, and finds this "interesting," and is speaking from his own "experience." My point is that something further is going on here than demonic cosmopolitanism. There is a sort of detachment, an apartness. It's like he is studying us. Is that Gene or the Demon?

Engaged detachment. Of the "Christie Sixteen" variety. Didn't strike me as all that creepy when that song came out. But then, I was only eighteen. I heard it upset a lot of people. Didn't think it was that great a song anyway.

J-Pop

So, KISS doesn't collaborate. Until they do. Of course. Business is business. One thing that really is different about this piece of the puzzle is that Chaim Witz (think of *him* what you will) is and always was a genuine comic-book nerd, and among his favorite flavors is Japanese. Lots of red-blooded American nerds love Japanese comics, and apparently some Israeli-Americans as well. The massive industry that has grown up around Japanese (often twisted) fantasies has been booming since Godzilla. Chaim was into this early. But it wasn't common in his generation like it is now.

The grown-up Chaim, in the process of becoming Gene, realized that some American bands got famous-er, outside the US, where the record companies were not so powerful and conservative. A few yen is as good as a buck or two. Numerous bands during this period got famous-er abroad, and then came back to the US with a vengeance—Jimi Hendrix,

Tom Petty and the Heartbreakers, and Cheap Trick come to mind. KISS certainly managed to poke their heads up without the help of Japan. Their first live album was pre-Japan for the band, if not exactly for Chaim and Gene. But arguably, Japan made them all what they became, in more ways than one.

There's a serious risk, with both kids and Japan. With kids, they outgrow what they liked and take on a certain shame over their foolishness. They don't want to remember that they had Donny Osmond posters on their walls. But some performers—not Donny Osmond or The Archies—such as Michael Jackson and Prince managed to appeal to kids and hold on to their coolness as the kids matured. So one has to navigate that thin line between pre-teen and early teen fandom, and remaining cool for adults. And here is where Japan helps. Apparently, like the coquette's absence (and Gene is sharp to notice this), Japanese kids are less likely to turn against their earlier selves. They are more at peace with the silliness of their youthful fandom and unashamed of that delicate relation between childhood and sexuality, and coolness.

So, one can see the barometer being built: if Japanese kids like something, chances are that, deep down, so do other kids, once they are liberated from all this guilt that the Western morality heaps upon them. They want to be liberated to love what they loved as kids, and it includes sexual liberation, *early*, and it's a dark secret. The sexual character of the comic books used to be more concealed than it is today, but less so in Japan. It is something Chaim surely noticed and remembered. The kids want a superhero, and superheroes have superpowers, and the Demon is a superhero.

Now the risk with Japan, and with letting that be your barometer: some would-be heroes went abroad and had to stay because they never really managed to capture the expected attention or boost back in the US. Elliott Murphy comes to mind. Rose to pre-stardom in New York, became famous in Europe, and finally had to move there to make a living. It's bit like baseball or basketball. The road from Texas to Tokyo is a lot shorter than the road from Tokyo back to Texas. You go over there, you may have to stay if you want to keep your professional career. But Gene was confident, other-worldly confidence, that his Demon would transcend the pigeonhole.

Nietzsche

I have consulted the many, so now a word on the wise. Considering what we have learned about Chaim/Gene/the Demon, was there ever such a philosopher? There was. Friedrich Nietzsche (1844–1900) was an uninhibited, cosmopolitan superhero. He wrote *Beyond Good and Evil*, and attacked everything in Western morality that tore down the deeper and more powerful (and more natural) human being within us: the true man, who wanted power because it is good, not something to be ashamed of. He wanted excellence, he wanted us to overcome our sniveling Christian guilt and become what we are. He wanted us to love our fate, to look into the abyss until it looked back, and to stand on the edge of our very mortality and find an aesthetic justification for our lives. He hated nationalism and anti-semitism, and he was regarded as satanic by millions of people. But he dreamed of a superhero he called the Overman.

And Nietzsche was a fine musician and a good (if not great) songwriter—like Gene. He wrote an autobiography, boldly entitled *Ecce Homo*, which is what Pontius Pilate said to the crowd while pointing at Jesus: "Behold the man." That book of Nietzsche's has subsections like "Why I Am so Wise," "Why I Am so Clever," and "Why I Write Such Excellent Books." Gene has a chapter called "Tonight I am a Legend," and the earliest picture in his autobiography has him holding a hammer, with the caption "For some reason I loved hammers." The subtitle of one of Nietzsche's books is *How to Philosophize with a Hammer*.

Nietzsche was, in short, Gene Simmons. Or the Demon in any case. Nietzsche said that what goes around comes around, an eternal return, and has a demon whispering in your ear "What if you had to live exactly the moment you are living now for all eternity?" Well? I hope you got something stronger than a beer. I actually had a bloody mary. Extra hot sauce. Go figure.

Like Gene, Nietzsche was uncommonly detached. He was studying us. Like a Demon would. With interest. And a few plans. But this *detachment* will come up in the next part, and the next, and the last. And it becomes the very point.

Puzzle Piece Number Two: The Starchild
A Decent Wine

But I'm switching to white wine now. Things will get a little more reserved, so a good estate reserve should be right. I've been saving this bottle a while. The aesthetics matter here.

The SS

Paul designed the KISS logo, based on some ideas Ace had sketched. Ace's sketches really did use the lightning bolts of the Nazi SS. Paul altered them, although not enough to suit his father, and not enough to keep the logo from being banned in Germany. And this brings us to a point about Paul that really is different from Gene. Paul knows what looks cool. He just isn't the sort to overthink something when he can see it looks good. He says that he just didn't really understand until he was much older what the big problem was with the logo and the way the S's were stylized (See *Face the Music*, pp. 118–19). We will revisit Ace at the end.

I'm not supposed to say this, but since we all know it, I will. Paul is good looking, *very* good looking. Gene, not so much. Ever. (And I am being gentle.) Peter and Ace, well, they stairstep down from Paul to Gene, if you get my image. And I don't know about you, but being a lot more like Gene than like Paul myself, in this regard, I have noticed that good looking people tend to notice, care about, learn about, and cultivate how things *look*. But for Stanley Eisen (let's call him Stan), who was trying to become Paul Stanley, the acquiring of these highly attuned aesthetic sensibilities about how things look did not come in through the front door. It was the side door, the right side door, of his head.

But first, a bit more about good-looking people. I mean, why not use what you've got? It is impossible not to notice that in his late sixties, Paul looks, well, very good. He has really kept himself fit and sexy, and that, folks, requires discipline. That shit doesn't happen by itself. It has always been fortunate for Gene that the band made it with make-up on, which

Paul didn't need (although he wore it very well). By the time anybody knew what Gene actually looked like, it didn't matter. It would be easy to think that Paul just breezed into his persona, but that isn't anywhere close to being true.

Paul and many others have written about this, but he was born with a really noticeable birth defect. He had microtia, which means that basically he had an ugly lump where his right ear should have been. It affected his hearing, which got corrected pretty early, but it absolutely determined his personality. He was born in 1952. Men and boys weren't allowed to wear their hair over their ears until about 1967. Stan was fifteen before he could cover his defect. We were talking about the balance between fate and luck, and here you have Exhibit A. If Stan had grown up as good looking as he became, we wouldn't have KISS. I will explain.

The Spitting Image

Paul tells of how he was always being stared at as a child, and how he developed a set of perceptual defenses, learning to see and not see, in response. He came to be someone who could see through and see past, and to understand the wide gap between how people see things and how they really are. He knew what it was like to be a "thing" as he puts it. He was not popular, not desirable, not cool, and certainly not good-looking. But he wasn't one to pity himself.

When he was five, another kid actually spat on Stan and called him awful names. Stan went home and told his mother. He thought she would call the kid's mother, force him to apologize. I admire Stan's mother. She said, "Don't come crying to me, Stanley. Fight your own battles." Seriously? Paul wrote, in italics: *"Fight my own battles? I'm five! I don't want to hurt anybody. I just want people to leave me alone"* (*Face the Music*, pp. 15–16). Holy shit, that sucks. Stan, in addition to having an uncool name, had a super-rough go of it. The stories will make you cringe if you have an ounce of compassion.

Ugly People

So, I won't wait so long to unveil the philosophical punch in this part of the story. Plato had Socrates say, in the immortal

Republic, that the only way a golden soul could ever become a philosopher was to have a defect. Socrates was famously ugly. Plato was no supermodel. And we, who are more frog-like and less godlike, have always consoled ourselves with the idea that beautiful people never get to be as deep and self-aware as we do. That smells like bullshit. But what of the changelings? Stan became Paul, and was such a being. When he became a rock icon, Stan-now-Paul couldn't believe he was so suddenly an object of desire, that girls were lining up to sleep with him.

Paul enjoyed it, but it didn't go to his head. It was too late. His soul was already formed under the conditions of detachment, of being thingified, of being alone and beyond. Paul's instincts were always communal—it pissed him off that in early interviews Gene kept saying "I-I-I" when Paul's basic nature was to say "we." But, as long habit had counseled, he ate the anger and pushed forward. Eventually Gene would have to accept Paul's viewpoint as equally valid, even if that came at the cost of the Catman and the Spaceman. Paul was smart, and he *did* have the discipline to think through things that required organization and structure.

Starchild Aesthetics vs. Demonic Morality

Those little Japanese girls probably favored Paul over Gene by five to one. I'll bet the most "interesting" ones favored Gene, but let's not go there. With the boys, I'm guessing it was the other way around. It certainly was in *my* neighborhood. We boys paid almost no attention to anyone but Gene. What would *he* do next? We may have wanted to be Paul, but Gene was safer for open praise, very manly, very unthreatening to our sexual identities as we were trying to be manly, like our fathers, who fought those ugly wars. But clearly the aesthetic was born of Gene and finished out by Paul.

Paul was the experimenter. He would try this, that, the other, and check for a response. Then he would hone. How big should the star be? He says that Neil Bogart, their manager from the record company, urged him to replace the star with a Lone Ranger or Zoro mask because the star was, well, too gay. Paul listened, experimented, played one show with a maskish make-up and said, and I quote, "Fuck this." He understood that he looked gay and didn't give a shit. He knew who he was, and what's the big deal anyway? So what if the queer ones found it exciting. As he put it, the people responded to the star and the star it would be. This is about the look, not the moral message. Androgynous works, aesthetically.

Detachment?

So what is this, in the puzzle, that enables Paul to be detached and engaged at the same time? I think that Socrates is right in saying that there is something about being the deformed one, the one-eared monster in Paul's case, that sets a person outside of fear. They have already done to you the worst they could do. You are a thing, an object, a monster. But you love music and you can play this guitar, and you can sing, and you can write, and they can't hurt you, and you want to be loved, and you want to be left alone. Your life is about the free cultivation of appearances, and you know the stable realities are not threatened by those appearances.

So, sipping my wine, I ask myself, "Who in the history of philosophy saw the world like that?" There was a guy. Epicurus was his name, unpolitical, lover of beauty, and music, creator of welcoming spaces, embracing the transience of existence, and thumbing his nose at fate. Paul's kind of freedom is *ataraxia*, which is freedom from fear, and peace of mind. That was the ultimate goal of Epicurus.

And secondly, there is *aponia*, the absence of pain. Pain is a given in mortal life, but it should be less rather than more. You have to embrace death, finitude, to gain this kind of happiness. Read his autobiography. Paul is so totally okay with his mortality, his limits, and the way that life goes on. *Therapeia* is also an Epicurean idea—therapy. Paul is devoted to it. See below. You can see that the "child" in Starchild is earned—he has managed to remain the child he was, while growing into the man he wanted to be, the star.

So Paul's detachment is a kind of calm, of peace, and of *joi de vivre*. He wouldn't see the world this way if he hadn't fought through his childhood, ostracized, deformed, learning to see how things really are against the way they appear, and deciding on beauty and friends and the transient good things about life. So, yes, he's good looking, but he is disciplined and focused on long-term, sustainable pleasures that come with being beautiful, and calm, and alive. I'm inferring this both from his way of telling his own story (a great fucking read), and from what he accomplished, and from what others say about him. I would have a longer conversation with Gene, but a better drink with Paul. You would too. You are reading a philosophy book. You are deformed, but you are not like . . .

Puzzle Piece Number Three: The Catman

A Couple of Shots

Before we move into a brief discussion of Catmen and Spacemen, let's share a couple of shots and see how close we are to an answer about why KISS succeeded so spectacularly. I have that vodka I was using for the bloody mary. It's cheap but it does the job. I wonder whether the Demon might have been able to use a high-end pure grain alcohol instead of kerosene. Yuck. Kerosene. Tastes like, well, hell. They say it's good for you in small amounts. Like everything else, I suppose.

Okay, so we have an uninhibited cosmopolitan Demon, who performs about the way Nietzsche philosophized. We have in the Starchild an aesthetically supercharged lover of humanity, life, and love who performs about the way Epicurus philosophized. They are superheroes. And we have kids. And sex. And rock music. Not necessarily in that order. I note that drugs are generally missing from this picture. That may have something to do with the longevity of these two superheroes, but it isn't the reason it worked. It may be the reason things didn't work out for the Catman and the Spaceman, as Gene reports.

One thing does begin to stick out: these guys are tough, emotionally, and tend to the calm (ataraxic) side of temperament. They are smart too. Obviously. And these things together give them an extraordinarily strong and centered sense of self. These guys know who they are and who they are not. They are able to compartmentalize Chaim/Gene/ Demon and Stan/Paul/Starchild. They know where the play ends and the work starts, they are disciplined, talented, and this power of centering and *seeing what's next* is their real superpower.

Some of the moves they made looked crazy at the time, but it seems like they never made a misstep. They knew when to show their faces and when to conceal them, when to go to Japan and when to come back. They exude confidence on stage, but that was an achievement for Paul where it was a native gift for Gene. And they are edgy, open, and experimental.

But their success was about the fans, always about the fans, always about knowing what we wanted. My first KISS album was the first *Alive!* Like so many other kids (well, I was fifteen). I faithfully lined up to buy every album, and yes, all four solo albums, proudly. I joined a band and tried to understand how to create the magic. It's hard.

But I do remember singing, over and over, playing my bass guitar in the clubs, what is still my favorite line, when Rick Neilson paid KISS the ultimate homage. He describes his own parents making mad passionate love on the couch while playing *his* KISS records. At first, when I heard "Surrender" I thought "ewwwww," but as time has gone on, well, I think that's the secret. It's about overcoming puritanical guilt and letting yourself enjoy life. How many KISS kids can *now* well imagine the scene depicted in that Cheap Trick song? I'm old enough to be a grandfather, and I'm a KISS kid. Of course, the weird part was that Rick's parents were of the World War Two generation, so the magic even goes backwards.

Take another shot with me. Everybody wants good sex. We just need to be relieved of our shame. And here you have a Demon on your left shoulder whispering about the eternal recurrence of the present moment, and a weird sort of angel on your right shoulder, whispering in the misshapen ear of your guilt that love is good and you're not a bad person when you love something for how it appears, so long as you also look deeper into what it really *is*. And both of them are saying, use your free will, but take care of yourself if you want to keep rocking into old age.

That, friends and neighbors, is why it worked to begin with and why it kept working, and why it still works. They know what we want to hear and they play it for us and they shout it out loud. Life's a party, don't miss it. On the other hand, it takes a peculiar power of detachment to recognize all of this, and to choose to engage the world on one's own terms, and not being driven into life on the terms the world offers. Not many people are able to do this—and win.

Beth

Cats. My absolute favorite beasts. I have four. Or they have me. Peter chose rightly. Cats do not care about yesterday and they don't care about tomorrow, but otherwise, they are all different. Paul says that he knew Peter would be their drummer the instant he heard Peter *sing*. Now that is an interesting criterion, for a *drummer*. But in fact, Paul was, as always, aesthetically correct. Anybody could play the drums. Only Peter sings like Peter. Well, Peter and Rod Stewart. The highest charting song for the band was "Beth," and even if Peter really had no part in writing it (as Paul says), it doesn't matter. He delivered it.

Gene didn't want that song on the *Destroyer* album. It wasn't a KISS-type song. It was a risk. Vulnerable, sweet-sounding. Orchestra. But look at the message. "I'm not coming home. I'm married to the music." There has never been a serious, or even semi-serious, male musician who didn't endure a girlfriend (or wife, or boyfriend—ask Elton) like Beth. The music is what makes them fall for you and then they want to try to *compete* with it. But that's not how it works. It's not a competition, although it is true that the music comes first and you're a close second, at best. Give it thirty or forty years, and I'll mature, *some*.

Gene relented, and I have little doubt it was a business decision. But at some level, he must have seen that "Beth" *is* a KISS song, and that it's because the Tomcat sings it (I know it's supposed to be "Catman," but Peter got that one wrong). This yowling for the mate is not Demon or Starchild stuff. This is Tomcat-out-all-night stuff. And Peter yowls well, all hoarse from shouting it out loud, and comes home a little battered. That song saved the sales of *Destroyer*, and the fans (including me) were a little stunned upon first hearing, but hey, it's a great fucking power ballad, minus the power. Excuse my language. I've been drinking. I had better quit soon. (Writing, not drinking.)

The official video for "Beth" is quite a study. Gene is clearly pretending to be pissed off at this interloper, trying to break in the band's scene and make a "good husband" of *his* drummer. I'm not sure how pissed he is at this moment, but every rock musician I know (the small-time ones like me) has been in a band with a dude whose chick was manipulating him this way. My band ended up canceling a six-month touring contract, literally as we were pulling out to go from Memphis (which was home) to Tucson, because our drummer's girlfriend said she wouldn't be waiting for him when he came back. The level of pissed off that this situation breeds is difficult to describe. So I won't try, but Gene wrote . . .

Burn Bitch Burn (It's the Demon Talking, Okay? You Look Up the Lyrics)

But I get this. Totally. You're trying to *do* something, to *be* somebody, to chase your dream, and some chick (not even your *own* chick—sorry for my sexist language, I've been drinking and I'm still pissed about that tour) sticks her unwelcome, well, let's say "nose" into the middle of everything. Yes, this is stuff for young males with too much testosterone, but it's hard to apologize for being young and male when you're, well, young and male. You feel for your buddy because, hey, you have a girl too, but the band comes first. It *has* to. It's what you *do*, and if she doesn't share the dream, then she needs to respect that this is the guy *she* chose and this is what *he* does, and for chrissake, that's *why* she went for him to begin with. Sheesh. (And that is not the word I want to use.)

So it's hard not to notice that this video for "Beth" is about the band, as a unit, and what *they* are trying to do. They do not focus on the kitty cat singing. In the opening tableau, the Demon is standing menacingly over Beth, all 6'2" of him, plus 5" heels (making him the actual height of his son Nick), and it is pretty hard not to notice that her face is awfully close to his crotch. In case that wasn't clear enough, a few moments later the Demon and the Starchild are in her front and rear, *way* too close, and not looking like they are going to be especially gentle with her. Then she is banished and they go on to do what they do.

Oh yes, this is definitely a KISS song. This is probably the point to mention that Paul sought and needed and depended on therapy, Epicurean that he was. He used to tell Gene that his attitude toward women, his unwillingness to make full commitments, and his way of life would eventually lead to a breakdown, and then Gene would have to go into therapy. Gene calls this view "bizarre" and doesn't seem to have come to a point of having that breakdown. So there is a shame differential between Paul and Gene, but I don't think it carries into the Demon and the Starchild. Therapy can be a powerful thing, if you need it. Epicurus said so.

Tomcats

The bookend to "Beth" is "Hard Luck Woman," which Paul wrote, but not for the band. He had Rod Stewart in mind. He was inspired by "Maggie May" and "You Wear It Well," and he sort of saw this as a third in a trilogy. He got the idea from the song "Brandy" by Looking Glass and executed a pretty unoriginal but perfectly crafted folk-pop song. But then Paul, ever the businessman, thinks: "hey, Peter sings the shit out of stuff like that, with an even rougher edge than Rod Stewart." Another hit. Ace playing a twelve-string guitar exactly like Roger McGuinn. And the fans have accepted that Peter, I mean the kitty cat, is the sweet one—and damned if that wasn't true. Peter was the one who smiled. He always does. He's not trying to be cool, he wants to be petted. He has no pride about that. Never did.

So when you have a friend like Peter, you let him in, feed him, and wait until he curls up in your lap. He'll go out chasing something later, when the notion takes him, but he is here now and that's all he cares about. And here is where his piece of the puzzle is. The man (and the persona) has a "lightness of being" that may be incompatible with serious thought, but it's not incompatible with making music. Gene remarks how Peter would breezily wander in and say "Hey, when are we gonna have a meeting about the tour?" to which Gene replies, "Yesterday, for two hours. You were there." Gene didn't report Peter's response, but I can guess it: "Oh, okay."

Now, that idea, "lightness of being." That reminds me of a book. It's a weird way of being philosophical. In Kundera's novel, the main character had this same way of floating in and out of life. People tried to put bonds on him, and that was okay, for a while, but he wore them lightly. It is consistent with loving deeply. Kazantzakis wrote about this too, in *Zorba the Greek*, where our protagonist learns, slowly and painfully from Zorba, how to bear existing lightly. And over by the door I have a cat napping, and another in the corner, in a cardboard box, and one up on top of the cat tree, sound asleep, and they haven't even had anything to drink.

So let's just say that having this gift of lightness isn't *un*-philosophical, even if it doesn't lead to writing much philosophy, or songs, or anything else. But it is a gift, not something earned, and it can be very hard on the serious people who have to make things happen. But, if you're detached enough (and I think I have made it clear who is and why), this quality in a person can be appreciated and guided to everyone's benefit. Up to a point. People who have this lightness also often have the heaviness of being in alternating turns, and so we have a name for this, and Peter was prone to depression in turns. It increasingly controlled him, along with the drugs and drinking, and when that point is reached, well, you get voted out of the band. But they still love you.

Last Puzzle Piece: The Spaceman

A Beer (Really, This Time)

I have had enough to drink, but I'll need it to bring this home. I think maybe an actual beer this time, to chase.

Odd

I quote from Paul: "Ace was odd." If you're odd in *this* band, you must *really* be odd. Praise from Caesar is praise indeed, as Horace said, sort of. Paul has just told the story of how he shared a bungalow with Ace on their first trip to LA (Gene had a bungalow with Peter), and the accommodations were generous, with several bedrooms and bathrooms, and Paul decides to take a shower the first day there. Halfway through, this awful stench comes to his nose and he thinks "wtf" (except they didn't have that phrase back then). He opens the shower curtain, and there is Ace, taking a shit, while Paul showers. Paul yells "what are you doing here?" Remember, there are other bathrooms in the house. Ace just shrugged. And Paul writes "Ace was odd" (*Face the Music*, pp. 138–39).

I'll be honest. I haven't read Ace's autobiography. I intend to. But this chapter is due and I'm pretty lit. I am going on what others said about him, and it may not be fair, but there is a consensus, and Paul has summarized it eloquently. The dude is just not quite all there, which is to say some of him is lost to the wider cosmos, and that is well matched by his choice of persona. I think there is consensus on that point as well.

Worrisome Aesthetics

So, Paul mentions but does not make too much of Ace's SS thunderbolts. He deflects the deeper issue by saying he came to understand later that Ace's fascination with such things runs a bit deeper than the way lightning bolt S's look cool. But Gene is not so coy. He tells about how on their first tour of Europe, Ace shows up, quite intoxicated, at his hotel room door, with a friend, both dressed in full Nazi regalia. They give the Nazi salute and say "Heil Hitler!" Now, this is being described by a man whose entire family, save two, was exterminated by Hitler.

This does not get Ace thrown out of the band. In fact, if it even made Gene mad, he doesn't say so. His point is that this space guy is that far out of touch with reality. Ace and his worrisome aesthetics, however, did not pose a threat. His main problems were with drugs and an uncooperative personality. But there could be no doubt about his contribution as a performer, a guitarist, and a fulfillment of the persona.

And the fact is that times have changed regarding people's sensitivity to the Holocaust and the horrors of the Nazis. I'm from the first generation of KISS fans. When I was growing up, we certainly pretended to kill Germans (we didn't call them Nazis) just as our fathers had actually done. I never even heard about the Holocaust until I was thirteen, and even then, I found it hard to believe that anything like that could have happened and *no one ever told me*. I assume that if I had grown up in New York or Chicago, someone would have mentioned it. Even then, it was so far beyond imagining that it was hard to know what the right attitude toward it would be.

There were a lot of kids like me, and I chalk it up to the fact that the world, sometime during the 1950s, decided that all that was over, the good guys won, and we just have to get on with life. We were getting on with life when Ace dressed as a Nazi, I think. Now we are more worried it could happen again. Now we have to be watchful. Now Ace needs to not do that, and it was a bad idea even then, but people donned Nazi uniforms during that time in ways they wouldn't now. Watch *Monty Python* or *Laugh-in* or *Bennie Hill* or *Hogan's Heroes*. People were allowed to make clowns of the Nazis then. It was an aesthetic response to something that had been beaten and defeated. That's part of the reason Paul didn't really take the SS seriously.

It's not just that KISS was detached, in both good and bad ways (which they were), but all of us, except in Germany, were detached from something too horrible to remember. What were we to do? Well, I have an answer: Rock and roll all night, and party every day. The *aporia* is done. The answer was obvious. KISS did what we all wanted to do, and they showed us how. I never joined the KISS Army (I did consider it), but I don't like military discipline and hierarchy, even if I understand its benefits. Maybe I'll send in my five bucks now. They can't do anything to me I haven't already done to myself. Just one more shot and off to bed . . . Oh, wait, no more vodka. Where did it go? Maybe the cat got it. Or Bob Dylan. Or Sharon Stone. Or Aristotle.

9
KISS the Ship of Theseus Goodbye!

Shane J. Ralston

The American rock band KISS is notorious. Its notoriety derives not only from the band's otherworldly costumes and masks (except for of course during the unmasked period), the fact that they were inducted into the Rock'n'Roll Hall of Fame, their numerous hit records or the amazing stage theatrics and pyrotechnics of their live shows.

It's also related to the band's constantly changing make-up (and I don't mean the kind on their faces!). Of the four members, only Paul Stanley and Gene Simmons were fixtures. With so many changes to the band's composition, has KISS always remained the same band?

Some see this head-scratcher as roughly similar to a conundrum in philosophical metaphysics (the area of philosophy addressing problems of existence): the puzzle of Theseus's ship. If you change one plank in the ship of Theseus, is it still the same ship? Two? Fifty? One hundred? When an object has any, most, or all of its parts replaced, does it remain the same object? Is its core identity preserved intact or does it become a different object altogether?

Many famous philosophers—Heraclitus, Plato, Thomas Hobbes, and Roderick Chisholm, to name a few—have contemplated different versions of the puzzle. It's left to us to answer the metaphysical question of whether KISS is still the same object, the best rock band ever, after so many band member changes, and granted that its most iconic version (Stanley, Simmons, Frehley, and Criss) no longer exists.

Shane J. Ralston

A Ship by Any Other Name

Greek historian Plutarch wrote the following about Theseus's ship:

> The ship wherein Theseus and the youth of Athens returned had
> thirty oars, and was preserved by the Athenians down even to the
> time of Demetrius Phalereus, for they took away the old planks as
> they decayed, putting in new and stronger timber in their place, in-
> somuch that this ship became a standing example among the
> philosophers, for the logical question of things that grow; one side
> holding that the ship remained the same, and the other contending
> that it was not the same. (Vita Thesei 22–23 at http://classics.mit
> .edu/Plutarch/theseus.html)

From Plutarch's account, we can imagine two puzzling
scenarios:

> **Scenario 1:** Theseus's original ship, call this ship B, is composed
> of one hundred planks. It takes a hundred years to rebuild it with
> all new planks (one per year). The philosophers' "logical ques-
> tion"—whether it's the same ship—can be asked at any point, from
> the first to the hundredth year. Most people agree that replacing
> one plank doesn't make a difference. It's still Theseus's ship! But
> at what point does its identity change . . . fifty planks, fifty-one, or
> all one hundred? Or does it always remain the same ship?

> **Scenario 2:** All one hundred planks of Theseus's ship are at once
> replaced with new ones, resulting in what we'll call ship A. The old
> planks are salvaged, stored in a warehouse, and then a second
> version of the ship is constructed out of the old planks, called ship
> C. The next question is a real zinger: Are ships A and C both the
> same as Theseus's ship, B? (This is Hobbes's version of the puz-
> zle, see his *De Corpore*).

Depending on the assumptions we make, different conclusions follow (so pay close attention to the reason for each):

> **1. Assumption 1:** Objects endure gradual change → **Conclusion
> 1:** A is the real ship of Theseus. (**Reason 1:** No matter how many
> original parts change, the identity of the object persists: it's still
> Theseus's ship, A = B.)

2. Assumption 2: An object is the same as its parts → **Conclusion 2:** The salvaged version is the real ship of Theseus. (**Reason 2**: So long as the totality of the original parts are preserved, the object they compose is the real deal, that is, C = B)

3. Assumption 3: The law of transitivity is true (that is, if A = B, B = C, therefore A = C) → **Conclusion 3:** A and C are the same ship because they are both identical to Theseus's ship, B. (**Reason 3**: logic.)

But how could two ships built at two different times in two separate locations with entirely distinct parts be the same ship? Sometimes metaphysics is logical, but not commonsensical!

The Band Is Breaking Up, Long Live the Band!

So, let's exit the weeds of logic and metaphysics for a moment to consider how KISS changed over time. The band's membership has been in a state of flux for at least thirty-five of its forty-five years of existence. For the first nine years— from KISS's founding in 1973 until Criss and Frehley left in 1982—the band was relatively stable (if you don't count Criss being fired in 1979). Each of the band members assumed their iconic roles with instrument, costume, hair, and make-up: Paul Stanley as the Starchild (vocals and rhythm guitar), Gene Simmons as the Demon (vocals and bass), Ace Frehley as the Spaceman or Space Ace (vocal and lead guitar), and Peter Criss as the Catman (vocals and drums).

Musician Eric Carr (assuming the stage name, persona, make-up and costume of the Fox) replaced Peter Criss in 1980. That year, Criss was fired during a band meeting when Stanley and Simmons voted for his ouster with Frehley against. For the next two years, Frehley would back off from his involvement with the band (he says because of creative differences, but the fact that he kept getting outvoted in band decisions didn't help), disappearing entirely by the time of the 1982 *Creatures of the Night* tour.

Vinnie Vincent (role and make-up of the Ankh Warrior) took his place. Gene Simmons denied that Vincent was ever an official member because of his penchant for self-destruction.

(He also refused to sign up for the band's liability insurance, which was probably related to him being a danger to himself and others.) Besides the *Creatures of the Night* album, Vincent also appeared on the 1983 *Lick It Up* record and co-wrote the 1992 *Revenge* album. In 1983 (not long after Frehley's departure), KISS started performing without make-up, which would last for an entire decade.

Even though Simmons claimed that Vincent was never a band member, he was fired and replaced by Mark St. John in 1984. St. John didn't stick around for long. He appeared on one album, *Animalize* (1984), before being diagnosed with Reiter's Syndrome and leaving. Besides Vincent, another on-again-off-again band member was guitarist Bruce Kulick who, after joining in 1984, appeared on multiple albums before being "permanently" exiled from the band in 1997 (his last album was *Carnival of Souls: The Final Sessions*, which came out in the same year).

In 1996, the original band reunited with nostalgic make-up and costumes. After Criss and Frehley left again, Singer returned as drummer and a new band member, Tommy Thayer, was added on guitar. Singer and Thayer assumed the identities of Catman and Spaceman, respectively.

With all these changes to the band's membership, Stanley and Simmons remained constants in the whole equation. Admittedly, both had personal problems requiring musicians like Vincent and Kulick to temporarily come on board. The saying "The king is dead, long live the king" suggests one plausible reason that the band endured so many changes. The idea behind the saying is not simply that there is always an heir to the throne in waiting. Instead, it's that the symbol and significance of the king outlasts whoever happens to be the living king. Indeed, the royal bloodline ensures that the death of a king, even a great king, does not end the royalty altogether. The same could be said about KISS. Even when Frehley and Criss were not members of the band, the symbol and significance of KISS lived on in their absence.

Is KISS Really the Ship of Theseus?

Following a blog post about the issue of band membership flux, and despite a flurry of comments about the Ship of Theseus, philosopher Greg Stadler denied that the puzzle bears any relation to the issue except in one remote situation:

> . . . what I was writing about focused on the identity of a band in terms of its membership, and the "Ship of Theseus" is a classic puzzle about a whole and its constituent parts. But as I pointed out to those commenters, that puzzle really has to do with a different kind of case.
>
> It's not as if there aren't some bands, though, to which the "Ship of Theseus" issue would apply. . . Simply put, the Ship of Theseus bears upon cases where none of the constituent parts of a whole are original to it. In terms of bands, this means we would be focused on bands that contain *none* of their original members. (heavymetalphilosopher.blogspot.com)

While there are cases where a band is reduced to no original members, KISS is not one of them. So, perhaps the changing membership of the band has nothing to do with the Ship of Theseus puzzle. If that's true, and Professor Stadler is right, then we can kiss Theseus's ship and all its logical and metaphysical headaches goodbye!

However, Professor Stadler's claim that the puzzle only pertains to "bands that contain *none* of their original members" is limited to a single version of scenario one and scenario two, when there is full replacement of all of the ship planks. It doesn't apply to Scenario 1 when at some point between the first year and the hundredth year (not including the hundredth year) the ship's identity changes because of the replacement of a single plank. Then Theseus's ship is relevant to KISS. Why? Imagine we decide that the next plank after replacing fifty planks changes the identity of Theseus's ship to another ship completely. It could be objected that this number (fifty-one) is arbitrary. Then someone might respond that it's not arbitrary because the principle is clear-cut: Replacing any more than half of an object's parts destroys its original identity, transforming it into something altogether new.

In the case of KISS, half of the band members stayed and the other half were in flux. On one interpretation, the band's identity was preserved purely in virtue of staying below this threshold mark (two, or fifty percent). Replacing three out of four members would have changed the band's identity. The band would have no longer been KISS. It would have become another band completely! On a second interpretation, it was not simply the quantity of band members replaced, but also their quality. In other words, Stanley and Simmons were two of the best and hardest to replace members of the band. Of course, Vincent and Kulick sometimes performed as substitutes, but this is only a minor distraction. Why? The best version of the band was always the original four. Also, Vincent and Kulick were never full members with voting privileges in band decisions.

The truth of the matter probably resides somewhere between the quality and quantity interpretations. Having two powerhouse musicians—Stanley and Simmons—always in the band preserved the core identity of KISS. Their constancy allowed the band's identity to persist despite the many changes in lead guitarists and drummers. What's also possible—as Stanley argues in his book *Face the Music: A Life Exposed* (2014)—is that the idea of KISS transcends time, place, and persons. No matter who the band members happen to be, the fans will always cling to the idea.

Will the Real KISS Please Stand Up?

Since KISS's farewell tour is supposed to end in 2021, it's easy to imagine a time when there will be zero original band members left. Philosophers like to use hypotheticals or imagined situations to work out the full implications of a problem and its solutions. So, imagine—hypothetically, of course—that a bunch of the original band members' relatives form a band under the KISS name in 2022. Putting aside the legal questions of trademark, imagine too that in 2025 the original band members decide to make a comeback as KISS and launch another tour. Two KISS bands would seem to exist simultaneously! Will the real KISS please stand up? Then we would have a situation analogous to scenario two and one that clearly satisfies Professor Stadler's requirements for a Ship of Theseus puzzle.

The easy answer to this conundrum is that there are two ships of Theseus or two KISS bands, but they are not the same. Following Roderick Chisholm, we can only say that the two are "identical" in a very "loose and popular sense" (see Chisholm's

1976 book *Person and Object*). Philosopher Ted Sider offers a more complicated solution. Professor Sider claims that time and space extend and partition into four dimensions. Any object is the sum of all its spatio-temporal parts—what Sider calls a "space-time worm" (see his 1997 essay "Four-dimensionalism" http://tedsider.org/papers/4d.pdf). So, objects like Theseus's ship or the band KISS, even multiple versions, can persist as the same entity, while differing in distinct "time slices."

However, it's still problematic when they appear in duplicate in identical time slices. Will the real KISS space-time worm please reveal itself? The move to four-dimensionalism lands us right back in the weeds of common-sense defying metaphysics!

Ultimately, and this is Chisholm's point, it's a very practical matter which ship is Theseus's or which band is truly KISS, a matter probably better left for courts of law, not armchair philosophers, to decide. On that note, it's about time we hit play on "Kissin' Time," turn up the volume and kiss the ship of Theseus goodbye![1]

---

[1] I would like to thank this book's editor, Courtland Lewis, for his invaluable assistance and my good friend, Chris Kelly, who is a guitarist and KISS fan, for his critical feedback.

III

The Starchild

10
KISS Was Made for Lovin' You

COURTLAND LEWIS

KISS is all about love. Except for songs like "God of Thunder" and "Detroit Rock City," KISS songs are mostly about making love, wanting love, or dreaming about love. It's one of the reasons we *love* KISS!

For those hoping to hook up with those not in the band, KISS provides courage that with enough rockin' and rollin' we too might woo a "Christine Sixteen" (assuming we're not over 18) or our own "Modern Day Delilah." For those hoping to rock-it with the band, KISS promises the opportunity of a lifetime with the Starchild, Space Ace, Demon, or Catman of their dreams. No matter your proclivities, KISS provides a twenty-album, Master's level course on love. All you need do is listen, pay attention, and learn the ins-and-outs.

It also helps if you're well-versed in the different types of love. So, if you're unaware of the myriad types that exist, I hope you're ready to have your world rocked, because the next few pages are going to be a full on lovemaking session that rivals the best backstage experience you can imagine. Philosophers and KISS fans love categorizing things, so in order to pleasure all readers, we're going to review just about every song featured on a KISS album, in order to figure out how KISS makes love.

I Stole Your Eros

Eros is the most common type of love portrayed in popular culture, and it's the main focus of most KISS songs. In fact, around fifty-six percent of KISS songs feature some sort of eros. So, what is eros? In Greek mythology, Eros was the god of sexual love and beauty, later adopted by the Romans as Cupid. In the twenty-first century, Eros appears as a chubby angel that brings lovers together on Valentine's Day each year, but this isn't the most common appearance of Eros. You see, Eros is the personification of a specific type of passionate, sexual love known as eros, and the word 'eros' is the root word of 'erotic'. So, when you hear 'eros', you should think 'erotic, passionate, love'. You know, the stuff of romantic comedies, steamy romance novels and movies, adult movies and magazines, and of course, KISS songs.

Defining 'eros' helps categorize KISS songs, but it's still too broad. To help us make the category more manageable, we should introduce a few more terms. Though Nick might be surprised to have his categories of love applied to KISS, Nicholas Wolterstorff suggests some important distinctions that are relevant to how we think of KISS songs. The first is what he calls activity love, which is when you relish and delight in a certain act and all of its components. When eros and the activity of love are combined, you end up with a type of love that delights in the activity of erotic love—in other words, it's when you put the 'X' in 'SEX'. Here are all of the songs that fit in this category:

"Tomorrow and Tonight"	"Turn On the Night"
"Any Way You Want It"	"When Your Walls Come Down"
"Rocket Ride"	"Keep Me Comin'"
"Burn Bitch Burn"	"Great Expectations"
"Heaven's on Fire"	"Sweet Pain"
"Lonely Is the Hunter"	"C'mon and Love Me"
"Murder in High-Heels"	"Love Her All I Can"
"Thrills in the Night"	"Room Service"
"Under the Gun"	"Read My Body"
"Any Way You Slice It"	"Rise to It"
"I'm Alive"	"You Love Me to Hate You"
"Love's a Deadly Weapon"	"Mainline"
"Radar for Love"	"Down on Your Knees"
"Secretly Cruel"	"100,000 Years"
"Uh! All Night"	"Deuce"
"No, No, No"	"Kissin' Time"

"Nothin' to Lose"	"Ladies Room"
"Exciter"	"Love 'Em and Leave 'Em"
"Gimme More"	"Makin' Love"
"Got Love for Sale"	"Tomorrow and Tonight"
"Shock Me"	"Mr. Speed"
"Then She Kissed Me"	"Take Me"
"Back to the Stone Age"	"(You Make Me) Rock Hard"
"Last Chance"	"Hot and Cold"
"Shout Mercy"	"Russian Roulette"
"Take Me Down Below"	"Say Yeah"
"I Just Wanna"	"Talk to Me"
"Tough Love"	"Torpedo Girl"
"Hard Luck Woman"	"Two Sides of the Coin"
"I Want You"	"Bang Bang You"

Each of these songs emphasize the erotic love that occurs during the activity of love. To illustrate, here a few prime examples to ponder. Songs like "Uh! All Night" and "Keep Me Comin'" obviously inspire images of lovemaking, as do "Makin' Love" and "C'mon and Love Me." Others, like "Room Service" and "Mr. Speed" imply lovemaking, but require a quick listening to confirm their meaning. "Room Service" is about groupies visiting the band in their hotel rooms, and "Mr. Speed" is about the velocity of Paul's gyrating hips, not the duration of Paul's love sessions. Songs like "Nothin' to Lose" and "Deuce" are obviously about lovemaking, but there is room for interpretation about what type of lovemaking. In "Nothin' to Lose," Peter and Eric are obviously trying to convince their lover to experiment with something sexual, and it's something she likes after giving it a try—I'll let you decide what exactly she likes. "Deuce" is similar. Gene has been working hard, and he needs a deuce. What's a deuce? Gene has said he doesn't know what it is, but it's obviously something he likes multiple times after work. The song "100,000 Years" is more subtle, describing a reunion between lovers where they reacquaint each other with their "styles." Paul is sorry that he's been gone for so long, and he wants them to spend some quality time together. So, the erotic activity in "100,000 Years" appears to be between lovers with a previous relationship, unlike "Heavens on Fire," where Paul is only concerned with the activity of heavy breathing—hah, hah, hah.

KISS's erotic activity songs contain several hits, but surprisingly, many of their most recognizable songs are missing from the category. Sure, there are many classics like the ones just discussed, but for one reason or another, songs of KISS getting it on with their fans or random strangers don't tend to inspire iconic hits. Let's look at some other categories to see where those occur.

Calling Dr. Attachment

The second type of love is that of attachment, which occurs when you relish and delight in the interaction between yourself and someone else. One of the difficult aspects of KISS songs is that many of them combine erotic attachment with erotic activity. The same will be true in the next section when we discuss erotic attraction. Nevertheless, erotic attachment is different from the others, because it focuses on the relationship between the lovers.

Instead of only being concerned with the erotic activity of lovemaking, erotic attachment delights in simply being with the other person. There seems to be a special connection that implies a certain level of mutual respect even if this respect is only superficial. Examples of this sort of erotic love include:

"Eat Your Heart Out"	"Sure Know Something"
"Nowhere to Run"	"Betrayed"
"Do You Love Me"	"Prisoner of Love"
"Rock Bottom"	"Calling Dr. Love"
"Good Girl Gone Bad"	"She"
"I'll Fight Hell to Hold You"	"Is That You?"
"Thief in the Night"	"What Makes the World Go 'Round"
"I Still Love You"	"You're All That I Want"
"Killer"	"Fits Like a Glove"
"Saint and Sinner"	"I Stole Your Love"
"Anything for My Baby"	"Danger Us"
"Two Timer"	"Modern Day Delilah"
"Magic Touch"	"She's So European"
"Save Your Love"	

The category of erotic attachment is full of fun examples. "Anything for My Baby" is about the dedication Paul has for his lover—he'll beg, borrow, and steal in order to keep his baby happy. "Is That You?" captures the anticipation of one's love coming over for a visit, while "Do You Love Me" expresses KISS's attachment to a lover, who is similarly attached to the band's seven-inch leather heels, but at least since the first reunion tour in 1996, it also expresses KISS's love for the fans. Paul often explains KISS's love of fans prior to playing the song live, and it's usually accompanied by a video retrospective that's meant to bring joy to the audience.

Not every example of erotic attachment is positive. In fact, most KISS songs in this category deal with breakups or relationships on the verge. "Rock Bottom," "Two Timer," and "I Stole Your Love" illustrate the complex emotions that occur when one is at risk of losing the person to whom they're attached. These songs often create a sense of pride and nonchalance about the breakup, often letting the former lover know they're the one who will suffer. However, several songs in this category show the pain and vulnerability of the band, especially Paul. In what I consider one of the greatest ballads, Paul's "I Still Love You" shows the devastating nature of losing a love of attachment. In fact, "I Still Love You" might be considered an example of pure attachment, but Paul's passion and desire create a sense of erotic longing that suggests it belongs in this category. Paul's willingness to make himself vulnerable allows him to explore erotic attachment in a more meaningful way than other band members. Ace's "Save Your Love" and Gene's "Eat Your Heart Out" have a sense of false bravado that suggests they don't care about their lovers. This bravado is what you expect from their personas, but it also keeps them from being able to explore the deeper emotions of attachment and loss—although, Gene will occasionally pull a few heartstrings when he wants. With songs like "I'll Fight Hell to Hold You" and "You're All That I Want," Paul uses his vulnerability to make fans feel the importance of attachment. With classics like "She" and "Calling Dr. Love," this section contains many fun and great songs to delight KISS fans, but we're still missing some important categories.

Welcome to the Firehouse

The third type of love discussed by Wolterstorff is attraction. Love of attraction involves the relishing and delighting in

the excellence of a thing or person. We could easily lump
songs of erotic attraction with those of erotic activity or attachment, but there are a few deserving of their own category. Here are the ones that exemplify erotic attraction:

"Ladies in Waiting"	"Watchin' You"
"I Was Made for Lovin' You"	"Firehouse"
"X-Ray Eyes"	"Strutter"
"Hide Your Heart"	"Hell or Hallelujah"
"Somewhere Between Heaven and Hell"	"Outta This World"
"All the Way"	"Boomerang"
"Got to Choose"	"Let Me Know"
"Hotter than Hell"	"Take It Off"

There are some great songs in this category, probably because fans can easily relate to a sense of attraction. We've
all seen someone "Hotter than Hell" and "Outta This World,"
and we've desired for them to "Take It Off" or go "All the
Way." Others have known times when we should "Hide Your
Heart," or seen a "Strutter" that took us to the "Firehouse."
These songs create a sense of excitement and anticipation
that we were made for loving the object of our attraction, so
it's no surprise this category contains several hits.

In addition to these songs of erotic attraction, there are
several songs that blend different types of eros. As a result,
they don't fit easily into any one category. For instance,
there's a sense in which eros strives to benefit the other person. Songs like "See You in Your Dreams," "Let's Put the X
in Sex," "Plaster Caster," "Shandi," "Tomorrow," and "Hell or
High Water" illustrate a type of erotic love focused on pleasing a partner, whether through a night of passion or via a
plaster replica. KISS is not only interested in pleasing others, but they also enjoy pleasing themselves. Songs like "All
American Man," "Larger than Life," "Charisma," "Love Gun,"
and "I'm a Legend Tonight" demonstrate an awareness of
one's own erotic prowess and a self-love of their own erotic
activities. Songs such as "King of Hearts," "Yes I Know (Nobody's Perfect)," "Who Wants to Be Lonely," "Partners in
Crime," and "Almost Human" blend erotic activity, attachment, and attraction. Finally, "King of the Night Time
World" and "Rock and Roll All Nite" combine erotic aspects

with the activity of living life. As will be discussed below, it should be no surprise that "Rock and Roll All Nite," KISS's biggest hit, presents a way of living life. KISS's way of life songs comprise one of the largest categories of songs and are some of the most popular; but we'll get to those in a couple of pages.

Let's end our discussion of the erotic with looking at a few songs that are difficult to categorize. They clearly fit in the category of eros, but there's a certain level of violence in each song that makes them fall outside of accepted forms of love. "Christine Sixteen," "Goin' Blind," and "Domino" all imply statutory rape. Gene has an insatiable attraction to young women, which "Christine Sixteen" illustrates perfectly. It's probably best he's not usually attracted to girls like her, but "Goin' Blind" implies that sixteen is his preferred age—"I'm ninety-three, you're sixteen." With its mystical overtone, "Goin' Blind" might be about something completely different, but I decided to leave it out of the mix nonetheless. "Domino" could go either way, but Gene is obviously ignorant of her age and a little concerned that she might not be old enough to vote. When combined with Gene's history of liking sixteen-year-olds, it's a safe bet she's on the younger side. Finally, "Dance All Over Your Face" wreaks of abuse. Sure, Gene is being boisterous, and there's an interesting interpretation that implies he's singing from the woman's perspective—the lipstick stain on the neck seems to have come from a woman, and if Gene's female lover is having an affair with another woman, then he's probably not going to be mad, unless they don't let him join. Regardless, with such ambiguity, I decided to exclude it from the eros category.

Love Is "Forever"

If we remove the erotic from our discussion, we get a type of love that many consider more pure. Eros tends to prevent us from thinking rationally—it gets us worked up like wild animals ("Make some noise!"). Without eros, we can focus on the pure attachment of lovers who relish and delight in the great good of interacting with one another. In other words, we get the basis for a great power ballad, love song. KISS's attachment songs include:

"Tears Are Falling"	"Stand"
"Childhood's End"	"A Million to One"
"I Confess"	"Journey of 1,000 Years"
"In the Mirror"	"Every Time I Look at You"
"Master & Slave"	"Reason to Live"
"Rain"	"Heart of Chrome"
"Forever"	"I Walk Alone"
"Comin' Home"	"Baby Driver"
"Parasite"	"Beth"

Though few in number, these songs touch on complex relationships that highlight the attachment of the singer to the object. You have your typical love songs, such as "Tears are Falling" and "Every Time I Look at You," but you also have songs like "Comin' Home" and "Beth," which deal with the difficulties of being in a band and maintaining relationships, and "Childhood's End," which deals with the loss of a friend—Gene being compassionate for once. Like "Baby Driver" and "Stand," "Childhood's End" might be described as a type of love grounded in philo—a feeling of mutual respect and admiration. 'Philo' is a love between equals, and is the root of the words 'philosophy' ('the love of wisdom') and 'Philadelphia' ('brotherly love'). This category also includes complex songs such as "A Million to One" and "Reason to Live." "A Million to One" is a song of self-affirmation in the wake of a devastating breakup, and "Reason to Live" tackles the threat of meaninglessness and suicide when a person's reason to live no longer exists. Some fans might scoff and says, "Those are just cheesy love songs," but KISS is actually dealing with some complex issues of love and attachment.

Crazy Crazy Life

So far, we've discussed the massive catalogue of KISS songs that deal with love in some way—all fifty-six percent of them. It's now time to shift our attention to the second largest category: songs that promote the love of a way of life. The meaning of life has been a topic of human interest for millennia, and an entire branch of philosophy known as ethics. For KISS, it comprises thirty-three percent of their songs, and as seen throughout this book, KISS offers a complex and intriguing perspective on how we should live our life. As hinted in the previous section, when discussing "Rock and Roll All Nite," this category contains some of KISS's biggest hits and concert staples:

"Rockin' in the U.S.A."
"Crazy Crazy Nights"
"And on the 8th Day"
"Get All You Can Take"
"I've Had Enough (Into the Fire)"
"While the City Sleeps"
"King of the Mountain"
"Trial by Fire"
"Hate"
"In My Head"
"It Never Goes Away"
"Jungle"
"Seduction of the Innocent"
"My Way"
"Creatures of the Night"
"Danger"
"I Love It Loud"
"Rock and Roll Hell"
"War Machine"
"Detroit Rock City"
"Flaming Youth"
"God of Thunder"
"Shout It Out Loud"
"Getaway"
"2,000 Man"
"Dirty Livin'"
"Hard Times"
"Cadillac Dreams"
"Little Caesar"
"Love's a Slap in the Face"
"Silver Spoon"
"The Street Giveth and the Street Taketh Away"
"Let Me Go, Rock 'n' Roll"
"Black Diamond"
"Cold Gin"
"All Hell's Breakin' Loose"
"Not for the Innocent"

"Young and Wasted"
"Hooligan"
"All for the Love of Rock & Roll"
"The Devil Is Me"
"Freak"
"Long Way Down"
"Wall of Sound"
"Dark Light"
"I"
"Just a Boy"
"Mr. Blackwell"
"The Oath"
"Odyssey"
"Only You"
"Under the Rose"
"A World Without Heroes"
"I Pledge Allegiance to the State of Rock & Roll"
"Into the Void"
"Psycho Circus"
"Raise Your Glasses"
"We Are One"
"Within"
"You Wanted the Best"
"God Gave Rock 'n' Roll to You II"
"Paralyzed"
"Spit"
"Thou Shalt Not"
"All for the Glory"
"I'm an Animal"
"Never Enough"
"When Lightning Strikes"
"Easy as It Seems"
"Naked City"
"Unholy"
"Lick It Up"

People who aren't fans, and those who mock KISS, are typically ignorant of KISS's positive message of self-affirmation, taking charge of one's life, and living life to its fullest. They see the make-up and theatrics as tricks to dupe fans into spending money, and fail to recognize the deeper messages of hope and inspiration. "Lick It Up" is an ideal example for how people often perceive KISS. From its name, "Lick It Up" sounds purely erotic, but when you actually listen to the words, you see it's an inspiring tale of taking charge of one's life. Inspired by a devastating breakup that left Paul pondering suicide, "Lick It Up" is his attempt to reclaim happiness.

That's KISS in a nutshell—instead of letting the world beat you down and make you sad, you've gotta believe in something real, believe in "I," whether you're a "Freak," "War Machine," "God of Thunder," or "Creature of the Night." No matter if you're from "Detroit Rock City" or the "Jungle," you gotta "Shout It Out Loud," and if someone tries to stop you, you gotta say, "I Love It Loud," "Let Me Go, Rock 'n' Roll." "God Gave Rock 'n' Roll to You," but you have to work real hard, and not just fanaticize about living the life you want. KISS's dedication to hard work, perseverance, and achieving goals is their greatest attribute, and it's what KISS fans love the most about the band. So, when life brings you down, remember, you gotta "rock and roll all nite, and party every day!" No one has said it any better.

Love It Loud

Philosophers such as Aristotle and Plato noted that if you're living the good life, then usually you'll enjoy the flourishing that results from such a pursuit. If lucky, you'll also enjoy many of the pleasures discussed in the section on eros. You might want to avoid some of them, since as each member of KISS discusses in their books, a life of excess can be devastating; but ultimately, it's up to you. One of KISS's most enduring lessons is that we have to decide for ourselves what is meaningful and then work hard for our own individual successes.

Another aspect of love that occurs while living our way of life, yet to be mentioned, is that of agape. Agape love is often described as the love between a parent and child, where the parent delights in sacrificing for the benefit of the child. A meaningful life often contains at least one instance of agape love, whether you are the parent or the child, and a life devoid of agape is often considered missing a necessary component of true flourishing. KISS has only one song dealing with agape, and it's "I Will Be There." Paul wrote "I Will Be There" for his son, and with its powerful message of agape love, some consider it his most meaningful—if not his greatest—writing achievement. High praise, indeed.

Regardless, one of the fun things about my analysis is that depending on what you emphasize in each song, you might come up with a different list in each category. Maybe "Take it Off" is better-placed under erotic attachment, if you think Paul is in love with the dancer. Or maybe "I'm a Legend Tonight" is not about Paul taking care of his lover, but is instead about his prowess in the sack. If so, then it should be placed under erotic activity. Regardless of where you think each song should appear, all you need do is provide good reasons for why it belongs. Philosophy and critical thinking let reason rule, and even if we're passionately discussing KISS, we've learned the skill of carefully considering the value of someone else's reasons. So, my challenge to you is if you disagree with my categories, then go through and develop your on list. "Rise to It" and make it your own!

In *In This World of Wonders*, Nicholas Wolterstorff describes our lives as being "shot through with love." Wolterstorff means that our lives have been "shot through with goodness and excellence." With this in mind, we shouldn't be surprised that almost every KISS song deals with love in some way.

Love is part of everything we do, motivating and providing our lives with meaning. Life is so full of love, it's as if someone pulled the trigger of the universe's love gun, infusing all creation with love, and creating KISS to provide the soundtrack for making sense of the world and all our activities within.[1]

---

[1] Many thanks to Matt Alschbach for turning me on to several KISS podcasts and the joy of making lists, which inspired me to spend some time making my own. Also, thanks for going on several KISS adventures!

11
EXCESS (I love it)

ROBERT S. VUCKOVICH

Examining KISS's lyrics philosophically might cause plenty of people's eyes to roll, because how profound can rock'n'rolling all night and partying every day be?

Since rock'n'roll is a euphemism for sexual intercourse, and since most of KISS's catalogue expresses this rock'n'roll sentiment, sex is assuredly a driving force for why this group carries on singing about it. Inserting sexual innuendos and stories into their songs for as long as this band has been around indicates that the rock'n'roll lifestyle has a worthwhile appeal. Even as philosophy has been described as a passion for wisdom, KISS's songs embrace a living passion for intimate physical relations.

Not all philosophers would think that passion is unsophisticated. Actually, a questionable student of Socrates, Aristippus of Cyrene (435–350 B.C.E.), was of the view that immediate sensual pleasures should not only be enjoyed, but deemed them as the most valued human activity, outshining any contemplative endeavor. Whatever stimulates a person's body pleasurably gives that person an appreciation of life. Specifically, life is best enjoyed as it happens. As R.D. Hicks translates Diogenes Laertius, a person can only derive "pleasure from what's present" and there's no point to "toil to procure the enjoyment of something not present." So when it comes to the enjoyment of sex, enjoy it now, not later.

Admitting to KISS's preoccupation with sex, in a 2016 interview with Greg Prato, Ace Frehley jokingly ponders which one of their songs "isn't about sex?" The suggestive admission does not explicitly state what it is about sex that preoccupies the band's fancies. It does allude to its being a principal fancy.

Ain't Talkin' 'Bout Love

It would be too bold to present KISS songs as a systematic philosophical body of work. Each song might be best regarded anecdotally as providing a snappy validation about one's partaking in pleasure. Besides, each member of the band, expressed in each composition, has a particular appetite for sex arising out of a unique and stimulating situation.

Since Aristippus belongs to a real old school of rock-'n'roll, something about his time period needs mentioning. The ancient Greeks had many different concepts of love. These accounts describe a specific type love that an individual has towards spiritual bliss (*agape*), oneself (*philautia*), another person or thing (*philia, pragma, ludus, eros, mania*), or a group of close persons (*storge*). In terms of sexual relations, *eros* best captures the passion that an individual experiences when drawn physically to another person.

Erotic passion overwhelmingly strikes an individual, causing one to immediately respond or react. Note the details Gene Simmons provides in such an undertaking in "Fits Like a Glove":

> Ain't no cardinal sin / baby let me in / girl, I'm gonna treat you right
> Well goodness sake / my snake's alive and ready to bite
> Hornet's nest /lay me down to rest / ooh, I wanna shed my skin
> I got the urge to merge / you're cold as ice /
>   baby, won't you let me in?

Being up front about how horny you are may come across as crass. What harm, however, is there in being honest in such soliciting? Sure, the man's dick and a woman's vulva are animalized, and the intended partner doesn't, initially though, share the same enthusiasm as the singer. Perhaps the determined nature for this *urge to merge* would've been a *cardinal sin* if his body were forced upon this girl. Instead of barging in like an unstoppable, corrupt force of nature, the Demon,

Gene's on-stage persona, exhibits self-control when asking this girl for permission to fit in. It's up to her.

Hurt So Good

Singing about the desire to be intimate with another person's body establishes a strong connection with attaining pleasure through physical contact. Pleasure is solely tangible. Though the analogies to a snakebite and hornets' nest imply an exposure to painful sensations, Aristippus would deem these lively descriptions as accurate, for "things which are productive of certain pleasures are often of a painful nature . . ." (*Lives of Eminent Philosophers*, Volume I, p. 219). Neither KISS nor Aristippus promote sadistic forms of pleasure in their hedonistic pursuits. For the sensual philosopher, gentle motions are conducive to bringing about pleasurable responses. Mentioning pain in such a manner helps to mark a threshold where intense physical interactions may either attract or repel a person from interacting with someone else's body.

A very tame reference to sadism is found in the song "Sweet Pain." Though it offers no exploration into sadomasochism as a method of generating pleasure, reference to the holstered whip signifies an assertive call, though not a domineering one, for sex. Interestingly, the woman, the song claims, will want *the same thing every day* and has no real interest in getting whipped.

There is nothing intimidating or one-sided about how this loving is initiated or what results from it. The singer of the track intends on sharing this sweet pain, so as to have the woman reach a level of ecstasy that will drive her crazy. Too bad, however, a more detailed description of such orgasmic bliss is left to the imagination. Perhaps it's better for someone to simply indulge, thus discovering the pleasures of the flesh and unleashing, as presented in the second single off *Animalize*, those thrills *that nobody sees living inside*.

Turn Me On

Enticing women into sexual relations isn't the least bit demeaning or lecherous, if they too have desires for and crave on occasion erotic encounters. Note that KISS's first single, "Nothin' to Lose," chronicles an attempt to get "a sweet thing" to experience anal sex. Her initial reluctance at the suggestion eventually turns, by the second verse, into a willingness to *do it anyway*. Is she concerned simply about pleasing the guy, or does she actually get her rocks off? If there is pleasure in it for her as well, then maybe she really has nothing to lose.

To think that women are sexualized for the sake of catering to some man's whim undermines the viewpoint that women have a flair for sex as men do. As noted in *Face the Music*, Paul Stanley came to learn that on KISS's promotional tour "girls wanted" sex, or, putting in mildly, to sleep with the band. Their willingness to indulge not only added a pleasurable dimension to rock'n'roll, it signified their consent to enjoy it as well.

Consent in this context focuses on one-time moments when the band isn't performing and can concentrate on more intimate and interactive activities. Performing live before a packed arena doesn't quite get the undivided attention as one person would when in private with another. "Room Service" presents in an arousing fashion this scenario. Withdrawing from the stage antics of song and dance, Paul, in the second verse, expresses his disappointment about the delays when traveling from show to show. Yet, a unique show takes place when *a stewardess in a tight blue dress* offers herself to the inconvenienced rock star. Declining this pleasure is preposterous, especially when this woman gladly performs a service on her knees twice. Take note of the effort to prolong this sexual experience, for it makes one's downtime all the more satisfying. Besides, she may not just be skilled at what she does, she may very much enjoy what she does to him.

Come Taste the Band

Not many expect to find a detailed analysis of cocksucking in philosophy. In Volume II of the *Lives of Philosophers*, the historian Diogenes Laertius (180–240 C.E.), however, alludes to the stoic Chrysippus (282–206 B.C.E.) as providing an "indecent," though vague, account of how one could "soil his lips" in positive terms. This activity not only pleases individuals with loose morals, there are those of higher standards who consider this intimate stimulation divine. Without letting our imagination run too wild to see a stoic squirm under such circumstances, we can presume that this thinker may've been implying that a man "soil his lips" on a woman too. That particular activity is not something that members of KISS would neglect.

In "Hotter than Hell," an offer to an extremely attractive woman consists of her interest in spending the night and having an extensive oral exploration of her body. Reference to taking her *all around the whole wide world* indicates a desire to engage in foreplay for an extended time, including cunnilingus, before capping the night off with intercourse. Getting to know this woman physically is the turn on. Not only does this woman, the lyrics suggest, appeal to the eyes, other parts of the male body are drawn to her body. Sexual pleasure is not restricted to certain body parts.

Though the encounter plays out as a one-time affair, there's a passion to savour the moment and prolong one's involvement with her body for as long as possible. A personal dilemma, though, arises at this tempting offer, for the woman, who does express an initial interest in getting physical, develops some reservation about being unfaithful to her husband.

Resolving the moral hang-up of infidelity is left unexplored, for sexual excursions aren't about committed relationships. Consent is all that's required for short-term encounters. Gene summarizes this hedonistic pursuit in a song from the fifth studio album, suggesting that it's best to "Love 'em and Leave 'em". It might seem discouraging to know that good things never last, but as indicated in "Room Service" and "Hotter than Hell," savoring the moment shows that pleasure, in spite of a short life span, is worth clinging onto. Perhaps a true appreciation of pleasure is one's giving that particular moment an enduring feel.

Pushed to the Limit

Time isn't the catalyst against one's passionate undertaking. As hinted in "Hotter than Hell," one seemingly committed member in a sexual liaison demonstrates some personal resistance to indulging. It definitely isn't anyone in KISS. Impressive is the married woman's showing restraint. Indulging isn't the same as overindulging. So when does too much of a pleasurable thing, in practice and not in song, become unpleasant for someone?

Without preaching, but providing a practical caution, Aristippus claims that there are situations where indulgences take control over a person. On a visit to a prostitute, the philosopher advises a chary youngster that "[it] is not going in that is dangerous, but being unable to go out." Similar to what the Eagles say at the end of "Hotel California," there's concern for when persons become too dependent on their bodies which provide pleasure.

Indulging is fine so as long as an individual is capable of exercising control over one's own passions. In the case of the woman in "Hotter than Hell," it's an example where an additional sexual relation, especially when she's skilled at leaving a guy *well done*, may be too much for that person to handle. Surely someone's going to get burned when a person's passion for pleasure becomes excessive. That hot married woman may have a genuine concern that either her or her lover, or both, may have more than a one night stand, creating needless friction should the affair become more than an indulgence, an obsession, perhaps, as characterized by *Mania*.

The sentiment in "Love 'em and Leave 'em" wouldn't apply to such drama. Aristippus avoided having his fancy possess him. Despite his frequent longing for and indulgence of the hot prostitute, Lais, Aristippus would not "prevent anyone else from [enjoying her]." Restricting the relationship to strictly a sexual one enables both the philosopher and the desirable young woman to focus on the pleasures that their bodies generate without having anyone dictate what another does with one's own and someone else's body.

Just remember that the seemingly aggressive demand for sex in "Fits Like a Glove" includes the stipulation of treating the woman right. Showing consideration towards your partner isn't uncommon during intense sexual intercourse. No exploitation or victimization is present. Notice how hedonistic activities reveal a moral dimension when pleasure is mutual.

Introducing morality also places a cap on how much passion goes into erotic encounters, especially when these relations presented in KISS songs and by Aristippus are not long term. It is as though those living the rock'n'roll lifestyle cannot embrace it continuously.

Enough Is Enough

Indulging hedonistically does vary among individuals. To recognize this difference in personal appetites, consider what appeals to the "senses" of the two mainstays in KISS, Gene and Paul. Gene's interest has always been about partaking in a steady influx of "girls." For Paul, though, according to David Leaf and Ken Sharp's *KISS Behind the Mask*, his appetite overtime has become refined, preferring "quality" sex over having many sexual partners. This slight disdain for excess doesn't make Paul less hedonistic than Gene, for one's craving of bodily pleasures, regardless of preferences or numbers, never diminishes entirely. A break from indulging is required now and then.

Aristippus can identify with Paul's refinement, for there's an occasion when the philosopher was given a choice to have his way with one of "three courtesans." Selecting all three was his immediate choice, but soon after, Aristippus abandons them without indulging. Perhaps three isn't the magic number, for a hedonist can set practical limits for oneself even when it's difficult to turn down so many temptations.

Turning down sexual pleasure has nothing to with wanting to abstain from pleasure and deeming it a vice. Consider it merely as giving your body some deserved rest when indulgences have reached a peak. As we find in *Nothin' to Lose*, Rusty Burns, the guitarist for Point Blank, a band which toured with KISS in the early 1970s, acknowledges that Gene graciously passed on a number of girls to his band after admitting that his indulging was "kind of done." Similar to Aristippus's reoccurring relation with Lais, Gene didn't deprive sexual pleasure to anyone. Allowing others to indulge helps KISS's bassist from overindulging so as to not become hedonistically worse or so sexually drained he may never indulge again.

Work Hard, Play Harder

Time away from bodily pleasures characterizes a shift in our priorities. Aristippus's mission into developing his philosophy alternates between activities: education and recreation. These recreational activities predominately revolve around sex. Yet one can't, presumably, live on sex alone. Capitalizing on his philosophical lessons enables this enterprising student, unlike his mentor Socrates (469–399 B.C.E.), to "charge fees" for teaching. Although, how much toil that a person goes through when receiving or administering an education can vary among early philosophers, philosophy is an active undertaking. For Aristippus, his philosophy of life commits himself to keeping his body active in both work and play, alternating between the two accordingly.

KISS too live this double life. Their preoccupation with physical pleasure is obvious, but that typically happens after rocking out. So when play time is over, its members go to work by creating and performing music. Yet no one sees what goes on when hearing a group's songs on the radio or listening to their record. Live performances of their songs put their physicality on display.

Alive! first showcases all the effort and hard work that KISS embodied when performing live vs. making records. Acknowledging this feat, in *Behind the Mask*, Peter Criss makes the distinction that KISS is "'great live'" and at the beginning not much of "a good studio band." Not only does a committed passion to play rock'n'roll manifest itself on stage, but there's a euphoric element to their liveliness. "No matter what kind of hassles I'm having, when I hit the stage, I blow them from my mind," Paul affirms in *Behind the Mask*—"It's fantasy and escape..., and it's no different for the audience than for me." Indeed, there's no time for thinking when you're up on the stage in a rage, for it's all about performing. Notice how getting whipped into this rock'n'roll frenzy is synonymous with how Aristippus figuratively blows away the mind, or rational activities, when bodily joys are impressionably intertwined with one's being active. It's here where KISS songs become entertainingly alive, for only what's physical is best made impressionable in the flesh.

It's All a Part of My Rock'n'Roll Fantasy

Leaving thoughts out of the rock'n'roll way of life puts KISS's approach on par with Aristippus. When all things physical generate pleasure, it produces value as well. Creating music illustrates a determination associated with getting work done. Having composed several rock anthems of their own, KISS's version of Argent's "God Gave Rock and Roll to You" revisits and stresses that active effort which made them successful, finding meaningfulness in terms of what they set out to accomplish through rock'n'roll.

Emphasis on the body is found in both renditions, but stands out more in the remake. Russ Ballard, the original composer, gives a spiritual account of what rock'n'roll does. He asserts: *Music can make your dreams unfold / How good it feels to be alive.* These uplifting lines come after the conditional component of how *you got to sweat or you won't get far.* Making music involves work. The alternative to the rock'n'roll lifestyle, according to Ballard, is for those who don't put forth an effort to sweat to return to the routine reality of *nine to five.* Though that reality also involves work, it offers no pleasurable sense of fulfilment. It's not stimulating.

Breaking a sweat means a lot more to KISS, for the sentiment is repeated in their version. Though the line about sweat remains unchanged, Paul and Gene contribute an additional disjunctive: *you can work real hard or just fantasize / but you don't start living till you realize.* This emphasis on demanding work encourages a continued effort to pursuing rock'n'roll success. KISS also separates mental longings, dreams to be exact, from a lived reality.

Relying on fantasies may keep the mind active and fantasies are part of lived reality, but the body stays inactive while daydreaming. Bodily skills develop and gradually improve over time through persistent work. Dreaming about exercising, for example, won't condition one's body; working out does.

Aristippus, without relaying anything specific, encourages bodily training, for it ensures that the individual concentrates on pleasurable benefits for the sake of one's body. A body must be conditioned so as to make the best of the pleasure it experiences. How much conditioning is required may depend on the pleasure one finds gratifying. Sometimes it's about exercising specific parts of the body, or a particular muscle, if you prefer.

In stark contrast to Aristippus's earlier point about how unnecessary it is to toil for pleasure, the toil that KISS values is about creating a musical experience for others to enjoy. Playing rock'n'roll is not about striving for an object for pleasure or attaining a certain goal. Rather, toiling in front an audience, especially on stage in either a club or an arena, excites pleasure on a mass scale, rousing everyone to cheer and sing along, then leaving them satisfied when all is said and done. Besides, since there are many types of love to experience, there too are many pleasures where exercising your body aren't sexual, but are ecstatic in nature.

Now the payoff for all of your work, especially with how KISS expresses it in song, is to give the body some well deserved recreation. KISS deduce that *when your body's been starved feed your appetite / when you work all day, you got to Uh! all night*. It's as though you can't separate the pairings of work and play or the body and pleasure. They complement each other in a positive manner.

Think! Let Your Mind Go, Let Yourself Be Free

As simplistic as this arrangement appears, KISS's line of work, performing rock'n'roll, operates as foreplay for those particular recreational indulgences. For a truly hedonistic philosophy, this is the life.

One clarification about KISS's love of rock'n'roll, though, is that because of their longevity, this love for creating and playing music live should be seen as *pragma*, a love that conveys a long-term interest and commitment. Interpolating *eros* with *pragma* then keeps the band's alternating activities grounded, regardless of whether they're rock'n'rolling literally or figuratively. If no love was involved, there wouldn't be any point in bothering for so long. In truth, KISS's determination to be the best, as announced at the beginning of each concert, is and must remain excessive.

Having so many loves to work with, as it were, is in keeping with KISS's libidinous way of life. Yet, despite such excessiveness, no one in the band professes to be a profound expert about sex; no doctor of love to be called upon for advice on any methodological approaches to getting laid. Singing about personal desires and episodic dalliances just candidly acquaint listeners with the satisfaction associated with a hedonistic lifestyle. That perspective summarizes the philosophy, similar to an innuendo, found in KISS's music.

KISS presents sexual pleasures through suggestive imagery, exaggerated accounts, *double entendres*, or blunt terms so as to make sex relatable as well as playful. Nothing scrupulous is needed to elucidate to others about bodily pangs and sensations. To get an impression of what they're all about, let people go experience them for themselves. Putting any thought into those intimate episodes would likely disrupt the peace of mind that one experiences while indulging in a piece of ass. There apparently is no room for philosophical discourse while two, or possibly more, people are engaged in intercourse, unless there's some previously unreleased material in KISS's catalogue stating the contrary.

The body, for Aristippus, serves as the epicenter for realizing which things in life bring about pleasure. Minimizing the importance of the mind and its preoccupations enables a person to enjoy bodily pleasures as if it were a virtue, because, as Cicero (106–43 B.C.E.) reports in the *Academica*, "the source of all things good is in the body—this is nature's canon and rule and injunction, to stray away from which will result in a man's never having an object to follow in life." To downplay the body like so is to deprive a person of purpose and value.

Perhaps when KISS sings "God Gave Rock'n'Roll to You II," they're reminding everyone that we possess those human urges and physical sensations to feel good. So for anyone who wants to live pleasurably, work hard until it's time to get the most out of life by indulging recreationally.

12
An Intimate Look at Paul Stanley's Love

ROBERT GRANT PRICE

Paul Stanley's stage persona, The Starchild, is effeminate yet masculine, vulnerable yet boastful. He is "The Lover" to Gene Simmons's "Demon" and the one most responsible for filling the KISS catalogue with so many love songs.

Love of Soul

"I'm in need of love," Ace Frehley sings on his solo album. It's a line that resonates because, as many philosophers will attest, it is part of our condition as humans to need love. Exactly what kind of love Frehley means becomes apparent in the verses, when he reveals that the sort of communion he needs is of the bodily, rather than spiritual, sort.

But that doesn't mean that the song's chorus loses force. The man needs love. And this love can be as easily read as romantic love, or the love between soulmates, as it can be read as sexual love. This kind of love, called *eros*, is the love that, as the cliché goes, "completes us." It is the "need-love"—the love we need.

One of the best illustrations of this love appears in Aristophanes's story of the soulmates. In this myth, found in Plato's *Symposium*, humans were originally creatures with two heads and eight limbs. Zeus, alarmed at the threat human beings posed to the gods, rips humans in half and scatters the pieces across the planet. Ever since, we have each sought after our other half, our soulmate, the one who will make us feel whole again.

This desire for wholeness aches. This love is rare—rare to the point that in poetry and song it achieves an almost sacred quality. The rock'n'roll songwriter, when he writes about this love, approaches with reverence and respect. No hip-thrusting boogies. Instead, he writes a ballad—a slow song.

Many ballads in Paul Stanley's canon reference this species of love explicitly. In songs like "Forever," "I Finally Found My Way," and "Every Time I look at You," the singer finds the love he needs through the person he loves. We know from the lyrics that the love he speaks about is a transcendent love. This love is not temporary. Rather, it is "forever," incorporeal, pure, and safe from corruption. Not only will this love survive time, it will bring the lovers a sense of unity. The soulmates will be as they were before Zeus cleaved humans in half: "together as one," as Stanley sings on his first solo album.

As a man prone to the dramatic, Stanley celebrates eros in fiery songs, too, like "I'll Fight Hell to Hold You" and "Anything for My Baby." These songs show the lengths a lover will go to find and keep the love of a soulmate. Love challenges us, as these songs suggest, and lovers must be heroic to sustain the love that completes them. They must give their lovers whatever they need to thrive, even if that means "stealing anything" or even going to war with hell. Stanley sounds characteristically hyperbolic in these songs, but he's not. Love is, in the Aristotelian sense, an act of profound giving, or as the philosopher Josef Pieper describes it, an act of total self-emptying.

Is the love that Paul Stanley sings about in these sings hard? Yes, it's very hard.

Love of Self

A second kind of love is self-love. Thomas Aquinas, the philosopher and Catholic saint, argued that there can be no love for others without self-love. Here, self-love is understood as a love for the common good, which includes the self. To love others well—to give them what they need to thrive—we must first give ourselves what we need to thrive. For example, if a band member loves his band and wants success for the band (a common good), he will first live a healthy life—or at least stay sober for the concert (a self good).

Plenty of Stanley's love songs—"A Million to One," "I'm a Legend Tonight," "King of the Mountain," and others—feature a narrator who praises himself. If romantic love contains a heroic quality—that of self-sacrifice for another, like a soldier who takes a bullet for his platoonmates or a rock star who saves his coke for after the show—these songs exhibit machismo, an extreme heroic posturing and self-adulation. Rather than praising the lover and the imperishable love between them, the lover admires what is most good about himself. These songs say, "The sacrifice that I'm called to make is enormous, but I am more than enough to satisfy, baby."

Self-love is essential to loving others. But, as Aquinas warned, self-love must be "rightly ordered." What he means is that self-love can easily become egomania if it's not shaped to fulfill a predestined role—that is, if it's not disciplined to a purpose. So, if I was made for loving you, then I must discipline myself so that I can do what I was made to do—love you and nobody else.

Self-love becomes disordered when it feeds the self without regards for others. A classic example is Gene Simmons's song "I." The narrator in this song lavishes praise on himself. He loves himself, and "believes" in himself so much that the song is "more" than the listener can even understand. This song is not so much a love song as it is a personal lubricant, since it says that "I" can complete myself and need no other. Such an understanding of self-love conflicts with eros. Self-love cannot exclude or remain a mystery to others. It must work to the betterment of self so that we can each love others well.

Proper self-love has a sensual quality about it, although Aquinas never put it in these terms. It's sensual in the sense that, when rightly ordered, self-love will please more people than just the one who loves himself. "It ain't a crime to be good to yourself," Stanley preaches. Indeed, it isn't. Being good to yourself—giving yourself what you need to thrive—can satisfy us both.

Love of Body

Sensual love is the default setting for rock'n'roll—and for KISS. The preponderance of sexual imagery and praise for lust explains why, since its beginnings, rock was so often denounced as degenerate. Lust is the lowest form of love, the most adolescent, the one most easily accessed, and the one most easily abused. It's also the most fun.

Paul Stanley, a sensualist, is most prolific as a writer of songs about lust. "Love Gun" (a song about his penis), "Makin Love" (a song about him using his penis), and "I Just Wanna" (a song about him wanting to use his penis), along with dozens of other songs, speak crudely, comically, and ironically about sex and sexual desire. Sex and sexual desire can be classically understood as "goods"—objects that can bring happiness: They feel good, and when shared between lovers, they can deepen eros.

But sensual love is only a good if it is well-directed, or to use Aquinas's language again, if it is "rightly ordered." If it is not well-directed, we can unwittingly end up desperately far from the happiness we seek. This is true with any good. Admiration can become envy. Courage is good to have, but too much can make a person reckless. Similarly, sex is good, and celebrating activities of the flesh in song is fun, but there is always the risk that such a celebration will objectify the other and reduce that person to a non-person.

In this way, rock can be rightly called degenerate if it reduces people (usually women) to sex objects, things to be used and tossed aside. The saving grace for Stanley's love music, and a lot of rock music, relates to how we're meant to read the lyrics. These songs are not instructions on how to objectify a woman. Rather, these songs should be understood as dramatic monologues, as the dirty talk that lovers trade with one another. What lovers say to one another assumes a desire to be acknowledged as flesh-and-blood beings. The songs are bawdy because the speaker and the listener want to talk bawdily. It's foreplay music; a call for intimacy. What is missing is his lover's response.

Love of Life

The highest form of love is a love that inspires a complete self-elimination by the lover for his beloved. The Greeks called this love *agape*. It is "gift-love"—a love that gives all that the other needs. When people say, "God is love," this is the kind of love they mean. It is the love behind all other loves. The one that deserves praise and gratitude.

Stanley is not a religious writer in the conventional sense, but there is little doubt that he writes songs of praise and plenty of evidence that he really does preach when he dons his guise as rock'n'roll preacher. But instead of praising God, Reverend Stanley praises love and its wellspring, life. To love life is a secularized way to indulge in religiously inspired agape, to experience that ineffable strangeness and beauty that is living.

The band has said in multiple interviews that they are glad they never wrote doom songs, like Black Sabbath. (Of course, they have written doom songs, like "Hate," that almost always appear near the bottom of fan favourites lists.) Instead, KISS, and Stanley in particular, wrote songs about the ecstasy of being alive. Case in point: "I'm Alive." While rife with innuendo and comedy, this song is essentially a gospel hymn praising life. In the chorus the narrator exclaims, with great pleasure, "I'm alive!"

We see the band praise life again in the 1976 song "Shout It Out Loud." The verses tell a story about teenagers gearing up for a party. It's going to be wild. And once it's started, the revellers will "shout it out loud." But what exactly will they shout? What is "it"? An early version of the song has lyrics that say the singer will shout his love for his girl to the world. In the refined 1976 song, the "it" that they will shout isn't a word but a feeling. It is cathartic joy. Like a choir, they will shout their love for life out loud.

Finally, it's worth noting that the band chose to name their live albums *Alive!* and not *Live!* The title does not advertise that the band is playing *live*; it says they are *alive*. The exclamation point lends an air of astonishment as well as volume to the word.

Why Love?

All this leads to a larger philosophical question: Why is love such a powerful inspiration for artists?

The easy answer is to say that not all artists make art about love. We know that many contemporary artists prefer to celebrate transgression over anything as sentimental as "love." And yet, as an audience wanting to understand what art is telling us, it's hard not to seek out what is common between various pieces of art. Invariably, the point of comparison—and the thing the artist holds in common with the audience—is some form of desire. This might be a desire for love, a desire to capture beauty, a desire to transgress boundaries of good taste and orthodoxy, or anything else.

Desire points to something always out of reach, a thing wanted by virtue of how it brings us happiness, and a thing loved because we see it as beautiful. Indeed, a school of aesthetics argues that art is art only when it captures beauty. Exactly what constitutes beauty remains a hotly contested argument. Some artists believe that what most people call "ugly" can itself be beautiful. In a famous documentary, the late philosopher Roger Scruton interrogates Michael Craig-Martin, an artist famous for his conventionally ugly and silly art, about what constitutes beauty. Craig-Martin argues that artists should strive to show the beauty in all that is around us. Scruton asks if a "can of shit" can be a beautiful work of art. That, too, can be art, replies Craig-Martin.

Is a medieval painting of the Madonna and Child beautiful because it captures the perfect love felt by a perfect mother towards her perfect son? Or is its piety a source of ugliness? And what about that can of shit? Is it ugly because shit is revolting and a can of shit in a gallery is insulting to people who appreciate "real" art? Or is a can of shit in an art gallery beautiful because it is repulsive to the pious people who would prefer to spend time with a gilded painting of Mary and Jesus?

By this understanding of beauty, the artist cannot help but reveal what she loves, and all that she writes and all that she paints aspires to preserve the love she holds for some object; to bridge the gap between herself and a love she desires; or to celebrate a love worthy of praise. At issue is whether there can be an objective definition for what constitutes beauty, a definition that allows us to say with confidence that a can of shit can never be art because it is not beautiful.

Beautiful Love

Whether words and concepts can have objective meaning puzzled ancient philosophers. Aristotle argued that since objects in the world always change, they can never fully express the meaning that supposedly defines them. As a result, we should treat universals with suspicion. In the same vein, some contemporary philosophers argue that there can be no definitive understandings of the concept "man" and "woman" without some party forcing the definition on others.

The counterpoint arises when we consider a concept like "truth." Can we say with confidence that truth exists? And I don't mean questions of ground-level truth, like whether it is true that KISS wears make-up (that's fact), or whether Ace is cooler than Paul (that's opinion), but higher-level questions of truth, like "Is a belief in God a true belief?" The answer to that question, whether answered in the affirmative or the negative, is objective in the sense that it exists outside of ourselves.

Mathematical truths lend credence to the idea of objective truth. 2 + 2 = 4. That's true, and any other answer will always be false. We might even say that the nature of this mathematical truth is *beautiful*. It's beautiful because it remains true, no matter how hard we try to prove the answer false. By this route of thinking, some philosophers and theologians have arrived at a belief that what is good and what is beautiful are also true. These transcendentals—the true, the good, the beautiful—awe us and inspire us. A right education, then, should help people distinguish between what is true, good, and beautiful and what is not, and all that we do—our actions, our words, our art—can be measured against these values. Art in particular, by this reasoning, involves love, since we will always love what is beautiful.

Critics who scoff at the idea that the members of KISS are artists surely turn their noses at the sentimentality of the lyrics—that is, by the naked celebration of love in all its forms. A real artist, the critic says, hides his love. Or better yet, he effaces beauty and mocks love's way of making us vulnerable. Sentimentalists, by contrast, show skin. Paul Stanley, in most of his lyrics, is buck naked. One struggle of the artist is to determine how much love—how much skin—is tasteful.

Stanley is most intriguing in those rare moments when he tries to hide his love like a "real" artist does. The "serious" music on *The Elder* and the dark sounds on *Carnival of Souls* strike fans as "not KISS" because love has been subverted and rendered joyless through the pained lyrics and dark tonalities of the songs.

Even a popular song like "I Stole Your Love" sits awkwardly in the Paul Stanley canon. Written during KISS's long zenith, the song features a narrator who brags to his lover that he has stolen her "love." It's not a love song, since he's mocking his lover, who lost something she did not apparently want to lose. The song is crass boasting and represents one of the few mis-steps in Stanley's canon of love songs that otherwise present love as a source of joy, communion, hope, and beauty.

Reason to Love

In the song "Reason to Live," Stanley tells his listeners that everybody has a reason to live—a dream, a hunger—but that reason for living "can't be your love." This song begs a response. Why can't "your love" be a reason for living? If we downgrade love to an opiate, or if we love poorly or incompletely—for example, if we stick around with somebody so we don't have to feel alone, or because our love is hotter than hell—then love can't be a reason to live.

A love that is an opiate and a love badly loved is probably not love. But if love is complete and rightly ordered, then it can be a reason to live. And not just a reason to live, but a source of joy and beauty and song.

13
You Wanted the Best, You've Got the *Right to the Best*

Mikko M. Puumala

The End of the Road tour is here, which means soon there'll be no more KISS to rock and roll all night and party every day. Yet, there's been some talk (and lots of rumors) that KISS could go on even after Gene Simmons and Paul Stanley choose to retire. Like Tommy Thayer and Eric Singer, who very successfully took the roles and outfits of the Spaceman and the Catman, someone else could step in to the boots of the Demon and the Starchild. The show could go on.

In fact, the idea of KISS continuing after Gene and Paul has been entertained by both in some recent interviews (for example, by Paul in *Rolling Stone* on May 30th 2019). In his book *Backstage Pass* Paul points out that KISS is more than the individual members playing in it. It seems safe enough to say that it is at least possible for KISS to continue without any original members. For at the very least, after the last encore, the confetti-covered audience will be hungry for more.

For the die-hard KISS fans (and the KISS Army!) the chance to take one's own children or grandchildren to a KISS show in the future would be great news. Even now, there can be multiple generations gathered to see their heroes play live. It is understandable that we want to convey such experiences to next generations. We already do it all the time. We want to leave the future generations things that we enjoy and value. We want to leave them beautiful places in nature, pass on the culture of our ancestors, and gift them the greatest achievements of our own generation.

Such emotions are an essential part of the motivation for any kind of culture or nature preservation or conservation efforts. In some cases, there is even a strong normative claim for preserving something. In these cases, it is argued that something *ought* to be preserved for future generations. Could a similar normative case be made for experiencing KISS?

The present generation always has a special power relation to the future generations: the future generations don't have a say on what we leave for them. Some things are necessary for their well-being, like leaving a healthy environment, and these are clearly the cases where the interests of future generations should be considered. But the interests don't have to have anything to do with fundamental needs or prerequisites of well-being. There are things that probably should be preserved for the future generations even though we can't be sure that the future generations will value them. The future generations don't *need* the Mona Lisa, for example, but a strong case can be made for preserving the Mona Lisa because at least we value it and perhaps the future generations will (or ought to) value it as well. It should be up to them to decide if they value it or not, and the present generation can't make that decision on behalf of the future ones.

In short, there are things that we ought to preserve or conserve for the future generations, even if only for their enjoyment. Is KISS, then, one of them?

Never Enough

We can easily imagine there being fans who'd demand more KISS in the future. To support the demand, an argument from preservation can be made. Let's assume that experiencing a live KISS show is at least as good as experiencing the visit to Niagara Falls or the Colosseum. Just as neglecting to preserve or destroying Niagara Falls or the Colosseum would violate the *rights of future generations*, does ending KISS violate the similar rights of the future KISS Army-would-be's? Is there a *corresponding duty* for Mr. Simmons and Mr. Stanley to ensure that their legacy rocks on? Do they owe it to the future?

For our purposes, let's call a fan making such claims about KISS's future the Preservationist. The Preservationist's argument could go somewhat like this: If possible, the future generations ought not to be denied chances for great experiences. Seeing KISS play live is a great experience. Therefore, if possible, future generations ought to be given the chance for the great experience of seeing KISS play live.

The notion of possibility takes into account that preserving something must be somehow realizable. The Preservationist should give us some account, then, of how KISS could be preserved. Also, the Preservationist should be able to tell us what exactly is *the* KISS that is to be preserved. We will look more closely into some possible accounts for those soon enough.

It should be noted that the argument only mentions the *chance* of seeing KISS. That is to say, it does not mean that there is a right to actually see KISS play. The mere chance for doing so is sufficient. Consider the Colosseum. Even though we owed the future generations the chance of experiencing the Colosseum, we owe them nothing about actually experiencing it. There doesn't have to be a general right to go and visit any of these landmarks, and the duty to preserve them doesn't seem to entail such a right. It is enough to preserve the chance for those who wish to see KISS.

Two Sides of the Coin

To gain further support for the case of demanding that KISS continues, the Preservationist can work with an analogy. An analogy is a method where a link between two different cases is made as a part of an argument, or just for demonstration. When used as a part of an argument, an analogy looks usually something like this: "if X and Y are analogous, and A is true in X, then A is also (probably) true in Y." If the purpose of the analogy is to demonstrate something, it is used as a tool to guide our intuitions in a more desirable direction. A good analogy usually serves both purposes.

The Preservationist can try to show that KISS ought to continue, because the future generations have a right to experience it. Analogously, the Colosseum ought to be preserved for the future generations because they have a right for the chance to experience it. Now we can look at the many justifications for preserving the Colosseum. If the analogy holds, then at least some of the justifications for preserving the Colosseum apply to preserving KISS as well.

The reasons for preserving something for future generations can vary from the inherent value and beauty of some place or structure to its being historically valuable or a good representation of some era or time period. The Colosseum and KISS share a few similarities that prompt justification for preservation in the case of the former, and therefore probably in the latter as well, if the analogy holds. For example, both represent some time period and are monumental in that respect. The Colosseum reminds us of Roman culture, the Roman way of life, and so on. KISS is similarly a monument of a certain epoch in rock music (which finally led them into the Rock'n'Roll Hall of Fame in 2014).

The reason for preservation can also be related to the qualities of the preserved things that inspire awe or give great experiences. Most natural monuments, like Niagara Falls, are preserved and sometimes repaired and restored so that the future generations could enjoy the experience of seeing and witnessing their beauty and power. So, reasons for preservation do not solely rest on historical value. The Preservationist can demand that KISS continues because analogously to Niagara Falls, such great experiences should be passed on to future generations. The live experience is stressed in these cases, so mere records and live videos of KISS playing are not enough, just as it is not enough to make a movie or a detailed record of Niagara Falls.

Got to Choose

Now that we have a rough idea about the Preservationist's case, we can move forward to discover some problems it faces. As much as we want to see KISS in the future, the Preservationist must be able to account for: 1. what is it exactly that should be preserved about KISS and 2. what can be changed about KISS before it ceases to be KISS.

Argument by analogy, *reductio ad absurdum* (more on that later), and so on, are some of the argumentative methods philosophers use. These philosophical methods used in this chapter are like guitar tricks, like the guitar licks used masterfully by Ace Frehley. Of course, it takes more than a few tricks to be a great guitar player like Ace but trying to nail the solo of "Love Gun" is a good place to start. Hence, we pay a little more attention to different tricks. If you want to learn the kind of guitar sweep picking, harmonics, and tapping philosophers use, I heartily recommend the second edition of *The Philosopher's Toolkit* by Julian Baggini and Peter S. Fosl.

So, let's continue with a face-melting trick called *reductio ad absurdum*. It is commonly used to show that if we follow some argument, we will end up in an absurdity. The user of the *reductio* accepts the initial argument only to show that accepting the argument leads into unacceptable consequences, usually unintended by the original proponent of the argument. It's an indirect way to point out that the argument is at least intuitively implausible. It's based on logic in the sense that it deals with the logical consequences of some argument, but its main power is psychological: the consequences are too ridiculous or absurd to accept, so it sheds doubt on the plausibility of the argument. Instead of insisting on making the argument, the proponent of the target of the *reductio* might want to look for other options to making a similar point.

Now, the opponent of the Preservationist can accept the Preservationist's argument but lead us to the awkward conclusion that if KISS ought to be preserved for the future generations, we must preserve all or most rock groups, since nearly all or most of them give their audiences great experiences. Also, most of them are an important instance of the rock music-related culture that ought to be preserved. That is because all great bands have dedicated fans and fan clubs, memories and merchandise, legendary songs and the ability to offer larger than life experiences. But clearly this is not what the (KISS) Preservationist had in mind.

It is problematic to apply this preservation argument to rock groups. How do we tell which bands to preserve this way? We want KISS on the list, but to avoid the absurd conclusion that *all* rock groups must be preserved, we must show that KISS is unique enough to exclude (most of) other groups. Here we can deepen the analogy to Niagara falls and the Colosseum. Just as we don't need to preserve every body of water and every building, we don't need to preserve *every* rock band. There must be some list of unique features that justify preservation efforts for certain old structures and certain places in nature, or some criteria for justifying demands for preservation.

Good candidates for unique features include the already mentioned different stage characters and their masks and outfits, the shows, the fan community (KISS army) and the richness in KISS-related artifacts (the mindboggling variety of merchandise). It is unlikely that one unique feature is enough to justify the claims of the preservationist. Other groups, like Slipknot and Lordi, wear masks. There are other groups, like Insane Clown Posse, who also have an impressive fan community (the Juggalos, who even made it to FBI's gang list). Some of these groups will probably make it to the preservationist's list even if we insist that it is a combination of these features that count.

On the other hand, being able to exclude most other groups can give a suitable enough list. We can demand preservation for Notre Dame and the Golden Gate Bridge on the same grounds that we demand preservation for the Colosseum. It doesn't make the case for preserving the Colosseum for the future generations any weaker. On the contrary, the preservationist can indeed conclude that all these groups should be preserved and be happy that KISS is in such good company. It is enough to separate them from most groups. *Reductio ad absurdum* only works if both parties agree on what is not an acceptable outcome. Sometimes a good counter strategy is to endorse the outcome. In this case, it is completely acceptable that the list of the Preservationist must include also other groups than KISS, although not necessarily all of them.

Further, we can note that some groups are easier to preserve than others. KISS is particularly easy to preserve, since very little changes on the outside. No matter who carries on that role, you can still see the Starchild fly across the room to play "Love Gun" in the middle of the audience, or the Demon spitting blood before "God of Thunder." And in our analogy, who cares if a few bricks are replaced in the Colosseum, if you can still imagine the gladiators fighting fiercely on the arena? Niagara Falls are restored and repaired every now and then, even to a point where it is not clear whether

it is a *natural* monument any longer. Yet, it should be preserved for future generations.

Back to the Stone Age

Even if we could produce an exclusive-enough list, we would
still face a problem of identifying what exactly is the KISS
that we are preserving.

To make the point, we can use another cool trick, namely,
a thought experiment. Thought experiments are imaginary
or real cases that we use to figure out what is a crucial or
important part or aspect in some phenomena, like the case
of preservation. Now, I'm using a thought experiment to unmask a type of a problem in preservation cases.

> *The Castle:* Imagine that an earthquake destroys most parts of a
> historical castle. The castle itself and the castle grounds had many
> layers of history built on top of each other. Different historical ar-
> chitectural styles were present, as were materials from different
> times. However, the earthquake also revealed areas of the castle
> that were unknown to the general public and even the archeolo-
> gists. The skillful restoration team says that they can, using the
> material left behind by the earthquake, restore the castle to its orig-
> inal form. However, with the finding of new layers, and the possi-
> bility to restore just about any historical era of the castle, it is not
> at all clear *which* castle the team should restore.

It was probably easier to do restorations in a castle that had
organically and continuously continued in its existence
through the ages, there being historical alterations here and
there. The restoration team only had to make sure it continues to exist as it is. But the earthquake caused a disconti-
uation, and after that they had to make a decision: repair
the castle and make it look like it was the day before the
earthquake, or, for example, restore it to the form of some
historical days of glory?

Now we can make an analogy to the case of the Castle.
Just as the earthquake disturbed the organic historical
process that brought it to this day, the End of the Road tour
seems to be doing something similar. Just like a castle, KISS
has seen many historical forms and responded (organically)

to many historical changes around them. They even took the masks off in the 1980s and continued being KISS. But after they call it quits, and a discontinuation similar to an earthquake in the Castle occurs, what KISS are the future members of KISS supposed to represent? All options seem equally plausible.

If the Preservationist's argument rests on an analogy with experience, different historical and generational experiences might be important to take into account. For example, for me, the earliest memories of KISS are from the 1990s reunion era, seeing them on TV in their full make-up. I was surprised to learn later that they had an unmasked era, but that was *the* KISS for my older cousin, who was an Eighties kid. When I was a teenager, he took me to my first KISS show, part of the *Alive/35* tour. After that, the most anticipated KISS album, for me, was *Sonic Boom*. In memories, that is *the* KISS for me. Some older KISS Army veteran might disagree with both me and my cousin, making a (very reasonable) claim that the *real* KISS was the original line-up, perhaps during the *Love Gun* tour. While all three of us might agree that all KISS eras have been great and important parts of KISStory, there's lots of ground for disagreement about the KISS that should be preserved for the future.

So, the problem remains, what exactly is the KISS that the Preservationist has in mind *after* the End of the Road? Is it the current one? The masked, original line-up from the Seventies? What about the unmasked Eighties? Should they try to accommodate features of each era, like in the castle?

The unmasked Eighties and early Nineties KISS might have to be excluded. This has to do with the possibilities for preservation. Something important would change if the stage characters, which arguably are tied to the masks and outfits, would be left out. What makes KISS uniquely fit for continuing the live experience in the future is that the whole KISS experience would remain intact even if some member would be changed (as has happened many times). Without the masks and the outfits, it is far easier to realize that some band members have changed. From the unmasked era, only the songs could remain.

Also, what would be an appropriate set list for this future KISS? Can they play anything from the *Music from "The*

Elder"? If, like in the Castle thought experiment, some historical state would be preserved, what should it be? For example, should they play only songs included in *Alive!*, the breakthrough album? This would exclude most hit songs they wrote much later. Or should the band pick up from where the previous lineup left? If they should, the Preservationist's case faces new problems.

Is That You?

In addition to questions of which KISS should continue after the End of the Road tour, the limits on future KISS members are unclear. To remain authentic, there's a danger that KISS becomes *museumized* in a sense that the band wouldn't be allowed or even able to evolve. In other words, the same features that make KISS unique and worthy of preserving can become a prison to the future starchildren and demons. Can the future members of KISS record new albums? What could they be like?

This problem of change is especially detrimental with KISS, even contradictory to real KISSness. They have always followed their time and changing trends in the music business. They've made movies, played disco and glam rock when it was cool (and perhaps a little longer), and they even made a grunge album in the 1990s. If *KISS Meets the Phantom of the Park* the movie wasn't particularly a success, going disco was, at least in the sense that they wrote one of their biggest hits, "I Was Made for Lovin' You," when taking that road. Many great hits emerged from the unmasked 1980s. Taking risks and making big changes are an integral part of the KISStory.

So, if folk music becomes mainstream, might we hear an acoustic KISS folk album? Could the future Demon play 30-minute-long bass jazz odysseys if that becomes a thing? If KISS couldn't change, that would imply a very ahistorical and static view of the group. Then again, would that KISS be authentic?

The danger is, then, that the KISS the Preservationist wants to preserve becomes a trap from which the band couldn't evolve any longer. What makes the band unique in the sense that it belongs to the Preservationists list may bind the future KISS unreasonably. There's a danger, then, that KISS becomes museumized, or a relic from the past. And as we've seen, that works against the very same things that kept KISS alive through the decades: they knew how to adapt. KISS has always responded to changes in music industry, for good and bad. Preserving KISS in a static way contradicts the spirit of these different eras in KISStory.

A World Without Heroes

The Preservationist has a hard time showing that there could be a *duty* to preserve KISS for future generations. By assuming that someone would make such an argument we have, however, unmasked some interesting problems regarding the possibility that KISS continues without any original members (in this sense the whole chapter was a thought experiment). These are questions about what is important in something being a group called KISS and continuing their legacy.

There is probably no special moral duty for Mr. Simmons and Mr. Stanley to allow KISS to continue without them, at least not in the sense the Preservationist might want to have it. But a brief utilitarian case could be made to favor the continuation of KISS. Utilitarianism is a moral theory that, roughly put, tells us that we should always pursue actions with the best overall outcomes. And as long as people are willing to go out and have a good time, the world would be a better place, overall, with KISS being around. It would certainly be a better one than the world without our heroes. [1]

[1] This chapter was written with the support of the Maj and Tor Nessling Foundation. Also, special thanks to Harri for taking me to my first KISS concert!

IV

The Catman

14
The Joyful Relativity of Kondoms and Kaskets

CASEY RENTMEESTER

Having sold more than one hundred million records worldwide, KISS has come to be one of the best selling bands of all time. From their over-the-top stage personas and theatrics to their eclectic merchandizing endeavors that span from condoms to caskets, KISS has lived up to their famous tagline as "the hottest band in the world."

This chapter analyzes the band—and the brand—that is KISS through the lenses of the philosophies of Friedrich Nietzsche and Mikhail Bakhtin.

KISS's music can be properly understood as an embodiment of what Friedrich Nietzsche in *The Birth of Tragedy* calls the Dionysian. As opposed to the measured and calm restraint that is found in Apollonian music, Dionysian music praises the raw, instinctual, and the libidinous aspects of life. Songs like "Rock and Roll All Nite" that embrace the party life and songs like "Love Gun" that celebrate sex are exemplars of the Dionysian.

KISS, however, is much more than their music. KISS brings to life what Mikhail Bakhtin refers to as carnival—what KISS might call a "Psycho Circus"—wherein ordinary social conventions are turned upside down and a freer, unrestricted, and playful world emerges that proclaims the joyful relativity of all order and structure.

The KISS Kondom, which is marketed as a condom that offers "Love Gun Protection," demonstrates the levity that often accompanies Bakhtinian carnival, as does the KISS

Kasket, a coffin licensed by the band that dons the famous KISS logo and pictures of the band members in their iconic make-up.

By manifesting carnival, KISS taps into what Bakhtin refers to as the latent sides of human nature that otherwise remain hidden and thereby teaches us all to lighten up a bit. While most of us can't "rock and roll all nite and party every day," KISS reminds us that the sometimes sterile status quo needs to be loosened up every once in a while and swapped out for a more playful world.

A Band for Everyone and No One

If there were one thinker who embodied the spirit and energy of KISS, it would clearly be the nineteenth-century philosopher Friedrich Nietzsche. Born to a pastor and a deeply devout Christian mother in small-town Germany, Nietzsche forswore his humble, pious beginnings to emerge as the "bad boy" of philosophy and, indeed, of Western civilization as such.

Having boldly proclaimed the death of God, Nietzsche would later in life refer to himself simply as "the Antichrist." He "philosophized with a hammer" and, in doing so, intellectually killed off what were once seemingly untouchable idols: religion, morality, and even truth itself. Think of KISS bassist Gene Simmons in his full-on Demon costume spitting blood and breathing fire to a packed audience: that is the equivalent of Friedrich Nietzsche in the world of philosophy. As Nietzsche aptly put it in his autobiography, *Ecce Homo*, he was no man: he was dynamite.

In Nietzsche's first work, *The Birth of Tragedy*, he examines two forces that can be recognized in all aspects of life, and particularly in artistic expressions like music: the Apollonian and the Dionysian. The Apollonian refers to the measured and calm restraint that evokes order, harmony, rationality, and symmetry, while the Dionysian refers to the raw, instinctual, and libidinous aspects of life that arouse chaos, untempered emotion, runaway passion, sex, madness, and drunkenness. Nietzsche referred to himself as a disciple of Dionysus, and he thought that a life devoted strictly to the Apollonian was a life not worth living. He famously wrote in

Twilight of the Idols or How to Philosophize with the Hammer that "without music life would be an error," and he made it very clear in one of his most famous works, *Thus Spake Zarathustra:A Book for Everyone and No One,* that he would only believe in a god who could dance, thus demonstrating his decided preference for the Dionysian over the Apollonian.

According to Nietzsche, the Apollonian took a strong grip on Western civilization in ancient Greece with the figure of Socrates, whom he interprets as the embodiment of reason. Nietzsche claims in *The Birth of Tragedy* that Socrates left his mark on Western civilization by showing that "the only true human vocation" is "to separate true knowledge from appearance and error." Since then, so argues Nietzsche, the Dionysian aspects of life were demonized and left to the wayside.

Lucky for us, the Demon and his fellow characters the Starchild, the Spaceman, and the Catman have been around since 1973 to keep the Dionysian ALIVE! The band's 1975 release *Alive!* catapulted KISS into stardom by featuring songs that celebrate the Dionysian. KISS had already gained a considerable cult following due to their legendary stage theatrics that included their signature stage personas, explosive pyrotechnics, band members flying across the stage, bombastic sound, stage elevators, and raw energy; however, their first three studio albums did not capture the energy that we've all come to associate with "the hottest band in the world."

The two-album *Alive!* release is KISS at its finest, as it showcases the over-the-top energy and superhero presence of its band members. Above and beyond the killer guitar riffs and pyrotechnic excitement comes the lyrics of the songs that celebrate and no doubt awaken the Dionysian aspects in us all. Songs like "Strutter," "Hotter than Hell," and "C'mon and Love Me" celebrate lustful passion and sex, while their hit "Rock and Roll All Nite" has become perhaps the most iconic party song in rock and roll history. *Alive!* was followed by *Alive II* just two years later, which featured even more tracks celebrating sex and lust like "Love Gun" and "Calling Dr. Love," as well as another legendary party anthem in "Shout It Out Loud." When Cheap Trick sings about mom and dad rolling on the couch "rolling numbers, rock and rollin'/Got my KISS records out" in the popular song

"Surrender," everyone knows what they are talking about. KISS is a party band that even mom and dad can embrace.

KISS's odes to Dionysus, of course, were not met with universal approval. In *No Regrets*, lead guitarist Ace Frehley recalls the reception the band received early in their careers: "I remember some of our early tours, there were religious fanatics outside the shows burning our records, saying we were devil worshippers." Some of this was fueled by the mistaken rumor that KISS stood for "Knights in Satan's Service," which has been repeatedly denied by KISS band members. Nevertheless, from a Nietzschean perspective, KISS is indeed a band for everyone and no one.

Nietzsche thinks that everyone has Dionysian aspects to themselves, but some people have forgotten to tap into their Dionysian elements and have indeed suppressed them altogether. The result is a conventional, prudent, and conservative existence. Purely Apollonian people fear what would happen if their wild sides were to make an appearance; some even try to cut off the Dionysian in us all, like the religious fanatics Frehley and his bandmates came across in their early years. These are the types of people who KISS would say are "too old to really understand" in their 1976 party anthem "Shout It Out Loud."

A healthier approach to life, so argues Nietzsche, would be a balance between the reasonable and tempered formalities of the Apollinian and the freer, less restrictive forms of life that open up when we stop being slaves to convention and allow ourselves to tap into the Dionysian. When we do so, Nietzsche states in *The Birth of Tragedy*, "Now the slave is a free man; now all the rigid, hostile barriers that necessity, caprice, or 'impudent convention' have fixed between man and man are broken. Now . . . each one feels himself not only united, reconciled, and fused with his neighbor, but as one with him." The Dionysian allows people to let down their guard and become unified with others. Anyone who has been to a KISS concert can verify that the spectacle induces a sense of unity with other members of the audience, as everyone—not only the notoriously loyal and I dare say *militant* KISS Army members donned in full-on KISS garb—simultaneously belts out KISS classics in unison. KISS allows people to open themselves up to a place where the wild and free aspects of themselves run freely, where "everybody's gonna move their feet" and "everybody's gonna leave their seat."

You Drive Us Wild, We'll Drive You Crazy

One of the reasons for the massive success of KISS is the band's larger-than-life stage personas that take on a super-hero presence. In his autobiography, *KISS and Make-Up*, Gene Simmons explains the metamorphosis that takes place when he transforms into his diabolical stage character, the Demon: "When I put on face paint, it was a kind of transformation. And when I took to the stage, it was the most profound transformation of them all. In the process, I managed to help steer KISS to the pinnacle of rock'n'roll."

Simmons not only acts as if he were another person when he performs on stage: he *becomes* the Demon, with all the full-blown arrogance and tongue-waggling indecencies that accompany the character. Fellow founding member Paul Stanley explains in *Face the Music* a similar transformation when he becomes the Starchild: "When I first put this make-up on, I had a sense of another person coming out . . . The character I created—the Starchild—would go up on stage and be *that guy*, the superhero, as opposed to the person I really was." When Stanley becomes the Starchild, he is more than the frontman and rhythm guitarist for the band; rather, he takes on an entirely different persona than his normal, everyday being. These transformations that take place as the band members mutate into KISS, as well as the transformations that often occur from members of the audience who temporarily leave their everyday existence, can be understood via the lens of Mikhail Bakhtin's notion of carnival.

Mikhail Bakhtin was a twentieth-century Russian philosopher who analyzed the way in which times of carnival functioned for persons in medieval Europe. Although much of a medieval person's life was guided by formal rules and regulations dictated by traditional rituals and hierarchical relationships, medieval European towns had carnival festivities wherein the normal, stable, and formal conventions were subverted and replaced with a freer, more open-ended reality that celebrated abundance, equality, and community. In times of carnival, what was conventionally considered to be taboo became permissible and even celebrated as townspeople donned masks and participated in lewd and downright crude behavior that included excessive alcohol consumption, sexually explicit acts, and overt mockery of authorities.

While some might think that carnival served merely as amusement for medieval persons, Bakhtin argues that carnival events played a much larger role. He states in *Rabelais and His World* that carnival "is by no means a purely artistic form nor a spectacle and does not, generally speaking, belong to the sphere of art. It belongs to the borderline between art and life .... Carnival is not a spectacle seen by the people; they live in it, and everyone participates because its very idea embraces all the people." In carnival, normal societal conventions are cast aside and swapped out for a less formal, more carefree way of being. In *Problems of Dostoevsky's Poetics*, Bakhtin argues that laughter plays an especially important role in these events, as participants make a mockery of the formality that exists in normal everyday life and embrace an "atmosphere of *joyful relativity*" where otherwise indecent words, expressions, and gestures are taken up with a sense of lightheartedness and indeed enthusiasm.

Simmons's and Stanley's description of the transformation that they experience when they become the Demon and the Starchild respectively fit nicely with what Bakhtin is referencing with regard to carnival. Importantly, when this transformation takes place, Bakhtin stresses that it is not as though the participants are merely acting a part; rather, the participants *become* the characters that they are acting. Despite the levity and humor that often accompanied carnival, the participants *lived* in their newly formed characters as if this were the *only* reality and, thus, there's a level of seriousness involved in the transition.

As KISS lead guitarist Ace Frehley put it in his reflection on becoming the Spaceman in *No Regrets*, "We might have looked like rejects from a science-fiction or horror movie, but we were deadly serious about what we were doing." In *Make-Up to Breakup*, drummer Peter Criss echoes this sentiment in reflecting on becoming the Catman: "When I put on that Cat make-up, I truly was transformed. Forget about Peter Criscuola, the kid from Brooklyn. He didn't exist. I believed

I was a superhero." The stern dedication involved in becoming their respective characters allowed the KISS band members to create a carnival experience that celebrated the Dionysian in ways unsurpassed by other bands.

Bakhtin argues that carnival allows participants to engage in topics and behaviors that are otherwise frowned upon. The themes of some of the most iconic KISS songs engage in subjects that are obviously taboo from the perspective of societal conventionality. In "Black Diamond," Stanley fantasizes about New York City prostitutes, while Simmons's "Christine Sixteen" and "Goin' Blind" are about an older man infatuated with a sixteen-year-old girl. Simmons outdoes the shock factor of "Goin' Blind" and "Christine Sixteen" with the concert favorite "God of Thunder," which is about being a devilish god who robs an innocent girl of her virgin soul and invariably includes the Demon's signature blood spitting and fire breathing antics when performed on stage.

In normal, everyday settings, persons might fantasize about similar things but they certainly do not talk about them, much less sing about them to thousands of people. According to Bakhtin's *Problems of Dostoevsky's Poetics*, in times of carnival, where freedom reigns supreme, "the latent sides of human nature . . . reveal and express themselves," and the crowd celebrates the liberation from the all-too-serious nature of normal life in the process while embracing the joyful relativity of order and structure. This may explain why KISS concerts bring out the wild and crazy in us all. What other concert event draws so many fans decked out in the face paint of their favorite band member, with the black leather and platforms to match?

I was lucky enough to experience KISS in concert in 2011 at a rodeo in Houston, Texas and in 2014 at Alpine Valley near Milwaukee, Wisconsin. At the first show in Houston, there were fans decked out in full-on KISS gear and face paint alongside cowboys and cowgirls in their ten-gallon hats. Normally the combination of glam metal fans and rodeo-goers would elicit a significant contrast, but everyone embraced the environment with a spirit of cheerfulness thanks to the carnival atmosphere that accompanies a KISS event. At Alpine Valley, I saw my father-in-law, a middle-aged man who analyzes investments all day in his suit and tie, joyfully belting out the lyrics of nearly every song as he alternated between pumping his fist to the beat and flashing the "rock on" hand horns that Gene Simmons has made so popular. At his side was his fifteen-year-old daughter doing the same. KISS is for everyone, because it brings out versions of ourselves that lie latent but need to be expressed every now and again if we are to heed the Apollonian-Dionysian balance that Nietzsche prescribed.

You Wanted the Best, You Got the Best!

More than perhaps any other band, KISS is far bigger than the music it produces: without question, KISS has become a brand in itself. Along with being America's number-one gold album record award winning band of all time, according to *Nothin' to Lose: The Making of KISS*, KISS has proven to be masterful in its merchandizing and marketing endeavors, as they boast a catalog of over three thousand products that has grossed them over five hundred million dollars. In the 1970s, in order to increase their popularity, the band launched KISS lunchboxes and pinball machines, which were not uncommon marketing tactics for bands at the time. KISS entered new terrain, though, in creating the KISS comic book in 1977, which was printed with the help of the blood of each band member—and, of course, marketed as such. The cover showcases the KISS logo and the four band members in action poses with fire rising in the background to help cement the superhero personas that we have come to know today. This opened KISS up to new merchandizing horizons that easily has a wider and more eclectic span than any other band in history.

Bakhtin argues that carnival often involves what he refers to as decrowning, wherein participants reveal a less serious, more playful side to even the most starkly serious matters, which KISS has successfully shown with their KISS Kondoms and KISS Kasket. The first KISS Kondom was released in 1991 and marketed as the "Rise to It" condom, an homage to the title of the opening track of the 1989 album, *Hot in the Shade*.

To understand the historical context, one should keep in mind that President Ronald Reagan made it very clear during his presidency that he thought the proper means of sexual education for high school children was to promote abstinence rather than promote the use of protection, as condoms were very much a social taboo at the time. In fact, according to Aine Collier's *The Humble Little Condom*, the first condom commercial advertisement on television wasn't aired until late 1991 by Fox Television, with NBC and CBS only following suit ten years later. KISS helped to break the social taboo surrounding condoms by slapping the famous KISS logo on the "Rise to It" condom, thereby helping to make condoms cool. This was followed by several other promotional endeavors in this realm, including the "Unholy" condom of 1992 and the three-style release of KISS Kondoms, billed playfully as "Rock 'N' Rubbers" in 2002: "Love Gun Protection," "Studded Paul," and "Tongue Lubricated." In doing so, KISS not only ventured into new merchandizing territory, but also helped to loosen up the stigma that condoms had at the time through their use of decrowning humor. In *The Sydney Morning Herald*'s article "KISS for Safe Sex" (June 3rd 2002), Gene Simmons explains this effect as follows: "Sex is always embarrassing for people, so when a guy whips out a KISS condom and there's Gene Simmons's tongue hanging out it lightens up the situation." Above all else, sex should be fun, and KISS has helped to remind ourselves of this fact.

Speaking of lightening up a situation, KISS controversially came out with the KISS Kasket in 2001, a casket that featured the KISS logo and images of the band members with the words "KISS Forever" on the side. The wording is an homage to the power ballad "Forever," their second single from *Hot in the Shade*, and most successful single since "I Was Made for Lovin' You" from 1979. Death, of course, is perhaps the most taboo subject in Western civilization. Many do not like to talk about death, much less think about it. This explains why so many people are so uncomfortable at funerals, as the confrontation with death is often a somber affair.

However, in *Thus Spake Zarathustra*, Nietzsche speaks about the possibility for persons to experience a free death in order to overcome the stigma that surrounds death in Western culture. He states, "Everyone regards dying as a great matter: but as yet death is not a festival . . . In your dying shall your spirit and your virtue still shine like an evening afterglow around the Earth: otherwise your dying has been unsatisfactory." From a Nietzschean perspective, funerals provide for an opportunity to celebrate a life, rather than mourn a death in the somber, sterile, and subdued manner that one typically does at a funeral. If there is no afterlife—and Nietzsche made it very clear that he didn't think there was one—then death is inevitable. And if death is inevitable, we should not avoid talking about it or thinking about it. Rather, we should seek to choose to have a free death that establishes the appropriate legacy of our spirit.

The KISS Kasket aims to do its part in alleviating some of the somberness that is associated with death, thereby opening up another possible narrative of celebration of life, instead of a mourning of death. We are all aware of the eerie lyric in "Detroit Rock City": "I got to laugh 'cause I know that I'm gonna die." The song is about how quickly a party can turn into a disaster (in this case a fatal car accident) and the senselessness that sometimes accompanies death. This senselessness was experienced firsthand by attendees at a heavy metal concert in December 2004.

Darrell "Dimebag" Abbott, who established himself as the heavy-hitting guitarist of the groove metal genre in the 1990s during his time with Pantera, was murdered by a deranged fan at a show in Columbus, Ohio. Zac Crain tells in *Black Tooth Grin* that Abbott had a tattoo of Ace Frehley's portrait and autograph on his chest, and was a self-proclaimed Frehley wannabe who "had KISS stuff everywhere" in his home. He was the kind of guy who loved to have a good time and made sure that everyone else was having a good time as well. Thus, it was fitting that Abbott's funeral was framed as a celebration of the life he led and included eulogies from heavy metal guitarist royalty, including Eddie Van Halen and Zakk Wylde (the lead guitarist for Ozzy Osbourne). Abbott was aptly buried in a KISS Kasket. This shows that while the KISS Kasket is certainly not for everyone, it is an appropriate way to establish the legacy of those "creatures of the night" like Abbott who live for the Dionysian.

Lick It Up

KISS have announced that their "End of the Road World Tour," will be the last tour with Gene Simmons and Paul

Stanley at the helm. Some have questioned whether or not KISS will survive beyond the tenure of Simmons and Stanley. From a Bakhtinian perspective, you could argue that as long as the persons taking up the personas of the Demon, the Starchild, the Spaceman, and the Catman embody them with the same spirit and dedication as the original KISS members, there's no reason why KISS can't keep the party going since KISS has undoubtedly become a cultural phenomenon that is bigger than the band itself.

By getting us all to tap into the Dionysian and opening ourselves up to the joyful relativity of carnival, KISS has offered us all a steady reminder to live life to the fullest and lick it up.

15
The Rashomon Effect in KISS's Autobiographies

Michael Forest and Matthew Mitchell

The more I hear, the more confused I get.

—Commoner in *Rashomon*

In the justly famous 1950 movie *Rashomon* by Akira Kurasawa, we are presented with different versions of an event by the four individuals who experienced it. The film proceeds, initially however, from the point of view of those supposedly on the outside of the event in question: a woodcutter who finds a body, a priest who sees a samurai and a lady, and a bounty hunter who finds the bandit Tajomaru. They, and the principal characters—the bandit, the samurai/husband, the lady/wife, and then again the woodcutter—generally speak directly into or just over the camera lens at the interrogator who's never on screen but implies that we the viewers are the ones who must determine the truth or falsity of the varying accounts. The movie has led to a popularized conception—the Rashomon Effect—in which varying accounts from different perspectives seem to block our access to what really happened.

What could be a better framework for reading the autobiographies of the four original band members of KISS as they recount events they all participated in but from varying perspectives? Each member gives differing accounts to us, the interrogators, and it's up to us to decide what is truth and what is fiction. Thankfully, we're aided in our survey by some philosophical concepts from two twentieth-century philosophers: the Canadian Bernard Lonergan and the famous French intellectual Jean-Paul Sartre. Our survey will show something like a Rashomon Effect for the original KISS members, with special focus on the recording of *Destroyer* (1976), but also importantly for ourselves as readers of the autobiographies, viewers of Kurosawa's movie, and as fans who still inexorably and naively want to know "how things happened."

Destroyer and "Beth"

The generally accepted understanding of the history of KISS on the eve of *Destroyer* runs as follows: three rapidly issued studio albums that failed to hit, and a financially struggling record label, led to a somewhat desperate counterintuitive move that paid off—the recording of the double live album *Alive!* This move may have saved Casablanca Records and the band, but it presented new challenges along with its opportunities. The new studio album needed to capitalize on the band's momentum, propel them forward, and could, for the first time, benefit from highly professional production support. As KISStory notes, the album's current status as a classic had to overcome the hurdles of an initially cool reception from some fans, suspicious of the strings and choral sections, before the unexpected hit song from the B side of "Detroit Rock City," "Beth," became wildly popular. This was also the launch of KISS as a cultural phenomenon throughout the late 1970s.

With the benefit of the passage of time, *Destroyer* is notable for a number of reasons beyond the story outlined above. It's the first collaboration with Bob Ezrin, who later produced *Music from "The Elder"* and *Revenge*, both widely seen as pivotal moments of disarray or re-ascendancy. It's an album whose recording, according to the testimony of the four members of the band, already saw the use of session guitarists, accusations of lackluster work, controlling behavior, frustrations over Peter's musical capabilities, and Peter's sense of not being given the respect he deserved, even as "his" song became the driving single for the band's success.

Thus, *Destroyer* is the album that cemented KISS in a trajectory of growing popularity while also strengthening the forces—though hidden at the time—that would lead to the dissolution of the original lineup. In *Face the Music*, Paul explicitly refers to "fatal fissures in the band" first opening at this time, although the fissures in his account are created by Ace and Peter. In this regard, it's notable that Gene's memoir adds an additional appendix in its paperback edition focused strictly on the process of recording *Destroyer*.

Sharing the Rashomon Effect

Ezrin's combination of vision, drug addiction, control, and perfectionism are commented upon by everyone. The harmony guitar solos on "Detroit Rock City," the voices of his children in the studio on "God of Thunder;" these stories are all recounted and shared. Additionally, a sympathetic reader can charitably see how a shared experience, such as recording an album, is not "the same experience" for everyone involved. One person sees only half of the band being competent or disciplined, and thus they end up doing "eighty percent of the work" (Paul). Another person lacks the confidence to present material and to meet the demands of a producer like Ezrin, so they withdraw (Ace). Someone else may take away the feeling of being shut-out, despite contributing the song that saved the album (Peter).

The actual detailed story of the composition and recording of "Beth," however, is another matter altogether. Trying to answer the simple question of "Who wrote the song?" leads us into a web of parallel narratives that seem tantalizingly similar, yet fail to cohere when we attempt to reconstruct a single series of events. Self-serving attributions of credit and accusations of fault are present in *all* accounts, and the hypothetical reader to whom the memoirs address themselves finds that, like the viewer/judge in *Rashomon*, they are unable to make a confident claim about one participant's perspective as somehow "the way it really was." To help us navigate some of these narratives, we will first look at some pertinent concepts by two twentieth-century philosophers who, like Kurasawa, worried about the veracity of our individual interpretations and perspectives.

Blind Spots . . .

It's human to lie. Most of the time we can't even be honest with ourselves.

—Commoner in *Rashomon*

Take out a sheet of paper. Place it in front of you 'sideways' so that the long edges run from left to right rather than up or down. Place a penny on the right edge of the paper. Cover your left eye with your left hand. Keep your right eye focused on the left edge of the paper. Now with your free hand slowly move the penny from the right side to the left. Somewhere near the middle of the page, the penny will "disappear." Congratulations. You've found your blind spot. The blind spot in our eye is called a 'scotoma', and the Canadian philosopher Bernard Lonergan called our tendency to have intellectual blind spots 'scotosis'—the condition of not being able to understand what we are experiencing.

For Lonergan, scotosis prevents us from having an insight—a grasping of elements in an act of understanding. We interpret our experiences through acts of understanding in ordinary moments—who took the cookies off the plate? I bet it was the dog!—and also in rarer moments such as the generation of a scientific hypothesis. These acts of understanding are not "truth makers," since we can have false interpretations—aha! it was the kids and not the dog—but they are the candidates for true statements, and without a lot of insights we have less chance of arriving at the most reasonable interpretation of any given phenomena. Having a blind spot means that we prevent insights from occurring and thus reduce our chances of seeing things from other perspectives and considering evidence against our own entrenched or preferred interpretation. In this sense, Lonergan notes that "scotosis is an aberration, not only of the understanding, but also of the censorship."

We saw this sort of interpretation and censorship in the varying accounts from Paul, Ace, and Peter previously discussed. They all have images and reputations to protect, so they interpret and construct memories that either support their self-image and/or diminish the reputation of the other members. This idea of wrongful self-censorship segues nicely into Sartre's idea of bad faith.

. . . and Bad Faith

Man just wants to forget the bad stuff and believe the made-up good stuff. It's easier that way.

—Commoner in *Rashomon*

While we focused on the intellectual problem of failing to understand because of blind spots through the texts of Bernard Lonergan, the idea of living in 'bad faith' comes through the philosophy of the French philosopher, novelist, and critic Jean-Paul Sartre. His fame goes well beyond the confines of philosophy. Sartre, just to properly distance himself from the four band members of KISS, was awarded the Nobel Prize for Literature in 1964. It came with a monetary award of what would roughly be $260,000 in 2019. Sartre rejected it because, as he explained in an open letter also published in the *New York Review of Books* on December 17th 1964, he thought that it unduly compromised him both as a free writer and as an advocate for socialism. It might be hard to find a figure more distant to our subjects than our French radical.

Sartre focuses on distinguishing bad faith from lying, which is actually quite difficult. In lying, I am fully aware of the truth but present myself with what Sartre calls "a cynical consciousness" that intends to deceive. Are the members aof KISS using their autobiographies to deceive fans, or are they misremembering, or have they deceived themselves about what happened? Deceiving others is fairly easy to understand, but how could I lie to myself?

In effect, bad faith is a kind of lying to oneself, but this seems logically impossible. If I know the truth but want to believe in something else, I am fully aware of this situation. As Sartre says in the section on bad faith in his most famous book *Being and Nothingness* published in 1943, "I must know what the truth is exactly *in order to* conceal it more carefully." So I present myself with something that I then hide from myself. As Sartre notes, "Our embarrassment then appears extreme since we can neither reject nor comprehend bad faith." By this he means that since bad faith appears to be a fact of our experience we cannot reject it, but because it makes no logical sense, we can't really understand how we do it.

Sartre gives an example of a woman on a date. Her date puts his hand on hers, implying physical intimacy and all that he hopes will follow. She doesn't want the relationship to become physical but she doesn't want the date to end either. So, she convinces herself that the hand holding is just a warm sign of friendship. This allows her to continue with what she wants—to spend an evening out with someone. But she lies to herself, because she also knows that the gesture implies a prelude to sexual intimacy. She might continue in the lie by denying that she accepted his advances, if the relationship moves toward this intimacy, and she might even convince herself of her interpretation of the act and become indignant. In this case, she is in bad faith.

So maybe the members of KISS are like the young woman on the date: they have deceived themselves into believing that their respective interpretation of events is correct. Given our presentation of scotosis and bad faith, we are ready to explore and draw conclusions about the four narratives of the original members a little more incisively, but as we do, let's also keep in mind that we as readers of the narratives can have our own blind spots and acts of bad faith.

The Four Narratives

This time I may finally lose my faith in the human soul.

—Priest in *Rashomon*

The simplest place to see this dynamic at play is with the question of who wrote "Beth." Here, let us follow the publication order of the memoirs. Gene attributes the "melody" to Peter, with producer Bob Ezrin doing much of the work (rewriting the lyrics and all the arrangements). Gene takes credit for changing the name of the song from "Beck" to "Beth," which occurred during a limousine ride. From *KISS and Make-up*, Gene says, "Peter brought this nice little melody into the studio and sang it for Bob. Immediately Bob sat down and fleshed it out."

Ace is characteristically vaguer and doesn't claim clarity of memory as to details, but in *No Regrets* says it was "Peter and someone else's" song that Bob Ezrin "put his stamp on." Ace claims Ezrin was responsible for the name change.

Peter's story is the most detailed, but mainly about the resistance he encountered from Gene and Paul about putting his song on the album in the first place, and also subsequently about releasing it as a single. During a limo ride, he sang Gene a version of a song he and Stan Penridge had written, but at a faster tempo as he knew that a ballad would be unacceptable. Ezrin, however, saw it as a hit record and ballad immediately. Peter credits Ezrin for the arrangement, and in *Makeup to Breakup*, he also attributes the name change from "Beck" to "Beth" to Ezrin, as the "one lyrical change" he made. Peter's narrative, however, is more concerned with the resistance to the song and releasing it as a single, claiming that Bill Aucoin recognized that while the song saved the album, he would be hated for it by Paul and Gene.

At this point things get a bit more pointed. Paul's memoir *Face the Music* claims that Bob Ezrin wrote the song based on "a few lines and a melody" from Peter and his co-writer. Ezrin wrote "the lion's share" and "most of it." Paul claims Peter always needed a co-writer, as "he couldn't really write."

Lastly (as though he needs both the first and last word) Gene's memoir, in its updated paperback edition, adds an appendix on the recording of *Destroyer* in which he echoes this line of attack. Gene now moves much more emphatically to seeing Peter's role as secondary. He says:

> "Beth" was written by Stan Penridge, mostly. It was credited to Stan Penridge, Peter Criss, and Bob Ezrin. In truth, Peter didn't play a musical instrument (drums are a percussive instrument) and I have never seen him write a single song. Peter may have contributed a line of lyric or two, but after hearing the original Penridge demo tape of the song, it's clear who came up with the original song . . . which, incidentally was called "Beck," as in Becky.

Rather than simply assess the accuracy of one version over another, it bears noting that the versions of the song's composition *after* Peter's memoir (Paul's story) consciously work harder to minimize Peter's role (and his abilities, for that matter). First-person narratives of the past are not, of course, simply fact-based, but are attempts at self-justification, explanation, or, in this case, seem to indicate elements of defensiveness and counter-attack. That many of the facts "agree" is less striking than that the points of disagreement are really about to whom honor and credit, praise or blame, ultimately belong. The reader is, like the viewer in *Rashomon*, fully aware that while nobody is a reliable narrator, nor is anyone simply an outright fabricator.

It's true that in most of Peter's songs he co-wrote while in KISS (eight of twelve), and on his first post-KISS album (nine of eleven), he made heavy use of Stan Penridge as a co-writer. It's *also* true that although Paul and Gene wrote most of the band's songs, "Beth" was the most successful single the band had ever released, and is featured prominently during the End of the Road tour, some four and a half decades later.

A View from Outside the Egos of KISS

What is a poor, helpless woman like me to do?

—Woman in *Rashomon*

In a review of *Rashomon*, the famous French film critic André Bazin wrote that "it serves to illustrate not so much the impossibility of knowing the truth through the vehicle of human consciousness as the difficulty in believing in the goodness of man. For in each of these versions . . . reveals an evil side." That evil side that Bazin noted in *Rashomon* is simply our selfish and self-serving version of the story. The version of the story that portrays us as morally blameless and generally the victim of circumstances or, in this case, the manipulations of others.

For the original bandmates of KISS, they all tell self-serving stories to us on the matter of "Beth," and each seeks to maximize their own profile while minimizing the role of others. Downplaying Peter's songwriting abilities and/or raising the profile of Stan Penridge to accomplish the same end, functions in these self-serving ways. The interesting point is not anything like the objective truth of the matter. The interesting point is the way each, especially Gene and Peter, portrays the story to their own effect.

That there's no objective view available should be clear by now, but there's one more narrative to add to the mix. Lydia Criss, Peter's ex-wife, has gone on record with her own memory of the song that had people occasionally calling her "Beth," as if she were the direct inspiration for the song. Her reminiscences are that the first version of the song was from Peter Criss and Stan Penridge. Rebecca, or "Beck," was a former bandmate's wife who constantly called during rehearsals or recordings. She remembers that the song was on tape for years, and when Peter wanted a song on the new album he presented this older song, and that their manager Bill Aucoin pushed for it to be recorded, while she suggested calling it "Beth." Her perspective affirms but complicates the versions we surveyed above, inasmuch as she also claims credit for the name change, although she alone has an explanation for the origin of the name "Beth." In an interview with Greg Prato, she says:

> Gene will never give me credit for this, because I know he takes credit for it, but it was me that named the song "Beth," because it was funny that Becky was a twin, and [head of Casablanca Records] Neil Bogart was married to a Beth, and she was a twin. It just kind of related. It got in my head, and I remember sitting in a limo one day . . . I don't think Ace was around and I'm not sure about Paul, but I know Gene and Peter were in the limo, and I was there. And I said, "How about 'Beth'?"

Reading in Bad Faith?

I don't care if it's a lie, as long as it's entertaining.

—Commoner in *Rashomon*

When we read these autobiographies, we might be in the same situation as the woodcutter and the priest who are disturbed by the bad faith and by the irreducible egoism of multiple perspectives. However, we may also be like the commoner in *Rashomon*. He doesn't care whether the stories are true or false, just that they be entertaining. Like a KISS concert, the more extreme the spectacle, the better it passes the time. In effect, the autobiographies put us in a similar situation. We can still love listening to *Destroyer*, no matter what actually happened in the studio. We're free to simply point and laugh at the situation, holding ourselves to no account for own blind spots or bad faith. Not that we're responsible in the same way as the band members for what happened in the 1970s, but that our willingness to ignore the truth behind the inner-workings of *Destroyer* and "Beth" marks a divide between the world of play and the personal interactions that define our lives.

Our tendency toward being genuine and honest is compared to the layers of an onion by Lonergan: "one is aloof with strangers, courteous with acquaintances, at ease with one's friends, occasionally unbosoms oneself to intimates, keeps some matters entirely to oneself, and refuses even to face others." At the center of the onion, it's not always clear how much or how accurately we are aware of our own actions and motivations.

Each of KISS's four narratives—or five narratives as we added Lydia Criss—reveals information to the outside world based on some sort of internal censorship. They reveal to us what they want us to know, but also what they want to believe about themselves as well, which is something we all do throughout our lives.

16
KISS Goes Disco and Boogies on Simmons's Bad Faith

CHRISTOPHER M. INNES

I'm holding in my hands a copy of a 1975 K-tel disco LP compilation, *Disco Mania*, on which KISS has one of its most famous tracks, "Rock and Roll All Nite." A KISS number on a disco LP—what a place to be! This reminds me of KISS's later 1979 disco single, "I Was Made for Lovin' You," from the album *Dynasty*. This hit got to Number Eleven on the Billboard Charts and sold over a million copies.

I'm tempted to laugh and jump on the bandwagon and pour scorn on KISS for *selling out*, or whatever it was that caused this "atrocity." Creating such an obviously commercial betrayal of their hallmark anthemic hard rock style is something that can't be accepted by anyone loyal to hard rock and certainly not to a fan of KISS.

I'm going to stop and think to myself for a moment. Is such a divergent musical expression really a betrayal of who they are as a hard rock band? I'm saying that KISS is hard rock because of its use of heavy rhythm, lead guitar, drums, and heavy bass, all amplified for the frenzy of the audience. This is their normal and *original* sound. Such an aesthetic diversion into disco might normally be seen as a betrayal; but is it really a betrayal, or an expression of their talent? Such a gift should be shown off to the audience.

We can look at a good example of KISS in their hard rock mood in "Detroit Rock City," from the album *Destroyer*. It's their anthemic type of music, with its strong electric guitar rhythm, bass, drums, and chorus. I listen and feel that there's a world of rock and I'm part of it. And in this mood, you go to one of their gigs and it's two hours of hard rock for you to enjoy and relish. There may be a slow love song number like "Reason to Live" from the album *Crazy Nights*, but it's mostly hard rock. Even this track has a distinct hard rock guitar solo.

The point we might have to accept is that even though KISS is mostly hard rock doesn't mean that KISS is just a hard rock band. So is there really a hard rock thing to be betrayed? Here we will ask if KISS can delve into other music genres. To say they have to remain hard rock is to say they have an essential self. This means that they are hard rock and nothing else. This is like saying that Gene Simmons is just a hard rock bass player and nothing else, but surely there is more to him than that. He has a number of university degrees, he's a father, an actor, and an entrepreneur. There's no one thing that makes Simmons who he is.

Likewise, can we say KISS has an essential self that makes them who they are? Isn't KISS talented enough to produce new and dynamic music? This can be imagined considering that KISS has had many lineup changes over the years, including Eric Carr, Vinnie Vincent, Bruce Kulick, and among others, Gary Corbett, the keyboardist on tour with KISS at the end of the Eighties. Disco might just be their new thing.

Maybe we should really be looking at those pointing their scornful finger at KISS, and instead pour scorn on them. Most of them haven't put too much thought into their argument and have simply jumped on the bandwagon of hating KISS and its flirtation with disco. To jump on a bandwagon is to commit what philosophers call a "fallacy." In this case it's when you agree with the majority view simply because you think it to be the right thing to do or you want to be cool. In fact, the majority view might be wrong. In our situation, I might say that KISS is hard rock and nothing else because Simmons and his fans says so. The fact that Simmons and his fans say so isn't evidence to support the conclusion that KISS is only hard rock. Of course, the irony is that Simmons is the most vocal critic of KISS's aesthetic meandering into the disco genre. He's not impressed. He's quite indignant and scornful and hates playing "I Was Made for Lovin' You" live.

Maybe the scorn for having a *thou must rock in a certain way* attitude should be pointed at Simmons.

This is where Jean-Paul Sartre's notion of "bad faith," as found in *Being and Nothingness*, might ring true in our ears. Bad faith is another philosophical argument that illustrates a fallacy in reasoning. Bad faith occurs when the existence of a group of people places someone under pressure to give up their beliefs and freedom of expression. They are forced to adopt false values. KISS is under pressure from fans to maintain a certain image and to follow a clan-like view that *thou must make music with hard rock values*. This view is seen as highly problematic by the bad faith argument. Following such a clan-like view prevents songwriters such as Paul Stanley, Desmond Child, and Vini Poncia from expressing their genuine aesthetic joy of music diversity. This freedom is inborn and undeniable, for Sartre. This freedom allows authentic expression and creativity, and this is needed in the creation of hard rock and any other types of music.

Let's Go Disco—I Feel the Beat!

Disco music is a guilty pleasure that Gene Simmons thinks no honest-to-goodness hard rock fan will ever enjoy. Dancing with your girlfriend at the office disco Christmas party is one thing, but seeing it as worthwhile music is another. No one who loves hard rock is going to sincerely get down to the sound of the Bee Gees. There may be a need to move with the times, but it must remain hard rock, and disco crosses that line.

This is the die-hard attitude of a hard rock critic like Simmons. Simmons is a music critic as well as a singer and bass player in KISS. In fact, we're all music critics, and rightfully so! Hard rock needs to be constantly evaluated to stop it from losing its way. Simmons says that he hates to croon "Do do do do do do do do do do" high pitched like a girl (the chorus line of "I Was Made for Lovin' You"), as told in David Leaf's and Ken Sharp's *KISS: Beyond the Mask*. A rather wimpy disco verse is surely not fitting for the likes of a committed hard rock band such as KISS

We can see the influence of Disco coming into being in the late 1960s and reaching its peak in the late 1970s, delivering what Alexis Petridis refers to as ground breaking, revolutionary, and "malleable and unfixed" aesthetic creativity. Noel Gallagher, of Oasis fame, gave up his obsession with clinging to the canon of rock by giving his album *Who Built the Moon?* some disco beats, in order to experience new musical avenues. This was a risky move, but it shows that artists can invent themselves anew by using disco. We'll see whether Gallagher is as successful as Pink Floyd's use of disco beat in the single "Another Brick in the Wall (Part 2)."

Floyd's disco beat is in tune with Floyd's over-all experimental approach to music. That's probably why Floyd's disco excursion was successful. The disco beat fit Floyd's "explore anything" identity. The disco beat also suited Queen who had a glam rock hallmark and took on disco with "Another One bites the Dust." Queen got no flack. This might be because they were notorious for playing around with different aesthetic outlooks. They played about with Shakespearean verse and operatic themes in "Bohemian Rhapsody" and religious chants in "Mustapha." Such a diverse repertoire both fit, and for some, was expected. Could KISS do the same?

KISS had an odd start to their career, which might partially explain what laid the path to their disco experiment. Detailed in the KISS biography *Behind the Mask*, KISS signed their first record contract with Casablanca Records in 1973. Previously being a music producer, Neil Bogart was the record executive who saw the showman qualities of KISS in their performances. He quickly signed KISS knowing that they had great merchandizing potential. Like KISS, he liked having fun and was a showman. It was Bogart who at the end of the day invented *bubble gum music*—ephemeral music that gives you a joyous feeling, as you get from chewing on bubble gum. The invention of bubble gum music paves the way for Bogart to be identified with and promoting the rise of disco. What could go wrong with making people happy? He even produced the first ever twelve-inch vinyl disco single in 1975, Donna Summer's "Love to Love You, Baby," and everyone was enraptured.

Here we have KISS in an atmosphere of aesthetic creation that might even influence the die-hard hard rocker such as Simmons. So why is it that disco and KISS don't get along and are forbidden to go out with each other? Why is it that KISS and the disco beat can't be together? Are we just going to agree with Gene Simmons? Is Corey Deiterman's view correct that their disco adventure was a betrayal of their talent, nothing more than a "glitzed-up schmaltz," and untrue to the essence of KISS? Must we accept this as the reality of KISS's musical adventure into disco?

Let Rock and Disco Unite

Let's go over the notion of bad faith. Donna Summer sang her ultimate disco song "I Feel Love" as an anthem, not just to sexual liberation, but to disco itself—it's for everyone no matter their race, gender, age, or sexuality. This is where the notion of inauthenticity comes into play. Sartre was an existentialist, which involves a philosophical critique of the inauthentic life. It argues that everything that gets in the way of authenticity is bad for people. We need to create new things in new ways. If we don't, we become empty and dull. We are by birth free to express ourselves, to choose and define our own actions, and to reject any action that isn't authentic. Summer's disco hit "I Feel Love" exemplifies Sartre's ideal of authenticity. What about KISS?

KISS's "I Love It Loud" expresses their authentic self as a rock band. The song is sung by Simmons as an example of KISS being KISS, but is this authentic or merely Simmons bowing to the pressure of fans? The same can be asked about "I Was Made for Lovin' You." We can certainly accept that Paul Stanley may say that he co-wrote "I Was Made for Lovin' You" as a whimsical poking fun at those who wrote disco music, but we should also recognize that it's still a worthy aesthetic diversion from his normal hard-rock guitar and lyric writing. It's difficult to stop doing what's worked in the past and even more difficult to try something new. KISS's original Self is a hard rock band, which is part of what Sartre would call their "facticity." This is to say that Simmons and his fans see KISS as hard rock and nothing else. It's like saying KISS is hard rock in the same way as $2 + 2 = 4$. It's a fact and anyone who denies that fact is wrong. Of course we know that $2 + 2 = 4$ is a fact, but is it a fact that KISS is only a hard rock band? To use Sartre's language, is being a hard rock band the "in-itself" of KISS—something that is naturally present and we have no choice but to accept it as it is? The answer to this is not as straight forward as the 2 + 2 = 4 example.

Fortunately, humans have the ability to reflect on any situation and think about how they can act in the future. They transcend as reflective conscious people who can reject past facts and choose to act in new, authentic ways. In this way it's KISS's responsibility to reflect and act in new and authentic ways. They have no excuse not to make new and adventurous choices. This might be difficult to accept for some fans, because hard rock fans tend to be reactionary and reject that which presents a challenge. It did it with punk in the late 1970s, as it did with disco at the same time. To simply remain the same because that is what's expected is an example of bad faith that prevents KISS from trying new types of musical expression.

We must make it clear that bad faith is not when a person says one thing but means something else. This is the common view of bad faith. Instead, bad faith is when a person says they are something they are not and they end up believing that they are that thing. Sartre uses an example of a waiter. Here the waiter acts like a waiter. This is no surprise. But, we have a problem in that he's not allowed to be anything else. The waiter is acting like a thing *in-itself*. He has expectations given to him by the guests. They want a waiter who is only a waiter. He in turn wants to be a good waiter and puts on the act—not to would insult the guests. He presents himself as a waiter resulting in himself being a waiter. He is not allowed to be a real person. *Nothing* separates him from himself and authenticity. It's this *nothingness* that has to be traversed for him to arrive at a state of being where he, as a person, becomes authentic.

Like an electric guitar that is incapable of being anything else, it lacks the ability for authenticity. The guitar has no state of *nothingness*. It is a guitar. People however have authenticity. This is where the *nothingness* comes into play. Human existence is an existence in the world of choice. It's a world where choices are to be made and there is nothing but ourselves to prevent them from making such choices. The world is our oyster, and anything preventing choice is bad for a person, because they need to express their aesthetic talent free from the narrow-minded wishes of others. So it is with the waiter, whose expectations are given to him by the guests, and so it is with KISS, if they feel compelled to accept the role of what others expect.

Something to Choose

KISS must continually choose what they authentically want to be, apart from the external pressures of fans. If they turn into the waiter who merely does what others want, then they're acting in *bad faith*. KISS was originally a hard rock band, but they are able to transcend this fact and become whatever they authentically choose—soft rock, pop, grunge, and yes, even disco. To act like an inanimate electric guitar is to deny authenticity and remain a thing *in-itself*. Political correctness pervades rock music, just as Sartre said bourgeoisie seriousness pervades the wider society, so we as fans also have a responsibility not to create a false notion of essence about what it means to be KISS. Instead of forcing KISS to be what we think they should be, we should accept that they are authentic beings that can be whatever they choose.

As Ace sings, there are "Two Sides of the Coin"; humans need authenticity, but they also mistakenly desire totality. Totality is Simmons wanting to play only hard rock—to be defined as only a hard-rock God. So, we are just a bit gobsmacked when we hear Simmons sing "When You Wish Upon a Star," like a flashback to his childhood days, and "Great Expectations" with its falsetto chorus. These glimmers of authenticity illustrate cracks in Simmons hard rock totality, and it's this struggle that represents for Sartre the complete human being. The human, like the hard rock band, is real if it recreates, invents anew, and is full of ingenuity to undo what it has done before. It shouldn't be a being that remains the same. As much as Simmons wants KISS to stay the same, at least as he argues that it should, it shouldn't.

To emphasize this point, we can look at bands like AC/DC who have been ridiculed for remaining the same and churning out the same heavy metal type of music over its four decades of life. KISS on the other hand is often self-conscious of its presence in the rock industry. It's aware of the trends of fans, the rock industry, and record companies; and is sometimes willing to explore new possibilities. Even though they thought of themselves as hard rock, there's an occasional feeling that they can be more. By being aware of others, KISS is aware of itself and its possibilities. The band can reject the image projected upon it by its fans and the record company and instead create anew. They can see the possibilities, even if they don't always follow through on exploring them. It seems that to be just a hard rock band is like telling a lie. To tell a lie is not the problem. It's believing the lie to be true that causes the *bad faith.* "I was Made for Lovin' You" shows that KISS is aware that the band can do other types of music. It's aware that KISS can go disco or grunge.

We can sympathize with KISS fans and with Simmons. They want a guaranteed two-hour hard rock concert. The fans see KISS as factual representation of hard rock, just as Simmons sees the band in a like manner. KISS fans are sincere in their judgment about KISS being a hard rock band, and it's this judgment that leads Simmons's into bad faith. The fans who hate "I Was Made for Lovin' You," however, fail to understand that to be aware of the band as authentic means that it's not subject to any one understanding, which means there's nothing inauthentic about KISS going disco, even though Simmons and some fans don't agree.

To Hell with Authenticity, I'm with Gene!

Even though we have been arguing in favor of KISS being authentic and diverse, we can also argue for why KISS should remain a hard rock band. Avoiding bad faith is not as easy as it sounds. We ask the question, can KISS really avoid bad faith, if what fans actually prefer is the rock steady beat? This is what the band presents and so is what we expect. Avoiding bad faith demands a constant rejection of what you did before. So, KISS the a hard rock band would need to reject their hard rock anthem to "Rock and Roll All Nite," go onto disco, then reject disco, go onto prog rock, then reject prog rock, go onto hair rock, then reject hair rock, and on and on—maybe spend some time being a ballet company, we might say jokingly. The band would be unrecognizable after a couple of tours and a few albums. Sartre says, there's "an imponderable difference separating being from non-being in the mode of being of human reality," which for KISS would mean an impossible spiral of authenticity that might end with KISS being an opera band. We've just said goodbye to KISS. They've vanished!

We have to remember that bad faith is a faith. It provides comfort and security. This might be a fake type of comfort, but it's comfort nonetheless. Bad faith is not a lie and it's not known by the assailant. This is to say that Simmons is not aware of his bad faith. We compare Simmons's view with that of the lead singer of Iron Maiden, Bruce Dickinson. He once said, "You can't play heavy metal with a synthesizer." This may well be a pompous remark and one that is subject to ridicule, especially due to the fact that Iron Maiden later did a synth-filled album, *Somewhere in Time,* with popular tracks like "Wasted Years." Dickinson was indeed in a state of bad faith. It might be beside the point that Iron Maiden deserted its heavy metal anthem roots, but the point is that Simmons and his fans are not going to be convinced by the argument that their hard rock anthem sound is to be deserted. An older and wiser Dickinson ridiculed his younger self. He said that keyboards were now accepted as a pallet of colors as Iron Maiden turned from a metal band into a progressive rock band. Simmons wants KISS and hard rock to remain guitar and drum based. The cherished comfort of hard rock is his security and his fans joy.

According to Sartre, we should take ownership of our nothingness—the gap between our consciousness and the world. You have to know both to be free. The person goes from the object that is *in-itself* to a conscious being that is *for-itself*. Nothingness is the gap. Maybe Simmons is more conscious than we give him credit. Individual persons should fill their nothingness with their own choices. Why not let Simmons fill his gap with predictable rock? It's his choice, isn't it? It's not what Sartre wants, but it's what Simmons wants. We might agree with Simmons and remind ourselves what Wayne Campbell said on *Wayne's World*: "I mean, Led Zeppelin didn't write tunes that everyone liked. They left that to the Bee Gees." Maybe Simmons is right and authentic in his choice to be hard rock, and that others should be left to do disco.

Even though there's pressure on people toward uniformity, there is an indication of a frustration when trying to be authentic in the presence of others. KISS should be free from the shackles of the expectations of hard rock, yet to be authentic, they need the rock world from which to be free. The band is responsible for being free, but only in relation to their roots as a hard rock band. It might be that a few fans will resist any change, but the band is responsible for its own fate, whatever that maybe. Disco, rock, or even opera?

Yeah, Simmons might be committing bad faith by saying KISS should only do hard rock. But to hell with that! Simmons likes KISS just the way it is, and who's to say he's wrong?! Who doesn't want "Lick It Up" to have its predicable vocals, strong bass, and lead guitar? Maybe hard rock is static and should always be the same. It has an internal core, an unchanging thing, a familiarity, a life of its own; and maybe we should respect it as authentic.

17
Forgive and Make Up?

COURTLAND LEWIS

We live in an imperfect world where we're bound to eventually wrong or be wronged by someone else. Add to the mix millions of dollars, alcohol, drugs, women, confined spaces, competing egos, fame, and a whole host of other things, and on a daily basis you're bound to wrong, be wronged, and at times simply have a mind full of imagined wrongs.

What are we to do in the face of being wronged? Should we fill our lives with hate and regret, never letting go of our resentment? Should we seek revenge by writing tell-all books and bashing each other in interviews? Should we seek forgiveness and reconciliation, realizing we're all likely to wrong others and at some time need to be forgiven?

KISS is famous for many things, including their image, stage show, sexual exploits, and of course, writing some of the greatest rock songs in human history. They are, however, also famous for their breakups, public feuds with former bandmates, and harsh criticism of anyone who threatens or dismisses the sacred name of KISS. When you read some of the stories that appear in magazines, interviews, and autobiographies, it's easy to understand why there's so much animosity between members and former members of KISS.

There are tales of drug use and petty disagreements that affected performances, stories of loves gone awry, and accusations of being cheated out of money. I would be upset too, if any of these things happened to me! Without weighing in on the specifics of who is right or wrong, I would like to discuss some of the animosity that exists throughout KISStory, in order to explore the nature of forgiveness.

I Was Made for Forgivin' You

Forgiveness is everywhere these days. It shows up in numerous movies and novels and is the bread and butter of pop-psychology, self-help books, and melodramas. Forgiveness is like the word 'love'—it's used all of the time, but rarely do people take time to consider what it actually means. 'Love' is used so much that it has lost most of its meaning, and the same is true of 'forgiveness'.

Jeffrie Murphy offers one of the easiest ways to understand forgiveness. In *Punishment and the Moral Emotions*, he maintains that forgiveness is the "overcoming, on moral grounds, of the intense negative reactive attitudes—the vindictive passions of resentment, anger, hatred, and the desire for revenge . . ." This intuitive approach to forgiveness can deal with most cases of wrongdoing. Take for instance the recent feud between Ace and Gene. Gene said Ace had been fired from the band three times and that, even if KISS wanted him on The End of the Road Tour, Ace wouldn't be capable of performing night after night for two hours. Ace got upset and fired back with accusations of dishonesty, assault, and a threat of litigation. Ace claims to have been sober for twelve years, he performs several hours a night on a regular basis, and he appears to have quit the band instead of being fired. If true, then Ace has been wronged by Gene's statements, and he must decide how to move forward.

Murphy's definition of forgiveness suggests that for Ace to forgive Gene, he would need to let go of the anger, resentment, and feelings of revenge that are apparent in his counterattack. Since Ace is obviously lashing out at Gene, he has not yet reached a point where he can forgive. He's angry at being wronged, and even though Ace has been quiet about the feud recently, as long as he holds on to feelings of resentment, then he has not forgiven. There would need to be more positive signs of letting go of resentment, such as Ace appearing on the tour or being featured on (hopefully) the next KISS album.

Charles Griswold offers a more complex definition, suggesting there are different levels of forgiveness, with the ultimate goal being what he calls "paradigmatic forgiveness." In his book *Forgiveness*, he argues that paradigmatic forgiveness occurs when wrongdoers fully repent for their misdeeds and victims forswear revenge, let go of resentment, reframe their understanding of themselves and the wrongdoer, and declare the wrongdoer forgiven.

Using the previous example of Ace's and Gene's feud, paradigmatic forgiveness occurs when:

1. Gene demonstrates he rejects his statements;

2. Gene repudiates his statements and promises never to do it again;

3. Gene experiences and expresses regret;

4. Gene commits to becoming the sort of person who does not wrong;

5. Gene shows he understands Ace's perspective; and

6. Gene gives an account and answer questions.

———

1. Ace forswears revenge;

2. Ace moderates his resentment;

3. Ace commits to letting go of resentment;

4. Ace refuses to see Gene as a "bad" person;

5. Ace refuses to see himself as "just" a victim; and

6. Ace addresses Gene and declares him forgiven.

As Griswold notes, this paradigmatic forgiveness is uncommon, but if both Gene and Ace went through this process, they would be changed individuals, able to work on projects, preform live, and live as friends. Since, such a state of affairs is probably unlikely for Ace and Gene, they should strive for a less stringent conception of forgiveness, either Murphy's discussed previously or one featured in the next few pages.

I Just Wanna Forgive You

Let's consider another instance of wrongdoing in KISS. Starting in the mid-1980s, Bruce Kulick established himself as a member of KISS, arguably the best KISS guitarist—both musically and creatively. In the early 1990s, Eric Singer became KISS's drummer and is the most technically proficient drummer that's ever been in the band. Yet, they were both excluded from the band when the opportunity to have a reunion and make many millions occurred. It would've been easy for both Kulick and Singer to feel resentment and bash Paul and Gene, as Ace and Peter did after leaving the band. Both were eventually asked to rejoin the band, but Kulick declined because he felt uncomfortable giving up being himself in order to mimic the Spaceman. Kulick, however, continues to attend KISS conventions, he's responsible for ensuring the release of *Carnival of Souls: The Final Sessions*, and he seems to harbor no resentment. Singer, on the other hand, took over drumming duties from Peter Criss in 2001, until he was replaced (again!) by Peter in 2002. In an interview with David Ling, Singer said, "I was definitely not happy," but he understood the nature of the music industry and economics. So, in 2004, he re-re-rejoined the band.

Kulick's and Singer's respective responses to being kicked out of the band illustrate the type of forgiveness discussed by Margaret Holmgren, in *Forgiveness and Retribution*. She argues for a type of forgiveness where individuals develop attitudes of forgiveness, where they treat wrongdoers with attitudes of respect, compassion, and real goodwill. Holmgren's type of forgiveness resembles a Buddhist approach to life where we teach ourselves to come to terms with the fact that we will be wronged throughout life. Instead of letting resentment control our actions, however, we live compassionately, forgiving all those who wrong us. Forgiveness becomes part of our character, and instead of letting wrongdoing destroy relationships, we strive to maintain positive relationships by forgiving. Forgiveness simply becomes part of who we are—our character.

Of course, I might be overestimating the character of Kulick and Singer. I don't know them personally, though I'd would be happy to change that fact—give me a call! Instead of having attitudes of forgiveness, they might simply be taking a utilitarian approach, where they recognize that nothing is gained by resenting Paul and Gene. In fact, a willingness to forgive ensures that they are asked back to perform, or gain other special treatment from the band (like being on the next KISS album, please), which ensures they have more exposure and gain more money. In *After Evil*, Geoffrey Scarre presents an account of forgiveness that focuses on maximizing the pleasure, money, and other benefits of victims. So, instead of forgiveness being some character trait, it becomes a calculation about what benefits ourselves.

I Need You

Since any discussion of forgiveness deals with what we should do, forgiveness is a matter of ethics. Philosophical ethics attempts to justify moral claims about what's right and wrong, and so, every conception of forgiveness is grounded in some sort of ethical theory. One ethical theory yet to be discussed is that of rights. Rights theory is a recent addition to the discussion of forgiveness, with my own book, *Repentance and the Right to Forgiveness*, suggesting new ways to think about forgiveness. So, let's consider what happens when forgiveness is grounded in a theory of rights designed to promote the peaceful flourishing of all those involved.

Eirenéism is the theory of rights that I argue best grounds forgiveness, because it takes into account the needs of all individuals involved, and it asks those individuals to seek the flourishing of all people. In other words, it seeks peace, what the ancient Hebrews called shalom. For simplicity, I will refer to eirenéism as peace-ethics. The foundational principle of peace-ethics is that each human has inherent moral worth that creates a set of corollary rights and obligations between all other moral agents. So, no matter the behaviors of Paul, Gene, Ace, Peter, and everyone else, we must always remember that each one them has inherent moral worth that should be respected. As a result, no matter how mad Gene might be at Vinnie and Ace, it's wrong to damage their life-goods (what they need in order to flourish), whether that be physical harm or harm to one's reputation. On the other side of the coin, Ace and Peter must remember that

Paul and Gene have moral worth too, and it's wrong for them to do the same. Even if Paul and Gene replace their on-stage characters with Tommy and Eric, they should recognize that fans enjoy seeing the make-up, even if it's not on the original member(s). In other words, Ace and Peter might have an obligation to let others use their characters' make-up and personae. In fact, and this might sound crazy, the needs of the fans might be enough to obligate Ace and Peter to live healthy lives that make them capable of being members of KISS, since doing so promotes everyone's flourishing—members and fans alike.

The previous sentence raises some deep ethical questions. What do we owe each other, and to what extent are we responsible for ensuring others peacefully flourish? Peace-ethics provides an account that maintains we have several obligations to ensure others flourish, if doing so promotes our own and others' flourishing. For instance, imagine a friend who is going through a difficult time in his life, such as when Eric Carr suffered with cancer. Eric's needs of friendship and consolation place an obligation on his friends to spend time with, to comfort, and to encourage his peace of mind. Ace's substance abuse obligates a compassionate response designed to promote a healthy life where he flourishes, whether he's part of KISS or not. Peace-ethics asks us to rethink the nature of all relationships. Treating friends with respect isn't merely a "gift," but a requirement of what it means to be a friend. Similar to the Confucian idea of living according to our Names, if I don't act like a friend, then I'm not a friend. Being named a friend requires I act in certain ways, which for peace-ethics means you promote your friends' flourishing.

Imagine a case where one person (call him Gene) steals from another person (call him Ace), but Gene's desire to steal is motivated by a desire to ensure that Ace can flourish. Imagine that both Ace and Gene are young and upcoming musicians, very talented, and both are highly capable of flourishing in their profession. Ace, however, begins using drugs, and begins to have difficulty writing, recording, and playing his songs. The drugs threaten not only to ruin Ace's musical career, but will probably cause his early death—maybe in a car wreck. Gene, on the other hand, is a concerned friend who recognizes Ace's problems and begins looking for ways to help Ace. After many failed attempts to help Ace break his addiction, Gene determines the only way to help Ace is to steal his drugs and prevent him from obtaining any more, which he hopes will force Ace to quit. If he doesn't quit, Gene will kick him out of the band, as a devastating message to get clean. Gene enacts his plan, and against all odds, his plan works: Ace is on the road to recovery and can resume his flourishing musical career. So, we have a case where a moral agent (Gene) steals some property (drugs) from another moral agent (Ace) in order to see him flourish.

For peace-ethics, the tension in this case is between the mistaken good of having drugs, which Ace improperly perceives as a life-good. The actual life-good is being able to flourish free from the negative effects of drugs. But in such a case, who or what decides which life-good is primary? Ace's judgment should be the best candidate for who gets to decide, but the effect of drugs seems to call into doubt his ability rationally to choose. While free from drugs, he might choose a life free from addiction, but if truly addicted, he'll lack the ability to refrain from using drugs. As an outsider, Gene seems in the best position to decide which life-good is primary, since as a friend, he cares deeply for Ace. To take this route, however, is to risk making Gene a parental figure who knows what's best for his "friend." To solve the riddle we must consider the trajectory of Ace's life on drugs vs. his life clean. Sure, Ace might live a happy flourishing life on drugs, but the drugs are more likely to harm his health and prevent him from flourishing. So, assuming Gene is motivated by the desire to see Ace flourish, then he's obligated to do something to help ensure Ace achieves the state of not having drugs, along with helping Ace during the withdrawal period.

Is it ethical for Gene to lie and steal in order to help Ace? Wouldn't Gene being doing something wrong? According to peace-ethics, such acts are morally permissible when doing so promotes the flourishing of others. If Ace is suffering from addiction, and Gene is a friend, then Gene is morally obligated to do something to help Ace free himself from his dependence on drugs; and if stealing Ace's drugs is his best option, then Gene is morally justified in stealing the drugs. More precisely, it's not the act of stealing that is morally permissible; it is Gene's making available to Ace a life free from drugs that is morally permissible, if not obligatory. At first, Ace might be angry with Gene, and consider what he did unforgiveable, but when Ace has a chance to sober up he will (hopefully) be thankful for Gene's help ensuring his flourishing—if Ace fails to stay sober, however, he might remain resentful.

What's more, since Gene's act was morally permissible, there is no need to ask for forgiveness since no wrong was done. As an act of kindness, Gene might ask for forgiveness to ensure there are no hurt feelings between them, but such a case does not qualify as a wrongdoing, so it doesn't require forgiveness. (Though we might, in fact, go so far as to say that Ace ought to ask Gene for forgiveness for putting him in a situation where he had to steal.)

Apply this conclusion to the case of Paul and Gene dismissing and excluding Ace and Peter. If Paul and Gene are motivated by a desire to help Ace and Peter, then Paul and Gene haven't wronged Ace and Peter, in regard to dismissing, excluding, and possibly even paying them less. As long as they aren't being greedy, and there's a true commitment to equality and promoting flourishing behaviors, then Ace and Peter aren't wronged. The same is true for having other musicians play their roles of the Spaceman and the Catman. If motivated by the right reasons, like promoting good behavior and delighting fans, then Paul and Gene are doing what promotes flourishing, and if anyone is wronged, it is Paul and Gene who suffer by having to play the "bad guys" in front of fans and to the media.

KISSin' Time

Peace-ethics doesn't give a particular definition of forgiveness, but it gives clarity about who is wronged and when we should forgive. Think of the relationship between Gene and Paul. They annoy each other and will often criticize one another in interviews. Gene makes fun of marriage and Paul's inability to sing like he could when they started. Paul doesn't invite Gene to his wedding and makes fun of Gene's "singing." Yet, no matter their criticism, they still find a way to get along. They're like a married couple who has incorporated the many lessons of forgiveness previously discussed. A married couple takes on certain obligations above and beyond those associated with strangers and friends. They share a love defined by their commitment to something greater than their individual desires. Their "marriage" is based on an agreement where they promise to respect the needs of all involved. This love is more than simply Paul and Gene giving each other the gift of their time and energy; it's a matter of carrying out obligations, as a way of demonstrating their love and respect for each other and fans. So, when they chose to carry on as KISS, even after criticizing each other, they're carrying out a promise to stay together, which promotes their flourishing and the flourishing of fans all over the world.

Therefore, KISS provides some valuable lessons about forgiveness. Sure, there are countless instances where members—present or former—have acted and said things that wrong others, but if we look closely enough, we find acts of forgiveness that are just as powerful as Paul's greatest love song—for me, that's "I Still Love You." KISS doesn't provide us with a clear definition of forgiveness either, but they provide many examples of complex moral relationships that shed light on the phenomena of forgiveness and its related concepts.

For example, in "On Forgiving Oneself," Paul Hughes suggests that forgiveness is simply a moral response—one among many, such as anger, hatred, and revenge—to being wronged by another. In "Forgiveness and Feminism," Joram Haber describes forgiveness as a personal response to moral injury that preserves self-respect. Unless we deny the existence of morality, there's not much to disagree with about these statements. They are helpful because they give us conceptual space to discuss forgiveness without getting bogged down with determining a specific definition. As a result, we might agree with Adam Morton's description of forgiveness, in "What is Forgiveness?", that it's simply a "bundle of mutually sustaining practices, ideas, and theories that center on people doing something roughly like forgiving one another for wrongs." Such an approach matches Geoffrey Scarre's definition from *After Evil* that forgiveness is a "multi-form phenomenon, a broad and varied family of practices," which include emotions like blame, responsibility, and excuse, and involve complex personal, interpersonal, and communal actions.

In the end, KISS echoes Jessica Wolfendale's conclusion in "The Hardened Heart." She suggests that we avoid taking on the idea that someone is unforgiveable. Seeing people as unforgiveable suggests they are somehow morally inferior, and if we see people as inferior, we are likely to treat them as such. Instead, we should always be open to forgiving others, which not only implies we see them as moral equals, but it also allows for their flourishing. In other words, forgiveness leaves open the possibility of Ace and Peter rejoining the band. In fact, it provides an atmosphere where Paul, Gene, Ace, Peter, Bruce, Vinnie, and Eric all come together as one, in order to create the most massive super-version of KISS imaginable, which truly promotes the flourishing of all.

V

The Fox

18
What Does It Mean if the Band Plays Forever?

ROBERT GRANT PRICE

So goodbye is only for now
'Cause I'm comin' back, I swear it somehow.

— PAUL STANLEY, "Goodbye"

KISS has lived through many endings and has had at least one *Second Coming* (make sure you see the documentary, if you haven't). The band famously took off the make-up in 1983, ending their tenure as Kabuki rock stars, until they put it back on in 1996.

They cycled through other beginnings and endings. In 2000, they traveled the globe with a 142-date tour called "The Farewell Tour." This was promoted as the last time to see the band. "It was the ethical way of closing the final chapter of the *live* band," explained Gene Simmons in David Leaf's and Ken Sharp's *KISS: Behind the Mask*.

But it turned out not to be the final chapter. The band went on to launch another *twelve* tours. Paul Stanley explained after the fact, in *Face the Music: A Life Exposed*, that the Farewell Tour wasn't the *last* last tour, but the last chance to see the original band on stage together. It was a farewell "to *drama*." The band launched a second farewell tour, the End of the Road Tour, in 2019. This tour wound around the globe and featured more than one "last" concert in several cities.

Cynics have called the false endings in KISS's career gimmicks and money grabs. Maybe they were. But the many double endings in the band's career also raise interesting questions for philosopher-fans about how we think about endings. What is an ending that never ends, and how can we know when to end something—a story, a song, a career—so that we exit with grace?

This chapter takes up these questions, and it does so hopefully with a sense of charity towards the band. After all, endings are notoriously hard to craft. Ask any novelist. Leo Tolstoy blemished his masterwork *Anna Karenina* by killing the protagonist at the end—surely an easier way out of the story for the novelist than the character. *Hamlet*, too, ends terribly, with everybody dying in the last scene. If Tolstoy and Shakespeare can bumble it, can we fault the Hottest Band in the World for botching the end of their storied career?

It's Forever

Narratives are defined by their structure: they have a beginning, a middle, and an end. The ending arrives when the conflict that initiated the story is resolved. Endings have inflated importance because they are the last scene we encounter, the last note we hear. And because they come last, they shape the narrative and augment its meaning. Think of murder mysteries: the identity of the killer will reveal the nature of crime and change the meaning of the story. If the husband killed his wife, it's a story of betrayal. If a stranger killed the woman, it's a story about the evil lurking in society. If the butler did it, it's a cliché.

Endings are hard to craft because they bracket off the story. Sometimes they appear too early and end the story before the resolution. We might call this the premature ending. Sometimes an ending provides resolution to the conflict but leaves questions hanging in the reader's mind. Call this the open ending. A closed ending, by contrast, ties up all the loose threads, like in most detective novels, where the last chapter is used to answer all outstanding questions the reader might have.

False endings occur when the conflict resolves but the story keeps going. A classic example in music is the hidden track. Back when albums were released on compact discs, musicians could "hide" songs at the end of the last track. The

hidden track shocked fans. You think the album is done—
but there's more!

False endings change the shape of a story. First, the false
ending changes the meaning of the story, since the story continues past the judgment the reader forms with the initial
end scene. Second, the false ending engages audiences with
the tease. The surge of knowing that the end is not the end
brings a surge of anticipation. Another story has not begun.
Rather, the story we love continues. And that's not always a
good idea.

KISS is guilty of false endings, most notably in their decision to tease fans with multiple farewell tours. If we treat
KISS's career as a story, what is the shape of this story, and
what does it mean? More pertinent to our discussion, how
might have KISS's story been different had it ended earlier?
Let's think through two counterfactual histories and consider how different endings change the meaning of the story.

Scenario 1: It's 1982. Ace Frehley, disappointed with the
band's direction and addled by drugs and drink, follows Peter
Criss out of the band. With two founding members gone,
Simmons and Stanley decide to fold the band out of respect
for what the original four had done.

For some fans, this ending might have had dignity, but
it's unsatisfying. The players were in their prime. They had
more to do, more songs to write as a band without make-up.
Regardless, such a story has meaning. It's a story of a band's
career cut short by the spoiling power of celebrity. It's a
tragedy, full of hubris.

Scenario 2: It's 2001. KISS finishes its Farewell Tour. In
keeping with the title of the tour, the members of the band
bid their fans farewell, hang up the armor, and retreat to retirement homes.

This ending creates a circular narrative: We end where
we begin, with the original players. The band retires while
still playing with skill and convincing vigour. We could read
such a story as a comedy—that is, as a story with a happy
ending: The bandmates overcome differences, reunite for a
champion finish, and, full of wisdom born of age and experience, quit before a steep decline in their powers.

Consider now the story the band gave us: After a series
of tours with and without founding members Criss and

Frehley, Simmons and Stanley continue playing into their late sixties and early seventies with replacement players Eric Singer and Tommy Thayer, also in their sixties. Despite efforts, they cannot help but look like old men in young men's clothing. At the risk of sounding uncharitable, this story is neither tragedy nor a comedy, but is instead a farce, a voluptuous burlesque.

But if we are to treat the band's career as a story, we must also determine the nature of the conflict and how that conflict resolves itself. That, in turn, forces us to consider the motivation of these characters.

Paint the Sky with Desire

Most of the band members have spoken candidly about why they do what they do. In the early years, Simmons and Stanley said they played rock to get girls. They also spoke about wanting to prove something. Still later, they said they wanted to become rich and famous. Each of these motives generates different readings of their careers. If they get what they want—fame, fortune, bragging rights—then, ultimately, we can judge the story of the band as a success. And, by this measurement, KISS really is a success—and a good story.

At first glance, KISS appears to have violated the show business rule that entertainers should always leave the audience wanting more. Fans can (and will) wonder why the band continues to play at an age when they qualify for seniors' discounts. If their main motive was to prove something, then they risk casting established proofs into doubt by playing past their prime. They cannot fairly claim to be cool if, in the final stage, they lower themselves to clowns—or as Peter Criss put it to KISS's official biographers: "I'd hate to see a star of mine who was aging and had a big belly . . . and had tits and had a problem making it up on stage. It would break my heart." If the motive is, as critics and cynics claim, only about the money, then the story loses its dramatic intensity. For KISS, the money is never in doubt.

KISS isn't fiction, of course. Even though the band present themselves as cartoon characters, they are still humans subject to the furry thinking of our deepest psychology. They might not know why they have let the story go on. But then, can we ever really know why we do the things we do?

Don't Want to Quit 'Cause It's Much Too Tough

A chapter about endings in rock'n'roll can't help but address the issue of the aging rock star. Rock'n'roll draws energy from youthful virility—sex is hardwired into the genre—and so the aging rock star is always at risk of self-parody as he strains to look and act virile, even though the sagging flesh and wigs testifies to the opposite.

KISS had long talked about the danger to their brand of playing past their prime. "Better to leave a little early than to stay too late," Stanley told an interviewer in 2000. Many critics, notably and most obnoxiously Mötley Crüe's bassist Nikki Sixx, argue that KISS did stay too late—so late, in fact, that they now use backing tracks in live concerts. Concert videos of a sixty-something Stanley singing with a strained voice—and even lip-syncing live on stage—offer strong evidence that the younger Stanley and his critics were right: The band played on too late.

But, as we have said, endings are notoriously difficult to write. Knowing when to end a chapter in a life—when to quit a job, when to give up a sport, when to end a business partnership—is never easy, especially if we've built our identity around that thing we have to give up. If we invest ourselves in our job, for example, we might never want to retire, since we would be giving up more than our job, we'd be giving up on ourselves.

This problem of identity has challenged philosophers since the beginning of philosophy. The question, "Who am I?" is the first question that the early Greeks said we must answer about ourselves. When religious traditions, from Judaism to Buddhism, counsel adherents to let go of their egos, they are following a similar logic. The high poetry of *Ecclesiastes*, in the Old Testament, reminds readers that they are but dust in the wind. All is vanity, even the pursuit of wisdom. Your career, your riches, your body, your art—it will all dissolve. We each must struggle with the question of what we will become when time and fortune strip us of the things we prize most. What lives under the flesh? What is the thing I call my Self? From what can I draw lasting meaning in a world of dust?

The challenge of aging lies in knowing when to give things up; and knowing when to quit requires wisdom. How does one become wise? According to the Stoics, wisdom follows from a person's command of the virtues of Prudence (also called Wisdom), Fortitude, Justice, and Temperance. One of the best-read Stoics, the philosopher king Marcus Aurelius, wrote in his *Meditations* that the wise person has self-control ("a mind free of passions is a fortress") and humility ("Vanity is the great seducer of wisdom"). The path to wisdom, then, begins with developing the inner strength needed to reject vanity and other distractions so that we can hold fast to the rigors of truth. In other words, wax on, wax off.

Traditionally, Stoic wisdom has been set apart from hedonism, a philosophy that sets pleasure as the highest good. Its most extreme form, libertinism, the unrestrained pursuit of sensual pleasure, actively rejects goods outside of those felt with the body and those goods that make unbridled sensual pleasure possible—goods like contraception, divorce laws, and legalized drugs. Rock lyrics, especially those originating in the hedonistic 1970s, speak infinitely about the search for sensual pleasure. Meatloaf, for example, says he found "paradise by the dashboard light." Kim Mitchell boasts that he is, himself, "a wild party." KISS, the kings of the night-time world, take a similar view of life in many of their lyrics. They speak about the imperative to party—that is, to live in the moment and to indulge in bodily pleasures. "Uh! All night," they advise listeners, and declare that, among all the things that they could do, they would prefer to "rock'n'roll all night and party every day."

The perfect pleasure that rockers say they want probably looks something like the expression found in Bernini's *Ecstasy of St. Teresa*. In this masterwork of statuary, we see the beloved saint enraptured by an angel with a fiery arrow. Lost in the pure goodness of the experience, she's beguiled like a virtuoso playing a killer guitar solo.

The problem facing the aging rock star is that the rational wisdom of Stoicism appears to stand at odds with the ecstatic nature of rock'n'roll. Rock is by nature sensual and irrational. Wisdom is intellectual and rational. A rock star must either never allow himself to grow wise, since wisdom might interfere with ecstatic experiences, or he must find pleasure in other forms of goodness, like the virtues. Like Courage. Or chastity, perhaps.

Given the bacchanalian thrust of rock, can there be such a thing as a wise rock star? And if a rock star is wise, can he truly be a *rock* star? If we take this logic to its end, we might conclude that the true rock star remains lost in the pleasure of the moment for eternity—just hanging on the perfect note, or lost forever in a deep, deep groove. He cannot possibly know when to quit or when he has made a fool of himself. Nor would he care. So long as there is a party, and he feels good, then he has found the ecstasy he seeks.

The fact that many rock bands try to transcend the sensuality of rock'n'roll by producing intellectualized concept albums might even be taken as an admission that hedonism is ultimately a folly or an impossibility. The human being wants wisdom, and intuitively, we each recognize that goodness includes the cardinal virtues. These are goods worth pursuing. (St. Teresa of Avila, featured in Bernini's orgiastic sculpture, herself concluded that constantly engaging in ecstatic communion with angels inhibits prayer life.)

Strikingly, KISS's ventures into "wise" music came midway through their career, with albums like *Music from "The Elder"* and *Carnival of Souls*. *The Elder* told a story about a hero with lyrics that spoke about the goodness of courage and justice. With *Carnival of Souls*, KISS took a metaphysical turn and spoke about other kinds of love, like the love between friends and parental love. In later music, found on *Sonic Boom* and *Monster*, they returned to the values of libertinism with songs about parties and penises (no more lyrics about being a good dad). The wisdom of KISS might be found in this decision to return to the philosophical foundation of rock'n'roll—sensual pleasure—rather than assaying on art and virtue. Rock, they understand, is in the pelvis, not the heart or head.

Still, wisdom is needed to shape a good ending to a story. What should the whole story look like? To answer that question we need to admit when it's over.

Told You that Forever Was a Word I Couldn't Say

At issue here is the choice we make to bring about an end. In art, in music, the end does not have to be the end—we can always sing another verse or launch a new tour. But in life, the end is often definitive. When we burn a bridge between us and a friend, we cannot raise it again. And there is no second curtain call for those who choose to euthanize themselves. Like KISS, we all must ask ourselves: Where should I place my ending? How does *this* end shape my story? How do we answer that question?

If life is a story (and that's debateable) the character's motivation to a large extent determines the character's development and resolution. What do you desire? And what *should* you desire? Or to put it another way, what is your "end," or your purpose? These are some of the foundational questions in philosophy. Indeed, philosophical debates about the nature of a good life arise from the directions our desires can take us—either to Heaven or Hell, in the Christian sense, or to "Hell and Halleluiah," in the way KISS frames the matter. Wisdom literature urges us to pursue goodness and to desire what is good—much like rock and roll does—but to define the good in such a way that goodness aligns with the cardinal virtues.

How very un-rock'n'roll.

Regardless, at the end of our lives, each of us will look back on what we've done. If we're lucky enough to have time to reflect on what we did with our time (or unlucky, depending on how we lived), we might consider the stories we wrote with our lives. Did you pursue what is good, and if you did, how did you define "good"? Did you have a purpose in life, an end that you strove to reach? And how did the story end? Did you leave the story unresolved, desire unfulfilled, or did you satisfy yourself and take all you could get of what is truly good?

That is the great thing about life. The story is yours. You have a choice. And you "Got to Choose."

19
Beauty of *The Elder*

COURTLAND LEWIS

Imagine you sit down to listen to your favorite alt-euro band The Blackwells' new album. It begins with an orchestral number that resembles the start of a medieval banquet. With rising horns, it crescendos into a moving song about a boy called to greatness, then continues by exploring the young man's journey preparing to live a life fighting evil. Will this boy remain lost, will he fail, or will he embrace his destiny to save the world? The only way to answer these questions is to set back and enjoy The Blackwells' epic concept album about a young boy's odyssey of self-discovery and greatness.

After finishing the album, you spend the rest of your evening pondering your own life, its meaning and purpose, and whether you're destined for some epic odyssey. This is exactly what great music is supposed to do. As Arthur Schopenhauer says in *The World as Will and Representation*, "The inexpressible depth of all music, by virtue of which it floats past us as a paradise quite familiar and yet eternally remote, and is so easy to understand and yet so inexplicable, is due to the fact that it reproduces all the emotions of our innermost being, but entirely without reality and remote from its pain."

Now, imagine you just finished blasting *Love Gun* and *Rock and Roll Over* through your four twelve-inch speakers, in preparation for KISS's latest album *Music from "The Elder."* With the excitement of a new drummer, and all of the press reports from the band about how the new album is a return to their rock'n'roll roots, you can't wait! Sure, the cover is a little strange, but it's the 1980s, and this is the new and improved KISS, produced by Bob Ezrin, the guy who not only produced *Destroyer*, but just finished producing Pink Floyd's epic *The Wall*.

So, you put the record on your turntable, and within seconds, you have crunching guitars, Paul's screams, and (wait a second) Paul singing falsetto?! Okay, that's a little different, but you keep going. Next up, however, you hear orchestras, acoustic songs about boys and heroes, and now you're just confused. Surely, the record company put KISS stickers on some other band's album, but no, that's Paul, Gene, and Ace singing. There has to be some sort of explanation, but as the minutes pass, and confusion turns to disgust, you come to terms with the fact that KISS just released a concept album that instead of rocking sounds like some alt-euro band's art album.

These two imagined stories are tales of what might have been vs. what happened. KISS's *Music from "The Elder"* might have a been an enjoyable record for fans of the genre, but as a KISS record, when compared to their earlier rock'n'roll masterpieces, *The Elder* falls disappointingly flat. Don't get me wrong, I thoroughly enjoy *The Elder*, and listen to it more than several of KISS's other albums, but this chapter is not about defending or bashing its greatness. Instead, I will use *The Elder* to explore aesthetics—the philosophical study of beauty. It is my hope, however, that through our exploration of aesthetics, you'll come to appreciate *The Elder* in ways you might previously have overlooked or thought impossible.

Under the Rose

Ask most people and they'll tell you that beauty is in the eye of the beholder, yet many of these same people will say that certain things are objectively ugly. This inconsistency is what makes *The Elder* such an interesting case study. It's not uncommon for there to be disagreement over the beauty of an album, but those who hate *The Elder* seem unwilling to accept the fact that others might find it enjoyable—the idea is as ludicrous as Gene having tongue reduction surgery. They seem to believe that *The Elder*'s ugliness is an objective fact—that beauty isn't in the eye of the beholder. Aesthetics attempts to settle such disputes by providing clear philosophical arguments to determine if beauty is in the eye of the beholder, or if there are certain standards of beauty as objective as $2 + 2 = 4$.

To say that beauty is objective is to claim that there's some sort of rational way to determine what is beautiful. This rationalist approach is supported by philosophers such as Plato and those who subscribe to contemporary accounts of the Golden Ratio, both of which suggest that beauty is determined by a sort of mathematical symmetry. To make sense of this, think of "Rock and Roll All Nite." The songs has a 4/4 beat, meaning the number of beats in the top bar is 4 and the individual notes in the bottom bar equal four. Or better yet, just listen to the beginning of the song and repeatedly count to four. If you have enough rhythm, your counting will follow Peter Criss's drumbeat—1, 2, 3, 4; 1, 2, 3, 4. Criss's signature drumbeat is a central component of what makes the song so memorable.

If Criss had tried something different, like 1, 2, 3; 1, 2, 3, "Rock and Roll All Nite" would be a waltz, which would completely change the song; or if he changed the beat each measure, the song would be more like jazz than rock'n'roll. The mathematical precision of the beat creates a rhythm in which songs are judged beautiful, or simply a mess. So, we can use objective standards to judge whether a song keeps a beat, but this is a different type of judgment than determining whether you like the song. *The Elder* does not contain dropped or inconsistent beats. In fact, one of the strengths of Bob Ezrin's production is that he's known to be militant about technical proficiency. He's not afraid to bring in hired musicians to do the work, if members are incapable of playing songs correctly. In terms of hitting the right notes and keeping the beat, *The Elder* meets the criteria of a good album.

The Oath

Since the eighteenth century, most philosophers have rejected the rationalist approach to defining beauty. Sure, there's a rational component to beauty, such as symmetry and having a consistent beat, but beauty also thrives with asymmetry and fluctuating beats. So, eventually philosophers developed new ways of thinking about beauty.

One of these new approaches was to distinguish between perceiving (seeing, hearing, tasting, feeling, and touching) something as beautiful and judging it beautiful. For instance, when I first listened to *Dressed to Kill* in 1988, I perceived many beautiful sounds. I was hooked, from the opening chords of "Room Service," to the final crescendo of "Rock and Roll All Nite." I didn't have to think about the music, I just loved it.

Later on, as I listened to it repeatedly, I began to analyze and appreciate the musicianship of the album, judging it great and comparing it to other albums. For this description to be true, humans must be capable of perceiving the world without instantly making judgments about the world. If judging is a rational process, and all we do is judge the world; then beauty would be inherently rational. To avoid this trap, we need a sort of internal sixth sense, what David Hume calls taste, or what Thomas Reid suggests is a lower level of knowing the world. Philosophers like David Hume and Immanuel Kant, therefore, argue for what's called the immediacy thesis of beauty. According to the immediacy thesis, my original perception of *Dressed to Kill* is *not* mediated by any mental inferences from principles or applications of concepts. In other words, there are no preconceived notions that interfere with me liking something. I simply like it because it matches up with my taste for music.

The same is true for *The Elder*. *The Elder* is beautiful, if I immediately perceive it to be beautiful. Sounds simple enough, but this is where analyzing *The Elder* is difficult. In fact, it's difficult for fans not to judge their favorite band's music. As the two cases that began this chapter show, both fans are excited to hear their favorite band's new album, and instead of sitting back and enjoying the music, they are listening closely, judging the merits of the new music.

Because *The Elder* wasn't KISS's first album, and because it's not usually the first KISS album fans hear, listening to it often occurs at the higher level of judgment. As Chuck Klosterman notes in "The Definitive, One-Size-Fits-All, Accept-No Substitutes, Massively Comprehensive Guide to the Life and Times of KISS," *The Elder* is "indisputably the most fascinating KISS album by a factor of ten," one that "signaled a permanent change within the band." As a result, the only way for us to determine the immediate enjoyment of *The Elder* would require finding someone who likes theatrical classical rock, yet has no knowledge of KISS. Only, then, could a person perceive and pass judgment on its beauty, free from preconceived notions of how it "should" sound. Without such an ideal observer, we're stuck with tainted judgments about *The Elder*'s beauty. Sure, we can enjoy the album, but our attempt to prove to others why they should judge it beautiful will always fall short. Of course, their attempts to tell us it's bad, will always fall short too.

Odyssey

Let's take a step back and look at the album itself. KISS rarely talks about *The Elder*, and when they do it's either flippant or dismissive. Paul has probably been the most vocal, but for the most part, he sees it as folly, with little depth. As he notes in *Backstage Pass*, KISS wasn't strongarmed, manipulated, or coerced during the making of *The Elder*; we simply sought validation from critics and wanted to make a grand musical statement. In *Face the Music*, he goes so far as to compare it to "Springtime for Hitler," from Mel Brooks's *The Producers*. To really gain perspective about the album, you must read Tim McPhate's and Julian Gill's *Odyssey: The Definitive Examination of "Music from* The Elder,*" KISS's Cult-Classic Album*.

McPhate and Gill illustrate how the record company rearranged the track listing, in order to highlight what they thought were possible hit songs. However, their interference affected the feel of the album. *The Elder* is a concept album that tells a story, so rearranging songs is akin to rearranging the chapters of a book. Imagine how disappointed you would be if the novel you're reading didn't go in order—you'd know the ending before the beginning! So, instead of a clear narrative about a boy's journey, fans received a hodgepodge of tracks on weird topics.

To illustrate, compare the rearranged track listing that appeared on *The Elder*'s original release with the band's original track listing:

Rearranged Track Listing	Band's Original Track Listing
1) The Oath	1) Fanfare
2) Fanfare	2) Just a Boy
3) Just a Boy	3) Odyssey
4) Dark Light	4) Only You
5) Only You	5) Under the Rose
6) Under the Rose	6) Dark Light
7) A World Without Heroes	7) A World Without Heroes
8) Mr. Blackwell	8) The Oath
9) Escape from the Island	9) Mr. Blackwell
10) Odyssey	10) Escape from the Island
11) I	11) I
12) Finale	

Originally, Fanfare served as an overture to set the tone of the album, signifying to fans: "This is something completely different from any other KISS album." The album then introduces the boy, talks about his odyssey, how only he can fight the evil present in the world, and takes listeners through the story of the boy's eventual acceptance of his destiny.

The rearranged tracks, however, make no sense. "The Oath," originally track 8, features the boy forged like steel and becoming a man. This is the climax of the story, which is why it appears near the end of the album. As track 1, it ruins the story. The rearranged story starts with the boy becoming a man, then offers the overture of "Fanfare," then begins the story of the boy. "Odyssey," which tells listeners what the story is about, was moved to the end, so fans get the beginning of the story at the end, and the end of the story at the beginning. It's just a jumbled mess that makes simply enjoying the album almost impossible, and shows why it's so easy for fans to judge the album poorly.

The remastered version restored the band's track listing, but by now, *The Elder*'s status as the "worst KISS album" is part of the collective memory of KISS fans. As Peter French discusses in *War and Moral Dissonance*, collective memories are stories that a group of people tell themselves that contribute to that group's identity. KISS and its critics have spent decades telling fans that *The Elder* is awful, and fans have parroted the same story. As a result, there's a long-standing narrative about *The Elder*, so that any new fan will automatically be inclined to accept the collective memory that *The Elder* sucks. In fact, to reject the narrative is to risk becoming an outsider—you're not a real fan if you like *The Elder*, or you simply have no taste in music. What's funny, however, is that fans of *The Elder* have started their own collective memory, counter-narrative, where appreciating and finding *The Elder* beautiful is the mark of a "true" KISS fan.

Dark Light

With disagreement between fans concerning the beauty of *The Elder*, who decides which group is right? First, we should recognize that notions of beauty are grounded in what philosophers call the disinterest thesis. The disinterest thesis maintains that all humans engage the world with a type of psychological egoism. According to psychological egoism, humans like and do things they find good or pleasurable. Even when you go to the dentist, you've decided that it's better to go now than to wait until your teeth rot. So, all human action is directed by self-interest. What makes aesthetic beliefs and judgments different from other types—such as ethical beliefs and judgments—is that pleasure in the beautiful is disinterested. Stated differently, ethical beliefs call us into action—we must do something to stop an injustice; whereas we don't have to do anything related to our aesthetic beliefs. We can just set back and enjoy our favorite album. Sure, we might be inspired to paint our faces and go to concerts, but there's nothing in an aesthetic belief requiring us to act.

Because of the disinterest thesis, we can say that there's nothing wrong or right with liking *The Elder*. It's simply a matter of enjoyment. If you love the album, that's great. If you hate the album, that's great too. Since there's no deep philosophical truth related to determining that beauty of *The Elder*, then we should be able to set back and simply enjoy—or avoid—the album. If we want to try to convince our friend of why *The Elder* is great (or awful), we should do so with the realization that our discussion is a matter of sharing a fun experience with a friend—not a fight to the death over ultimate truth.

To help understanding why—and how—we can have fun disagreeing, think of how we interpret works of art, including musical works. KISS had specific intentions when creating *The Elder*. They wanted critics and fans to react a certain way, wanted to create some songs that would make them proud, and so on. Such intentions are the focus of the philosophical discussion of intentionalism. Should KISS's intentions decide how we judge *The Elder*, or are the fans the only people who get to decide?

Noel Carroll distinguishes between three types of intentionalism, with two being relevant to our purposes. First, there is anti-intentionalism, which maintains that the author's intentions don't matter. So, if Gene meant "I" as an anti-drug song, it doesn't matter. We, the listeners, get to decide the meaning of the song. Second, there is actual intentionalism, which maintains that the author's intentions are relevant to determining meaning. Of course, there are two types of actual intentionalism. Extreme actual intentionalism suggests that only the fans' intentions matter, while moderate actual intentionalism suggests that the fans' intentions matter, but are tempered by external factors—like what the author intended.

For Carroll, anti-intentionalism fails because it doesn't allow for irony and ignores that artists create works with specific intentions. KISS's intentions were for *The Elder* to be a massive success for fans and critics. The songs have specific meaning and tell a particular story. If anti-intentionalism were true, then we as fans could simply say, "*The Elder* was meant as a joke album, making fun of the pretentious prog groups of the time," and it would be true. But such a claim would be false. KISS was serious about the album, and to simply ignore their intentions creates a state of affairs where either the truth doesn't matter or there is no truth. On the other hand, extreme actual intentionalism undermines the relational nature of art.

As consumers of art, we don't simply appreciate the artist's creation. We make it our own, interweaving the author's intentions with our own. As Jerrold Levinson says, in "What a Musical Work Is," composers are creators, their music is always personalized, and their "musical composition could not fail to be seen as a historically rooted activity whose products must be understood with reference to their points of origin." However, "the pure sound structure of a musical work, while graspable in isolation, does not exhaust the work structurally, and thus that the underlying means of performance must be taken into account as well if the work is to be correctly assessed." What I take Levinson to mean is that there's a relationship between composers and listeners, and that even though we make songs our own by adding meaning to them, we must never forget that the composer imbued the song with meaning first.

Therefore, we should understand songs as containing a mixture of the composer's and our own meaning. For Carroll, this is why moderate actual intentionalism is our best approach to interpreting music. It allows both types of meaning to coexist and enrich each other. We can accept KISS's good-faith effort to push themselves towards new creative territory, and we can map our own meaning onto the project. Whether we like it or not, *The Elder* is what it is—a well-performed and well-produced album, focused on a young boy's odyssey. How we perceive and judge the beauty of the album is up to each person, and fans who love and fans who hate *The Elder* should avoid acting as if their judgment of the album somehow makes it objectively great, or garbage.

Escape from the Island

In *The World as Will and Representation*, Arthur Schopenhauer makes many wonderful insights into the nature of music. Ponder the following: "How full of meaning and significance the language of music is . . . which would be intolerable in the case of works composed in the language of words. In music, however, they are very appropriate and beneficial; for to comprehend it fully, we must hear it twice."

As Schopenhauer eloquently says, unlike the written word, where repetition is criticized, music requires repetition to be fully grasped. There's something deep (and mystical?) about music that requires we hear beats, rhythms, and lyrics repeatedly, and instead of becoming tedious, we find ourselves entranced. To quote Schopenhauer again, "Music expresses in an exceedingly universal language, in a homogeneous material, that is, in mere tones, and with the greatest distinctness and truth, the inner being, the in-itself, of the world, which we think of under the concept of will, according to its most distinct manifestation." In other words, music is the not only truth, but it is the soul of the world.

For the haters of *The Elder*, they will never experience this distinctness and inner being of the album. Thankfully, KISS has many other great songs and albums that provide such a deeply moving experience. For fans of *The Elder*, they perceive the focus, intensity, and unity of one of KISS's grandest experiments in expanding their sound in new directions.

Unlike detractors, not only can fans of *The Elder* enjoy KISS's other great albums, but they have a "bonus" album in which to delight. Instead of letting collective memory dictate their judgments of beauty, they have broken away from the pack and found something to believe in. They have found *The Elder* beautiful, and their lives are enriched because of it.

VI

KISStory

Band Configurations

Mark I: 1973–1979

Paul Stanley
Gene Simmons
Ace Frehley
Peter Criss

Mark II: 1980–1982

Paul Stanley
Gene Simmons
Ace Frehley
Eric Carr

Mark III: 1982–1984

Paul Stanley
Gene Simmons
Vinnie Vincent
Eric Carr

Mark IV: 1984

Paul Stanley
Gene Simmons
Mark St. John
Eric Carr

Mark V: 1984–1991

Paul Stanley
Gene Simmons
Bruce Kulick
Eric Carr

Mark VI: 1991–1996

Paul Stanley
Gene Simmons
Bruce Kulick
Eric Singer

Mark I (Reprise): 1996–2001

Paul Stanley
Gene Simmons
Ace Frehley
Peter Criss

Mark VII: 2001–2002

Paul Stanley
Gene Simmons
Ace Frehley
Eric Singer

Mark VIII: 2002–2004

Paul Stanley
Gene Simmons
Tommy Thayer
Peter Criss

Mark IX: 2004–Present

Paul Stanley
Gene Simmons
Tommy Thayer
Eric Singer

Other Notable Contributors: 1974–Present

Dick Wagner (*Destroyer* and *Revenge*)
Eddie Kramer (*Love Gun*)
Bob Kulick (*Alive II, Unmasked, Creatures of the Night,* and *Psycho Circus*)
Anton Fig (*Dynasty* and *Unmasked*)
Tony Powers (*Music from' the Elder'*)
Vinnie Vincent (*Creatures of the Night,* songwriter on *Revenge*)
Rick Derringer (*Lick It Up*)
Bruce Kulick (*Animalize* and *Psycho Circus*)
Phil Ashley (*Crazy Nights* and *Hot in the Shade*)
Gary Corbett (Keyboardist on "Crazy Nights Tour")
Tommy Thayer (*Hot in the Shade, Revenge,* and *Psycho Circus*)
Bob Ezrin (producer *Destroyer, Music from "the Elder,"* *Revenge*)
Adam Mitchell (songwriter *Killers, Creatures, Crazy Nights, Hot in the* Shade)
Desmond Child (songwriter *Dynasty, Animalize, Asylum, Crazy Nights, Smashes, Thrashes, Hot in the Shade, Live to Win*)
Vini Poncia (producer *Dynasty* and *Unmasked*, and co-writer, "I Was Made for Lovin' You")

Official Album Releases (Studio, Live, and Compilations)

Kiss (1974)

Strutter
Nothin' to Lose
Firehouse
Cold Gin
Let Me Know
Kissin' Time
   (not included on first
      pressing)
Deuce
Love Theme From KISS
1000,000 Years
Black Diamond

Hotter than Hell (1974)

Got to Choose
Parasite
Goin' Blind
Hotter Than Hell
Let Me Go, Rock 'n' Roll
All the Way
Watchin' You
Mainline
Comin' Home
Strange Ways

Dressed to Kill (1975)

Room Service
Two Timer
Ladies in Waiting
Getaway
Rock Bottom

C'mon and Love Me
Anything for My Baby
She
Lover Her All I Can
Rock and Roll All Nite

Alive! (1975)

Deuce
Strutter
Got to Choose
Hotter Than Hell
Firehouse
Nothin' to Lose
C'mon and Love Me
Parasite
She
Watchin' You
1000,000 Years
Black Diamond
Rock Bottom
Cold Gin
Rock and Roll All Nite
Let Me Go, Rock 'n' Roll

Destroyer (1976)

Detroit Rock City
King of the Night Time
   World
God of Thunder
Great Expectations
Flaming Youth
Sweet Pain
Shout It Out Loud

Beth
Do You Love Me
Rock and Roll Party

Rock and Roll Over (1976)

I Want You
Take Me
Calling Dr. Love
Ladies Room
Baby Driver
Love 'Em and Leave 'Em
Mr. Speed
See You in Your Dreams
Hard Luck Woman
Makin' Love

Love Gun (1977)

I Stoll Your Love
Christine Sixteen
Got Love for Sale
Shock Me
Tomorrow and Tonight
Love Gun
Hooligan
Almost Human
Plaster Caster
Then She Kissed Me

Alive II (1977)

Detroit Rock City
King of the Night Time
    World
Ladies Room
Makin' Love
Love Gun
Calling Dr. Love
Christine Sixteen
Shock Me
Hard Luck Woman

Tomorrow and Tonight
I Stole Your Love
Beth
God of Thunder
I Want You
Shout It Our Loud
All American Man
Rockin' in the USA
Larger Than Life
Rocket Ride
Any Way You Want It

Double Platinum (1978)

Strutter '78
Do You Love Me
Hard Luck Woman
Calling Dr. Love
Let Me Go, Rock 'n' Roll
Love Gun
God of Thunder
Firehouse
Hotter Than Hell
I Want You
Deuce
100,000 Years
Detroit Rock City
Rock Bottom (Intro)
She
Rock and Roll All Nite
Beth
Makin' Love
C'mon and Love Me
Cold Gin
Black Diamond

Paul Stanley (1978)

Tonight You Belong to Me
Move On
Ain't Quite Right
Wouldn't You Like to Know

Me
Take Me Away (Together
   as One)
It's Alright
Hold Me, Touch Me
(Think of Me When We're
   Apart)
Love in Chains
Goodbye

Gene Simmons (1978)

Radioactive
Burning Up with Fever
See You Tonite
Tunnel of Love
True Confessions
Living in Sin
Always Near
You/Nowhere to Hide
Man of 1,000 Faces
Mr. Make Believe
See You in Your Dreams
When You Wish Upon A
   Star

Ace Frehley (1978)

Rip It Out
Speedin' Back to My Baby
Snow Blind
Ozone
What's on Your Mind?
New York Groove
I'm In Need of Love
Wiped-Out
Fractured Mirror

Peter Criss (1978)

I'm Gonna Love You
You Matter to Me

Tossin' and Turnin'
Don't You Let Me Down
That's the Kind of Sugar
Papa Likes
Easy Thing
Rock Me, Baby
Kiss the Girl Goodbye
Hooked on Rock 'n' Roll
I Can't Stop the Rain

Dynasty (1979)

I Was Made for Lovin' You
2,000 Man
Sure Know Something
Dirty Livin'
Charisma
Magic Touch
Hard Times
X-Ray Eyes
Save Your Love

Unmasked (1980)

Is That You?
Shandi
Talk to Me
Naked City
What Makes the World Go
   'Round
Tomorrow
Two Sides of the Coin
She's So European
Easy as It Seems
Torpedo Girl
You're All That I Want

Music from "The Elder" 1981)

Fanfare
Just a Boy
Odyssey

Only You
Under the Rose
Dark Light
A World Without Heroes
The Oath
Mr. Blackwell
Escape from the Island
I

Killers (1982)

I'm a Legend Tonight
Down on Your Knees
Cold Gin
Love Gun
Shout it Out Loud
Sure Know Something
Nowhere to Run
Partners in Crime
Detroit Rock City
God of Thunder
I Was Made For Lovin'
    You
Rock and Roll All Nite

Creatures of the Night (1982)

Creatures of the Night
Saint and Sinner
Keep Me Comin'
Rock and Roll Hell
Danger
I Love It Loud
I Still Love You
Killer
War Machine

Lick It Up (1983)

Exciter
Not for the Innocent
Lick It Up

Young and Wasted
Gimmie More
All Hell's Breakin' Loose
A Million to One
Fits Like A Glove
Dance All Over Your Face
And on the 8th Day

Animalize (1984)

I've Had Enough (Into the
    Fire)
Heaven's on Fire
Burn Bitch Burn
Get All You Can Take
Lonely Is the Hunter
Under the Gun
Thrills in the Night
While the City Sleeps
Murder in High-Heels

Asylum (1985)

King of the Mountain
Any Way You Slice It
Who Wants to Be Lonely
Trial by Fire
I'm Alive
Love's a Deadly Weapon
Tears Are Falling
Secretly Cruel
Radar for Love
Uh! All Night

Crazy Nights (1987)

Crazy Crazy Nights
I'll Fight Hell to Hold You
Bang Bang You
No, No, No
Hell or High Water
My Way

When Your Walls Come
Down
Reason to Live
Good Girl Gone Bad
Sword and Stone
Turn On the Night
Thief in the Night

Smashes, Thrashes, and Hits
(1988)

Let's Put the X in Sex
Rock Hard
Love Gun
Detroit Rock City
I Love It Loud
Deuce
Lick It Up
Heavens on Fire
Calling Dr. Love
Strutter
Beth (Eric Carr Vocals)
Tears Are Falling
I Was Made For Lovin' You
Rock and Roll All Nite
Shout It Out Loud

Hot in the Shade (1989)

Rise to It
Betrayed
Hide Your Heart
Prisoner of Love
Read My Body
Love's a Slap in the Face
Forever
Silver Spoon
Cadillac Dreams
King of Hearts
The Street Giveth and the
Street Taketh Away
You Love Me to Hate You

Somewhere Between
Heaven and Hell
Little Caesar
Boomerang

Revenge (1992)

Unholy
Take It Off
Tough Love
Spit
God Gave Rock 'n' Roll To
You II
Domino
Heart of Chrome
Thou Shall Not
Every Time I Look at You
Paralyzed
I Just Wanna
Car Jam 1981

Alive III (1993)

Creatures of the Night
Deuce
I Just Wanna
Unholy
Heaven's on Fire
Watchin' You
Domino
I Was Made For Lovin'
You
I Still Love You
Rock and Roll All Nite
Lick It Up
Forever
Take It Off
I Love It Loud
Detroit Rock City
God Gave Rock 'n' Roll To
You II
The Star-Spangled Banner

KISS Unplugged (1996)

Comin' Home
Plaster Caster
Goin' Blind
Do You Love Me?
Domino
Sure Know Something
A World Without Heroes
Rock Bottom
See You Tonite
I Still Love You
Every Time I Look at You
2,000 Man
Beth
Nothin' to Lose
Rock and Roll All Nite

You Wanted the Best, You Got the Best!! (1996)

Room Service
Two Timer
Let Me Know
Rock Bottom
Parasite
Firehouse
I Stole Your Love
Calling Dr. Love
Take Me
Shout It Out Loud
Beth
Rock and Roll All Nite
KISS Tells All (with Jay Leno)

Greatest KISS (1997)

Detroit Rock City
Hard Luck Woman
Sure Know Something
Deuce

Do You Love Me?
I Was Made For Lovin' You
Calling Dr. Love
Christine Sixteen
Beth
Strutter
Cold Gin
Plaster Caster
Rock and Roll All Nite
Flaming Youth
Two Sides of the Coin
Shout it Out Live (Live 96)

Carnival of Souls: The Final Sessions (1997)

Hate
Rain
Master & Slave
Childhood's End
I Will Be There
Jungle
In My Head
It Never Goes Away
Seduction of the Innocent
I Confess
In the Mirror
I Walk Alone

Psycho Circus (1998)

Psycho Circus
Within
I Pledge Allegiance to the State of Rock & Roll
Into the Void
We Are One
You Wanted the Best
Raise Your Glasses
I Finally Found My Way
Dreamin'
Journey of 1,000 Years

KISS: The Box Set

Disc 1
Strutter (Demo)
Deuce (Demo)
Keep Me Waiting (Wicked
    Lester)
She (Wicked Lester)
Love Her All I Can
    (Wicked Lester)
Let Me Know (Demo)
100,000 Years (Demo)
Stop, Look to Listen
    (Demo)
Leeta (Demo)
Let Me Go, Rock 'n' Roll
    (Demo)
Acrobat (Live)
Firehouse (Demo)
Nothin' to Lose
Black Diamond
Hotter Than Hell
Strange Ways
Parasite
Goin' Blind
Anything for My Baby
Ladies in Waiting
Rock and Roll All Nite

Disc 2
C'mon and Love Me (Live)
Rock Bottom (Live)
Cold Gin (Live)
Watchin' You (Live)
Doncha Hesitate (Demo)
Mad Dog (Demo)
God of Thunder (Demo)
Great Expectations
Beth
Do You Love Me?
Bad, Bad Lovin' (Demo)
Calling Dr. Love

Mr. Speed (Demo)
Christine Sixteen
Hard Luck Woman
Shock Me
I Stole Your Love
I Want You (Sound check)
Love Gun (Demo)
Love Is Blind (Demo)

Disc 3
Detroit Rock City
King of the Night Time
    World (Live)
Larger Than Life
Rocket Ride
Tonight You Belong to Me
New York Groove
Radioactive (Demo)
Don't You Let Me Down
I Was Made for Lovin' You
Sure Know Something
Shandi
You're All That I Want,
    You're All That I Need
    (Demo)
Talk to Me (Live)
A World Without Heroes
The Oath
Nowhere to Run
Creatures of the Night
War Machine
I Love It Loud

Disc 4
Lick It Up
All Hell's Breakin' Loose
Heaven's on Fire
Get All You Can Take
Thrills in the Night
Tears Are Falling
Uh! All Night
Time Traveler (Demo)

Hell or High Water
Crazy Crazy Nights
Reason to Live
Let's Put the X in Sex
Hide Your Heart
Ain't That Peculiar (Demo)
Silver Spoon
Forever

Disc 5
God Gave Rock'n'Roll to
   You II
Unholy
Domino (Demo)
Every Time I Look at You
Comin' Home (Unplugged)
Got to Choose (Unplugged)
I Still Love You
   (Unplugged)
Nothin' to Lose
   (Unplugged)
Childhood's End
I Will Be There
Psycho Circus
Into the Void
Within
I Pledge Allegiance to the
   State of Rock & Roll
Nothing Can Keep Me
   from You
It's My Life
Shout It Out Loud (Live)
Rock and Roll All Nite
   (Live)

The Very Best of KISS (2002)

Strutter
Deuce
Got to Choose
Hotter than Hell

C'mon and Love Me
Rock and Roll All Nite
Detroit Rock City
Shout It Out Loud
Beth
I Want You
Calling Dr. Love
Hard Luck Woman
I Stole Your Love
Christine Sixteen
Love Gun
New York Groove
I Was Made For Lovin' You
I Love It Loud
Lick It Up
Forever
God Gave Rock'n'Roll To
   You II

KISS Symphony: Alive IV
(2003)

Deuce
Strutter
Let Me Go, Rock'n'Roll
Lick It Up
Calling Dr. Love
Psycho Circus
Beth
Forever
Goin' Blind
Sure Know Something
Shandi
Detroit Rock City
King of the Night Time
   World
Do You Love Me?
Shout It Out Loud
God of Thunder
Love Gun
Black Diamond

Great Expectations
I Was Made For Lovin'
   You
Rock and Roll All Nite

The Millennium Collection:
The Best of KISS (2003)

Strutter
Deuce
Hotter Than Hell
C'mon and Love Me
Rock and Roll All Nite
Detroit Rock City
Beth
Hard Luck Woman
Calling Dr. Love
Love Gun
Christine Sixteen
I Was Made For Lovin' You

The Best of KISS, Volume 2:
The Millennium Collection
(2004)

Creatures of the Night
I Love It Loud
Lick It Up
All Hell's Breakin' Loose
Heaven's On Fire
Thrills in the Night
Tears are Falling
Uh! All Night
Crazy Crazy Nights
Reason to Live
Hide Your Heart
Forever

Gold (2005)

Strutter
Nothin' to Loose

Firehouse
Deuce
Black Diamond
Got to Choose
Parasite
Hotter Than Hell
C'mon and Love Me
She
Anything for my Baby
Rock Bottom
Cold Gin
Rock and Roll All Nite
Let Me Go, Rock 'n' Roll
Detroit Rock City
King of the Night Time
   World
Shout It Out Loud
Beth
Do You Love Me?
I Want You
Calling Dr. Love
Hard Luck Woman
I Stole Your Love
Love Gun
Christine Sixteen
Shock Me
Makin' Love
God of Thunder
Tonight You Belong to
   Me
New York Groove
Radioactive
Don't You Let Me Down
I Was Made For Lovin'
   You
Sure Know Something
Shandi
Talk to Me
A World Without Heroes
Nowhere to Run
I'm A Legend Tonight

The Best of KISS, Volume 3: The Millennium Collection (2006)

God Gave Rock'n'Roll to You II
Unholy
Domino
Hate
Childhood's End
I Will Be There
Comin' Home
Got to Choose
Psycho Circus
Into the Void
I Pledge Allegiance to the State of Rock and Roll
Nothing Can Keep Me from You

Alive! The Millennium Concert (2006)

Psycho Circus
Shout It Out Loud
Deuce
Heaven's On Fire
Into the Void
Firehouse
Do You Love Me?
Let Me Go, Rock 'n' Roll
I Love It Loud
Lick It Up
100,000 Years
Love Gun
Black Diamond
Beth
Rock and Roll All Nite

Sonic Boom (2009)

Modern Day Delilah
Russian Roulette

Never Enough
Yes I Know (Nobody's Perfect)
Stand
Hot and Cold
All for the Glory
Danger Us
I'm an Animal
When Lighting Strikes
Say Yeah

Monster (2012)

Hell or Hallelujah
Wall of Sound
Freak
Back to the Stone Age
Shout Mercy
Long Way Down
Eat Your Heart Out
The Devil is Me
Outta This World
All for the Love of Rock & Roll
Last Chance

KISS 40 (2014)

Nothin' to Lose
Let Me Go, Rock'n'Roll
C'mon and Love Me
Rock and Roll All Nite
God of Thunder
Beth
Hard Luck Woman
Reputation
Christine Sixteen
Shout It Out Loud
Strutter
You Matter to Me
Radioactive
New York Groove

Hold Me, Touch Me (Think of Me When We're Apart)
I Was Made for Lovin' You
Shandi
A World Without Heroes
I Love it Loud
Down on Your Knees
Lick It Up
Heavens on Fire
Tears are Falling
Reason to Live
Let's Put the X in Sex
Forever
God Gave Rock 'n'Roll to You II
Unholy
Do You Love Me?
Room Service
Jungle
Psycho Circus
Nothing Can Keep Me from You
Detroit Rock City

Deuce
Firehouse
Modern Day Delilah
Cold Gin
Crazy Crazy Nights
Hell or Hallelujah.

KISS Rocks Vegas (2016)

Detroit Rock City
Creatures of the Night
Psycho Circus
Parasite
War Machine
Tears are Falling
Deuce
Lick It Up
I Love it Loud
Hell or Hallelujah
God of Thunder
Do You Love Me?
Love Gun
Black Diamond
Shout It Out Loud
Rock and Roll All Nite

Movies and other Video Releases

KISS Meets the Phantom of the Park (1978)
Animalize Live Uncensored (1985)
Exposed (1987)
Crazy Nights (1988)
X-treme Close-Up (1992)
Kiss Konfidential (1993)
Kiss My Ass: The Video (1994)
Kiss Unplugged (1996)
Psycho Circus 3-D Video (1998)
The Second Coming (1998)
Detroit Rock City (1999)
Kiss Symphony: The DVD (2003)
Rock the Nation Live! (2005)
Kissology Volume One: 1974–1977 (2006)
Kissology Volume Two: 1978–1991 (2007)
Kissology Volume Three: 1992–2000 (2007)
Scooby-Doo! and Kiss: Rock and Roll Mystery (2015)
Kiss Rocks Vegas (2016)

Books

Paul Stanley

Face the Music: A Life Exposed
Backstage Pass

Gene Simmons

Me, Inc.: Build an Army of One, Unleash Your Inner
*   Rock God, Win in Life and Business*
KISS and Make-Up
Sex Money KISS
Ladies of the Night: A Historical and Personal
*   Perspective on the Oldest Profession in the World*
27: The Legend & Mythology of the 27 Club

Ace Frehley

No Regrets: A Rock'n' Roll Memoir

Peter Criss

Makeup to Breakup: My Life In and Out of KISS

Other Books of Interest

KISStory I
KISStory II
Nothin' To Lose: The Making of KISS 1972-1975
*   (Ken Sharp, Gene Simmons, and Paul Stanley)*
KISS: Behind the Mask—The Official Authorized
*   Biography (David Leaf and Ken Sharp)*
KISS: 1977–1980 (Lynn Goldsmith, Gene Simmons,
*   and Paul Stanley)*
KISS and Sell: The Making of a Supergroup
*   (C.K. Lendt)*
Odyssey: The Definitive Examination of "Music From
*   The Elder," KISS's Cult-Classic Concept Album*
*   (Tim McPhate and Julian Gill)*
Danger Zone: An Exploration of KISS's Crazy Nights
*   (Julian Gill)*

Books

Take it Off: KISS Truly Unmasked (Greg Prato)

The Eric Carr Story (Greg Prato)

KISS Kompendium (Gene Simmons and Paul Stanley, editors)

Shout It Out Loud: The Story of KISS's Destroyer and the Making of an American Icon (James Campion)

Out on the Streets: The True Story of Life on the Road with the Hottest Band in the Land—KISS! (Peter Oreckinto, J.R. Smalling, Rick Munroe, and Mike Campion)

Contributors from the Elder (AKA "The Destroyers")

MATT ALSCHBACH is an Associate Professor of history at Owens-boro Community and Technical college. Over the past fifteen years, he has taught college-level history courses in Southern California and Western Kentucky. He specializes in US history, World War II history, and the history of Kentucky. He has presented his research at numerous conferences and events discussing topics such as Eleanor Roosevelt, Muhammad Ali, the Salem Witch Trials, temperance and prohibition, the US Constitution, and Japanese internment. In the fourth grade, he dressed as Gene Simmons for Halloween, complete with makeup, wig, and platform shoes. He claims that this was likely the greatest moment of his young life, but falls short because his mother neglected to capture the epic moment with photos. He is still a little upset about it.

By day, **RANDALL E. AUXIER** teaches philosophy and rhetoric at Southern Illinois University Carbondale. But he is King of the Night-time World, stalking cornfields and small-town honky tonks with his bass guitar and his believable persona as an aging and not very successful rock musician. He gets not very many girls this way, in fact none, and has a following of one wife (so long as he is well behaved), four cats (so long as he feeds them), and two (or so) dissertation students (so long as he reads and returns their pages in timely fashion). Come to think of it, that's really all the same thing. So, a following of five to seven. He actually does drink beer, bloody marys, and wine, but never shots. That was just for show. He is a devoted epicurean. Except that he has a habit of running for office, which is very un-epi-curean. Please talk him out of it. He'll never be elected with a following of seven, four of which can't vote and two of which can but won't.

PETER FINOCCHIARO is an Associate Professorial Research Fel-low at Wuhan University. When he's not practicing his bass licks, he writes about the methodology of metaphysics, espe-cially the differences between the metaphysics of natural reality and the metaphysics of social reality. When he first moved to China, he was shocked to find how many people were missing out on the hottest band in the world. Now, he introduces his stu-dents to both American philosophy and American rock. Turns out, "Lick It Up" is a hit!

MICHAEL FOREST teaches philosophy at Canisius College in Buffalo, New York. Lately his publications have been on aes-thetics and popular media. His first memorable encounter with KISS was going to grade school the day after the band appeared on the *Tomorrow* show and hearing from older students that "Ace was high." Indeed! His main connection however is having an office next to his co-author, a human encyclopedia of KISS information.

CHRISTOPHER M. INNES got his PhD from Goldsmiths College. This is the coolest college in the University of London. It's where Kate Tempest, Esmé Bianco, Beatie Wolfe, Amelia Warner, Katy B., and other singers got their inspiration. He now teaches phi-losophy at Boise State University in Idaho. The US is a creative haven for the KISS fan. The fans rule and the band plays on! Dr. Innes remembers well, as an undergraduate, KISS playing on the radio reminding him that study is not all there is to life. Rocking hard and heavy is needed as well. The dream of dressing up with his face made up like a wolf and rocking it up on stage like KISS is always more than just a fantasy. (This is when he was an un-dergraduate at Hull University gaining his BA, later to gain his MA at Kent at Canterbury University) It is now with the funda-mentals of philosophy understood that he can now talk about KISS in his undergraduate philosophy classes. The authenticity and essentialism of what is rock music is still perplexing.

COURTLAND LEWIS is author of *Repentance and the Right to For-giveness*, co-editor of *Doctor Who and Philosophy* and *More Doc-tor Who and Philosophy* (with Paula Smithka), and editor of

Futurama and Philosophy (recently translated into both Spanish and Italian). Courtland is Associate Professor at Pellissippi State Community College in Knoxville, Tennessee. He is a proud father and husband who spends his free time playing music with his band Court and the Jesters, mentoring, and enjoying life. He's primarily a Starchild, with a little Demon and Fox to make things interesting. Courtland has seen KISS eleven times, often in the make-up of the Demon, Starchild, or Fox, and has only been kicked out of one show for supposedly stalking Gene Simmons. He was merely trying to deliver a letter inviting the band to his apartment for an after-party gathering.

MATTHEW W. MITCHELL is Professor of Religious Studies at Canisius College of Buffalo. He first encountered original-era KISS visually on posters and album covers at a young age, even though his own auditory fandom took root in the Eric Carr and Bruce Kulick era. The first album he bought as a new release was *Asylum*, often since wondering if its cover art should qualify as a rival set of "make-up" characters. His oddest and proudest KISS moment was passing by Paul Stanley in an art museum in St. Petersburg, Russia, and managing not to disturb his viewing of the Dutch masters with any lame fan antics.

DONALD PRESLEY is an independent scholar who specializes in occult and evil studies. When not dressing up as the Demon and scarring "civilized" folk, he reads, talks with his parrot, and avoids worrying about the future of the human race by listening to KISS.

ROBERT GRANT PRICE, PhD, lectures at the University of Toronto, Mississauga. His research interests include narrative, pedagogy, and personhood. In his youth, he subscribed to *Firehouse Magazine* (the finest KISS fanzine that ever was) and later formed a short-lived chapter of the KISS Army at Erindale College.

MIKKO M. PUUMALA is a Doctoral student in philosophy in University of Turku, Finland. He is writing his PhD dissertation on moral demandingness, moral psychology and climate ethics with the funding of the Maj and Tor Nessling Foundation. Mikko appreciates long drum solos and a second encore. He would definitely use Paul Stanley's old 'bandit' make-up and start the show with "I Stole Your Love."

SHANE J. RALSTON is forced by circumstance to serve as Assistant Dean and Teaching Faculty at Woolf University, but has a vivid fantasy life, wherein he is the most expendable member of a KISS cover band and assumes the role and make-up of Owlman. He plays the air guitar.

L.A. RECODER is an internationally acclaimed visual artist, independent scholar, and proud veteran of the KISS ARMY (1977–1980). His reflections on the golden years of the original KISS lineup were conceived under the contagious influence of Ace Frehley's hysterical laughter. The thought is that by tuning into the critical wavelength of this cosmic clown's sonic outburst we can determine with utter precision whether the hi-fi philosophical remastering of KISS is well-equipped to survive the blast. Recoder lives and works in the "New York Groove" with his Gibson SG.

CASEY RENTMEESTER is the Director of General Education and Associate Professor of Philosophy at Bellin College in Green Bay, Wisconsin. He is author of the book *Heidegger and the Environment* (2016) and twenty peer-reviewed articles and book chapters. When he is not teaching, writing, or spending time with his amazing family, he can be found listening to his extensive vinyl record collection, which includes a whole lotta KISS. He strives for the Nietzschean balance between his Dionysian tendencies, which surface less frequently as he has three young children, and his Apollonian tendencies, which guide a lot of his professional work. His wife, Cassandra, is an avid KISS fan, which Casey finds "hot, hot, hotter than hell." They have strong disagreements as to the value of the KISS song, "Beth," and their children generally think that "Mommy's alright, Daddy's alright—they just seem a little weird."

R. ALAN SILER is an author, publisher, librarian, and drummer/percussionist who has performed in rock bands, jazz combos, folk groups, orchestras and operas. Currently the drummer in a Heart tribute band (Heartisans), he has played in two previous KISS bands. In 2011, to commemorate the twentieth anniversary of Eric Carr's passing, he organized a tribute concert called Night of the Fox, which featured songs from throughout Eric's time in KISS as well as songs he wrote or co-wrote for other artists. A second Night of the Fox, themed around the thirtieth anniversary of *Lick it Up*, was staged in July of 2013 with the intention of making it an annual birthday bash.

ROBERT S VUCKOVICH is a former rock soldier whose interest in rock music waned once drawn to the diabolical clutches of philosophy, even though he occasionally listens to Deep Purple (especially the Mark III and IV line-ups), the Monkees, Band Maid, and K-Pop groups, T-ara and 2ne1. Having written articles on pop culture and philosophy (*SpongeBob SquarePants* and the *Twilight Zone*), rhetoric, bioethics, Diogenes of Sinope, and education, he has become a loyal fan of the Stoics—especially the original CCR—Cleanthes, Chrysippus, and Musonius Rufus. His one connection to KISS was of a performance of "Shout It Out Loud" as Gene Simmons's Demon in a high school air-band competition, which was photographed and preserved in Grand River Collegiate Institute's 1986 yearbook.

Index